Measurement of Trends in Wellbeing, Poverty, and Inequality
with Case Studies from Bolivia and Colombia

Göttinger Studien zur Entwicklungsökonomik
Göttingen Studies in Development Economics
Herausgegeben von/ Edited by Hermann Sautter und/and Stephan Klasen

Bd./Vol. 32

PETER LANG
Frankfurt am Main · Berlin · Bern · Bruxelles · New York · Oxford · Wien

Melanie Grosse

Measurement of Trends in Wellbeing, Poverty, and Inequality with Case Studies from Bolivia and Colombia

PETER LANG
Internationaler Verlag der Wissenschaften

Bibliographic Information published by the Deutsche Nationalbibliothek
The Deutsche Nationalbibliothek lists this publication in the Deutsche Nationalbibliografie; detailed bibliographic data is available in the internet at http://dnb.d-nb.de.

Zugl.: Göttingen, Univ., Diss., 2010

Cover design:
Olaf Glöckler, Atelier Platen, Friedberg

Cover illustration by Rolf Schinke

Gratefully acknowledging financial support
by Ibero-Amerika-Institut
für Wirtschaftsforschung,Göttingen.

D 7
ISSN 1439-3395
ISBN 978-3-631-61376-4

www.peterlang.de

Für meine Eltern

Editor's Preface

Reducing poverty and increasing wellbeing in developing countries have become one of the central aims of both the national policy-makers as well as the international community. With the Millennium Development Declaration of 2000, the international community has agreed to focus on the poverty reduction and the reduction of deprivation in its many dimensions. These dimensions of life include, besides income, health, eduction, nutrition, as well as participation, and security. It has become widely agreed that it is necessary to take a multi-dimensional approach when investigating poverty and designing policies for poverty reduction.

The literature on poverty and inequality reduction has generated tools to follow the wellbeing of the poor over time. One of the tools is econometric survey matching techniques known as poverty mapping. With this micro-econometric approach it is possible to fill gaps in microeconomic household surveys over time with imputed data from surveys originally designed for different purposes. The second important tool is to look beyond national (or regional) averages when investigating poverty reduction but to focus on the relation between income growth, poverty reduction, and inequality reduction over time. The concept of pro-poor growth has emerged from the aim of going beyond averages by looking at growth of different quantiles of the income and non-income distribution.

In the present book entitled *Measurement of Trends in Wellbeing, Poverty, and Inequality with Case Studies from Bolivia and Colombia*, Melanie Grosse contributes to filling some gaps in this literature with four essays on dynamic aspects of wellbeing, poverty, and inequality measurement. In the first essay entitled *Matching Household Surveys with DHS Data to Create Nationally Representative Time Series of Poverty: An Application to Bolivia*, Grosse extends the literature on poverty mapping by introducing a dynamic component in the micro-econometric simulation procedure that underlies the poverty mapping approach. She uses the various different data sources that are available in many developing countries—such as recent national Living Standard Measurement Surveys, series of national Demographic and Health Surveys, National Accounts, and early or spotty (urban) Household Income Surveys—and combines them in several ways. In doing so, she is able to generated more information by this data combination compared to the information the data sets deliver when being analyzed separately from each other. For the Bolivian example, she is able to extend the time series of comparable national income data 10 years back in time compared to what has been available without the data combination. Poverty and inequality trends in rural areas, that had formerly been uncovered by income household surveys, can be investigated more deeply. Detailed poverty profiles and poverty trends over time for the urban–rural divide and for socio-economic characteristics of the population reveal how important it is to track poverty trends over time.

In the second essay entitled *Estimating the Stability of Poverty Analysis: Out-of-Sample Predictions in Dynamic Poverty Mapping*, Grosse deepens the analysis carried out in the first essay to judge the stability of poverty mapping results by using out-of-sample predictions. Grosse fills the gap in verification of results and contrasts poverty and inequality outcomes using two different assumptions in the regression underlying the mapping procedure and using two different base years. She finds that results can vary considerably for the example of Bolivia, both concerning levels and trends over poverty and inequality indices.

Whereas the first two essays are mainly using income as the main wellbeing indicator, Grosse turns to non-income dimensions of poverty and inequality in the third and fourth essay. In the third essay entitled *Measuring Pro-Poor Growth in Non-Income Dimensions*, she extends one of the tools of the pro-poor growth literature—the growth incidence curve—to non-income dimensions of wellbeing. In doing so, she overcomes the shortcoming of pro-poor growth concepts that have only focussed on income changes over the income distribution. Grosse applies this logic to non-income dimensions using Bolivian data and is able to answer the question if the poor were able to expand their outcomes in non-income dimensions such as education or health, thus, if non-income poverty and inequality were reduced or not.

Using Colombian Quality of Life Survey data, which is rich both in income or consumption and in non-income dimensions, Grosse extends the analysis of non-income pro-poor growth in the fourth essay, entitled *Pro-Poor Growth in Multidimensional Poverty Indicators: An Application to Colombia*. She turns to the question of how to aggregate several indicators into one single index using two different weighting systems. By contrasting findings from normatively selected and statistically determined methods to determine the weights of the variables entering the indices, she presents a solid empirical application on how to construct and interpret trends in multidimensional poverty over time. The Colombian case is an interesting one because it encompasses a period of deep economic contraction which has affected income and non-income dimensions of wellbeing differently from each other.

Melanie Grosse investigates conceptual and empirical issues on the measurement of trends in wellbeing, poverty, and inequality and nicely illustrates her approaches for Bolivia and Colombia. She has contributed significantly to filling data gaps by combining existing data in a new way. Furthermore, her book presents an important step forward in the direction of focussing more on multidimensional outcomes of wellbeing rather than on monetary inputs. The essays are important contributions to the economic literature on developing tools to monitor the progress in achieving the Millennium Development Goals.

Prof. Stephan Klasen, Ph.D.
Göttingen, October 2010

Author's Preface—Or: My Ph.D. thesis in 3 Steps...

Ever tried. Ever failed. No matter. Try Again. Fail again. Fail better.
Samuel Beckett (1906–1989)

... 1: the Start. The most important part of a Ph.D. thesis (and maybe the most important reason to finish it) is to write the acknowledgements. So thanks to all for giving me a good start. I "always" wanted to write a Ph.D. thesis, and I am very grateful for having been given this opportunity by the Chair of Development Economics at the University of Göttingen. I have started with an enormous amount of ambition, motivation, and enthusiasm. And I have been able to observe a steep learning curve on everything I had hardly any idea about before: Econometrics, STATA, LaTeX, teaching classes, contributing to organize the chair, supervising students, and having good times and research collaborations with colleagues. And, last but not least, having a lot of fun at the chair.

My deepest thanks go to my supervisors, above all to Prof. Stephan Klasen for supporting me throughout all the time that it took me to finish this thesis. He was always able to find the right motivating words and to provide stimulating inputs whenever I needed them. His scientific and practical advice have been invaluable to me and his insistence from the very beginning until the very end has been my safeguard to stay on track. I am also deeply thankful for the freedom he gave me to finish my Ph.D. and for the trust in my capacities to really do it. I would also like to thank Prof. Michael Grimm for his readiness and his perseverance to keep on supervising my thesis, even after he has left Göttingen in favor of The Hague. Furthermore, I would like to thank him for the friendship and nice work atmosphere that evolved by working in the offices next to each other, having a cup of tea together from time to time, and by sharing some evening working hours at office. My thanks also go to Prof. Walter Zucchini for his patience in teaching me the beauty that statistics can have and for his availability to comment on my research with stimulating questions and valuable suggestions.

... 2: the Middle. Thanks to all who kept on believing that I would do it. The list of people to thank (mentioned in non-systematic order) feels nearly endless, so felt the time I spent in "the Middle". Thanks to those who have hosted me from time to time for an "Arbeitsurlaub" at their place, mainly my "idol" and friend Andrea Schertler at the University of Kiel who kept on teasing me even harder than my supervisor; my former room mate and old crony Nicolé Evensson for a nice work atmosphere combined with fun in Amsterdam and Järvsö; my friend and former colleague Isabel Günther hosting me at ETH in Zürich and keeping the balance between fun and research (and providing numerous invaluable, but sometimes unfortunately unreadable), suggestions to my thesis; and my cousin Thorsten Grosse welcoming me at IP Exchange in Nürnberg, also motivating me with potential prospects at the job market; and most importantly to Max Bönisch and Frauke Siegmüller to constantly and frequently satisfying my basic needs for food, clothes, shelter, firewood, and participation during wonderful and innumerable times in front of the fireplace and TV in Echte.

Many friends have crossed my way at office and made my time a lot nicer, namely my friend Kenneth Harttgen with whom I have been sharing doubts and ambitions about the Ph.D. thesis and with whom working together was really really fun; Eva Söbbeke with whom I have been sharing similar positions and passions such as being at office during late-night and week-end sessions, loving to have dinner outside, and procrastinating by studying www.phdcomics.com (thanks also to Jorge Cham for writing them); Silke Woltermann with whom I am sharing the love for Brazil (including Cachaça) and for development economics and development cooperation; Iris Butzlaff with whom I was sharing the challenging, but funny, times in our office in Büsgenweg as well as during nice dinners at home; and Axel Buschmann for allowing me to join him to the worst mensa ever: Nordmensa.

Other friends have crossed my way after office hours and have made the way much more pleasant, namely my room mate Jan Niessen giving me support in the day to day life (and not to forget night to night life with wine & beer and pizza & pasta); Katja Töpfer and Andreas Röder sharing their sofa, dinner, and TV each Sunday for Tatort; Beatrice Radecke for coming over to share week-end breakfasts which forced me to wake up "early" even Saturdays and Sundays and to do research afterwards; Femke Schäfer and Sybille Mai for sharing sports ambitions and the love for good food; Felix Hammermann for constantly being worried about the unlikely outcome that I would not do it and for giving me good advice on where to focus in the career planning and in life; Matthias Stenger and Katharina Scholz for having gone through the same ups and downs and having shared these experiences in frequent meetings and endless phone calls; my former class mates Julia Schultz and Sophie Rotter for having fun together, going out for dancing and drinking, and keeping in touch all the time; and my sandbox friend

Sandra Ziep for continuing our long history of friedship in endless tea time and dinner events.

... 3: the Finish. Thanks to all who finally pushed me to the end. After several years and after some cumbersome, turbulent, and challenging times, I am thankful to all who believed in me during all the time: my supervisors, my colleagues, and my friends. But my special thanks go to my family who might have never really understood what I was doing, why I was doing it, and why it took me so long to do it, but who kept on believing that I would do it! And I did it. I am deeply thankful to my parents who gave me the feeling of being loved and supported ... "come hell or high water".

Melanie Grosse
Göttingen, October 2010

Contents

List of Tables

List of Figures

List of Abbreviations

BCG	Tuberculosis vaccine (Bacillus Calmette-Guerin)
BMI	Body Mass Index
CHIM	Change in Mean
CI	Confidence Interval
Cov	Covariance
CPI	Consumer Price Index
CWI	Composite Welfare Index
DANE	Departamento Administrativo Nacional de Estadistica (Colombia), National Administrative Department of Statistics
DHS	Demographic and Health Survey
DNP	Departamento Nacional de Planeacion (Colombia), National Planning Department
DPT	Diphtheria, Pertussis, and Tetanus vaccine
EAP	East Asia and Pacific
ECH	Encuesta Continua de Hogares (Bolivia), Household Survey
ECV	Encuesta de Calidad de Vida (Colombia), Household Survey
EH	Encuesta de Hogares (Colombia), Household Survey
EIH	Encuesta Integrada de Hogares (Bolivia), Household Survey
FARC	Fuerzas Armadas Revolucionarias de Colombia, Revolutionary Armed Forces of Colombia
FDI	Foreign Direct Investment
FGT	Foster Greer Thorebecke (Set of Poverty Measures)
GDP	Gross Domestic Product
GIC	Growth Incidence Curve
GNI	Gross National Income
GRIM	Growth Rate in Mean
HDI	Human Development Index
HDR	Human Development Report
HIPC	Heavily Indebted Poor Countries
ICV	Indice de Condiciones de Vida, Life Conditions Index
IMF	International Monetary Fund

INE	Instituto Nacional de Estadistica (Bolivia), National Statistics Institute
LAC	Latin America and the Caribbean
Lhs	Left hand scale
LLDC	Least Developed Countries
LSMS	Living Standard Measurement Survey
MDG	Millennium Development Goals
MIC	Middle Income Countries
n.a.	Not available
NBI	Unmet Basic Needs Index
n.d.	Not defined
NIGIC	Non Income Growth Incidence Curve
OLS	Ordinary Least Squares
PCA	Principal Component Analysis
PPCA	Polychoric Principal Component Analysis
PPCH	Pro-Poor Change
PPGR	Pro-Poor Growth Rate
PPP	Purchasing Power Parity
SSA	Sub-Saharan Africa
Rhs	Right hand scale
SD	Standard Deviation
TV	Television
UDAPE	Unidad de Analisis de Politicas Sociales y Economicas (Bolivia), Social and Economic Policy Analysis Unit
UNDP	United Nations Development Program
USAID	U.S. Agency for International Development
USD	United States Dollar
Var	Variance
WIDER	World Institute for Development Economics Research
YOS	Years of Schooling

Introduction and Overview

Have compassion for all beings, rich and poor alike; each has their suffering. Some suffer too much, others too little.
Buddha (563BC–483BC)

Fighting poverty and inequality is among the goals upon which the international community has agreed. The issue of lifting the poor out of poverty and enhancing the wellbeing of the deprived and marginalized is on top of the international agenda of researchers, policy makers, and the general public. This broad agreement becomes well visible by the Millennium Development Goals (MDG) which have been set by the international community in 2000 in the Millennium Development Declaration (UN, 2000). By setting these goals, which are inspired by the seminal work of Sen (1985), several aspects of development have become more important for researchers and policy makers alike.

The first aspect is that development and poverty need to be understood as multidimensional phenomena. By setting 8 goals (and specifying 21 concrete targets and 60 indicators to be measured and monitored) the view has become wider than just looking at money-metric goals such as increasing per capita income. Besides income poverty, which is one target of MDG1, the other goals focus on eradicating hunger (second target of MDG1), enhancing education (MDG2), increasing gender equality and empowerment of women (MDG3), reducing child mortality (MDG4), improving maternal health (MDG5), combating diseases such as HIV/AIDS and malaria (MDG6), ensuring environmental sustainability (MDG7), and developing a global partnership for development (MDG8). The second aspect besides setting these goals is that they should be measured and monitored regularly until 2015.

The essays presented in this book deal with the measurement and trends of poverty and inequality and follow the spirit of the MDGs in several aspects. **Essay 1** deals with data generation out of incomplete data to being able to monitor the trends in (income) poverty and inequality over a longer time period. **Essay 2** deepens the analysis of the first essay by determining the stability of poverty and inequality estimates using different methods of data generation. **Essay 3** deals with the measurement of multidimensional poverty and inequality and its monitoring over time. **Essay 4** deepens this analysis by comparing different methods for data weighting and aggregation of multidimensional indicators.

Trends of Worldwide Poverty and Inequality

After the second world war, hopes were strong that the development (or catch-up) of the poorer parts of the world would take just a few years or at maximum some one or two decades—inspired by the success in economic development of post-war Europe. The believe was that by setting the overall macroeconomic conditions and by providing enough "money", development would result nearly automatically (Kiely and Marfleet, 1998). With the end of the cold war, a market-based economic system became the "winner model" in the world, and policy recommendations for developing countries consisted of structural reforms, also called the "Washington consensus" (Williamson, 1990; Rodrik, 2003; Lora, 2001; Schweickert and Thiele, 2004). However, hopes did not materialize everywhere, but the effect on enhancing growth and reducing poverty and inequality were at best mixed (World Bank, 2005; Chen and Ravallion, 2008; Rodrik, 2006). Thus, since the 1990s, the focus of research and policy shifted back to answering the very essential questions why poverty and inequality persist in so many countries.

In this vein, the first Human Development Report (HDR) from 1990 has "the single goal of putting people back at the center of the development process in terms of economic debate, policy and advocacy ... [and addresses] the question of how economic growth translates—or fails to translate—into human development."[1] Also, since the mid to late 1980s, measuring poverty and inequality and their trends have become easier. Household surveys have been conducted more frequently and in more countries, for example in a standardized way under the Living Standard Measurement Survey (LSMS) project of the World Bank. In parallel, the Demographic and Health Surveys, funded by USAID, have started collecting data on health and population trends that has led to more data collection. The literature on the trends in worldwide poverty in the 1990s using this data suggests that inroads into poverty have been made, however, not everywhere (Chen and Ravallion, 2008). This finding continues in the 2000s as well, and the latest MDG monitoring report (UN, 2009) raises the fear that the recent economic crisis together with rising food prices would increase vulnerability and lead to rising poverty, in some regions more (Africa) than others (East Asia).

In general, Latin America and the Caribbean (LAC) does on average better than other regions for the time period of investigation of the essays in this book. As shown in Appendix Table A.1, the region has, compared to other regions or

[1] http://hdr.undp.org/en/reports/global/hdr1990/.

groups of countries, the highest GDP per capita in 1990 and 2005, even higher than the group of Middle Income Countries (MIC). Concerning non-income indicators, LAC is leading in, e.g., life expectancy, female literacy, and the Human Development Index (HDI). For most of the other selected indicators presented here, such as immunization, male literacy, school enrollment, infrastructure (roads, telephone connection), it is among the leading regions. Also the structure of the economy is in LAC relatively advanced with the lowest share of agriculture in GDP and the highest share of services. Concerning the ratio of exports to GDP, LAC is in the middle group. Inflation was still high in the 1990s, but has been substantially reduced to more sustainable levels, but it is still the highest compared to all other regions. GDP growth rates are rather low and even decreasing, in contrast to high and even increasing growth rates in East Asia and the Pacific (EAP) and South Asia. The MIC group also outperformed LAC in the 2000s. On the other hand, LAC still does better than Sub-Saharan Africa (SSA) and than the group of Least Developed Countries (LLDC) in levels as well as growth rates. The same holds for the selected non-income indicators.

Poverty, Inequality, and Policy in Bolivia and Colombia

The period of investigation of the essays in this book covers the 1990s and the beginning of the 2000s: For Bolivia the time period studied is from 1989 to 2002 and for Colombia from 1997 to 2003. This period also marks the beginning of the monitoring and reference years for achieving the MDGs: 1990 is the reference year for all goals set by the international community in 2000 (UN, 2000), that should be reached until 2015. For LAC countries, it marks the turning point of the focus of national and international policies. Leaving the so-called "lost decade" of the 1980s behind, the countries had gone through policies suggested by the "Washington consensus" which included the deregulation of product and capital markets, the liberalization of trade and FDI policies, fiscal reforms including tax reforms and decentralization efforts as well as increased public spending on health, education, and infrastructure, combined with the restructuring of publicly-owned firms, mainly by privatization (Klasen et al., 2005; Schweickert and Thiele, 2004).

In Appendix Table A.2, Bolivia and Colombia are shown in a comparative perspective with neighboring countries, i.e., some of the Andean countries (Chile, Ecuador, Peru).[2] Bolivia is among the three poorest economies in Latin America, together with the struggling countries Nicaragua and Haiti. In per capita income, Bolivia is growing on the LAC average, whereas Colombia is growing a little faster. Both have higher population growth, Bolivia shows even in an in-

[2]See Klasen et al. (2005) for more LAC countries.

ternational comparison a high level (Appendix Table A.1). Both countries have achieved moderate inflation rates. Bolivia is struggling from a rather low population density and problematic geographic conditions due to the difficult terrain. The structures of the Bolivian and Colombian economies are relatively similar at the first glance, having above average agricultural participation and a high share of services. For indicators measuring human development, Bolivia shows weak outcomes and is receiving quite high aid inflows compared not only to LAC but also to other regions.[3] It is doing worse on life expectancy, immunization, infrastructure (roads, telephones), and also on the overall HDI value. For many of these aspects, Bolivia is doing similarly badly as countries in SSA or South Asia, except for education. Colombia, however, is very close to the average of LAC countries, both looking at income levels as well as non-income indicators.

Turning to the political and social stability of the countries, Bolivia was mainly under military rule in the 1970s and early 1980s, but a democratic regime was established in 1982 and has persisted ever since. The 1980s and 1990s were dominated by changing coalitions of parties representing the Spanish-speaking population but with little representation from indigenous groups.[4] The early to mid-2000s were driven by protest, civil unrest, and political instability. From 2001 onwards, each Bolivian president remained in charge for approximately only a year (Klasen et al., 2005). At the end of 2005, the candidate of the "Movement for Socialism", Evo Morales, won the election, being the first indigenous head of state. The situation in the country remained unstable with protest from the middle class and the richer lowland departments against the leftist policies[5] (some regions even declared autonomy) but Morales was able to win a recall referendum in 2008, to get approved the new constitution in 2009 (allowing reelection), and to actually be reelected in December 2009 in the first round.

Colombia had only a short time under military rule in the mid-1950s, being under democratic rule ever since, with either conservative or liberal presidents. However, since the 1960s, Colombia has been suffering from the internal armed conflict with the Revolutionary Armed Forces of Colombia (Fuerzas Armadas Revolucionarias de Colombia, FARC), other paramilitary groups, and the drug cartels. The conflict became worse every decade, which up to today places Colombia internationally in the "leading group" for homicides with 45–61 homicides in 100,000 people (compared to 3–4 for Bolivia), only "outperformed" by

[3] Bolivia is taking part in the HIPC initiative.

[4] Bolivia has a very large indigenous population and is one of the most ethnically diverse countries in Latin America.

[5] These include a strengthening of the rights of the indigenous people, partly nationalization of the natural resource sector (mainly gas) and/or stronger control over foreign firms, and a less restrictive approach towards coca growing.

South Africa.[6] The same holds for internally displaced people with 2.6–4.7 Mio. people, only "outperformed" by Sudan with 4.6–4.9 Mio. people.[7] Since 2002, Colombia has been ruled by Alvaro Uribe, an independent liberal candidate. He was able to win great public support due to his strong priority to end the internal armed conflict, following the so called "democratic security policy" with a rather tough approach to overcome the violence and to stabilize the country. Stabilizing the country and achieving increased economic growth made it possible for him to initiate and push trough a constitutional reform (allowing reelection), and actually Uribe was reelected in 2006 in the first round. He was only stopped by the Colombian Constitutional Court to run for a third term.[8] Instead, his political heir Juan Manuel Santos was able to clearly win the selections, expected to continue the most of the politics adopted under Uribe.[9]

Comparing the two countries presented in this book reveals how poverty and inequality might harm growth and cause social turmoil and political change (as suggested by the case of Bolivia) and how political and social instability might harm growth and non-income wellbeing such as subjective perceptions on life satisfaction and personal safety (as suggested by the case of Colombia). The political and social struggle of the 1990s and 2000s shows how important policies directed to enhancing wellbeing are. The long-lasting segmentation of Bolivia along the ethnic divide, which strongly coincides with the divide between highlands agriculture and lowlands resource-based economy, led to turmoil (Klasen et al., 2005) and finally to the succcss of the leftist government of Evo Morales. The burden of the internal armed conflict hinders Colombia to grow beyond the Latin American average and to converge towards the richer neighbors with similar initial conditions.

Measurement of Wellbeing, Poverty, and Inequality

Many different measures have been proposed to measure and monitor poverty and inequality. The essays in this book apply several measures and thereby shed light on different aspects of poverty and inequality. From the Foster-Greer-Thorbecke set of decomposable poverty measures (Foster et al., 1984), we use the poverty headcount or poverty incidence (abbreviated FGT0 or P0) that measures the proportion of poor people in the total population, the poverty gap (FGT1 or P1) that measures the depth or intensity of poverty showing how far the population is on average from the poverty line, and the poverty severity (FGT2 or P2) that takes

[6] http://www.unodc.org/unodc/en/data-and-analysis/ihs.html.
[7] http://www.internal-displacement.org.
[8] http://www.nytimes.com/2010/02/27/world/americas/27colombia.html?ref=colombia.
[9] http://www.nytimes.com/2010/06/21/world/americas/21colombia.html.

the inequality of incomes among the poor into account. The FGT measures, especially FGT0, are the most frequently calculated and best available measures.

For measuring inequality, we use the Gini coefficient, the Atkinson indices, the Theil index, and Quantile-Ratios (Sen and Foster, 1997). The Gini coefficient can be derived from the Lorenz curve[10] and measures how close the Lorenz curve is to the curve of total equality. The Gini is lower the closer the Lorenz curve is to the equality curve: it would be 0 for perfect equality and 1 for perfect inequality.[11] Its intuitive interpretation and the availability of data for many developing countries makes it the most widely used inequality measure. The Atkinson index can be made more sensitive to the lower end of the income distribution by increasing the "inequality aversion" parameter in the Atkinson formula. The Theil Index offers the advantage, in contrast to the Gini, to be additively decomposable over subgroups of all observations N (as the weighted average of inequality within subgroups plus inequality between those subgroups) and ranges from 0 to $\ln N$. The last inequality measure used is the quantile ratio, defined as the ratio of the richest quantile to the poorest quantile (for example the richest decile to the poorest decile), sometimes also called Kuznets ratio. It is the easiest to calculate and also the most intuitive to understand.

All these poverty and inequality measures require household survey micro data. Especially for inequality, the data should be of high quality because the inequality measures take the whole distribution into account for calculating the indices, and some of them are sensitive to data at the tails of the distribution. For poverty, only the lower end of the distribution is relevant, i.e., the people up to the poverty line.[12] To follow poverty and inequality trends, this data needs to be comparable over time. Unfortunately, household survey design often change over time (e.g., in sampling, questions, recall periods) making sound analysis and clear statements difficult. **Essay 1** and especially **Essay 2** come up with some suggestions how to deal with some aspects of data generation and data comparison.

Specific methods to follow the trends of poverty and inequality jointly over time have evolved and have been applied to a range of countries, some of which are also applied in this book. A special group of methods can be grouped under the topic of "pro-poor growth" which is, generally speaking, growth that is beneficial to the poor of the income distribution. Questions addressed by pro-poor growth methods are, for example: How can a poverty decline be decomposed in

[10]The Lorenz curve depicts on the x-axis the cumulative share of people ordered by increasing income and on the y-axis the cumulative share of income. The total equality curve is the 45 degree line.

[11]It is calculated as the area between the Lorenz curve and the equality curve divided by the total area under the equality curve.

[12]For inequality, it would matter if you had a very rich person, e.g., Bill Gates, in the sample, but for poverty, it would not since only persons below the poverty line enter the calculations.

rising incomes and falling inequality (growth-inequality decomposition of Datt and Ravallion (1992))? What is the required growth rate to achieve the same poverty decrease as observed if the income distribution had remained constant (poverty equivalent growth rate of Kakwani and Son (2006))? How much does each quantile of the income distribution benefit from growth (growth incidence curve of Ravallion and Chen (2003))? Did the poor grow faster than the non-poor (pro-poor growth rate of Ravallion and Chen (2003))? The standard data used to apply the described poverty and inequality measures and their trends over time as well as the pro-poorness of the trends are income or expenditures data, as done in **Essay 1**. Wellbeing, however, goes beyond income as outlined above. For this purpose, standard pro-poor growth methods are applied to non-income indicators, which are similar to the MDGs or multidimensional (composite) measures such as the HDI, in **Essay 3**. These analysis are extended and different aggregation weighting schemes in multidimensional indices are discussed and applied in **Essay 4** putting normative and also subjective aspects in the center of analysis.

How to Overcome Missing Data Problems?

Essay 1, based on joint work with Stephan Klasen and Julius Spatz, and **Essay 2**, based on joint work with Boris Branisa, address the question how to overcome the problem of missing data by using household survey matching techniques. In many developing countries, a time series of nationally representative household budget or income surveys does not exist, while there often are urban household surveys as well as nationally representative Demographic and Health Surveys (DHS) which lack information on incomes. This makes an analysis of trends and determinants of income poverty and inequality over a longer time period impossible.

Using these data sets nevertheless for poverty and inequality analysis, these analysis have to be either restricted to urban areas only, or these analysis have to rely on alternative wellbeing measures such as asset indices, that can be created using the DHS data (Sahn and Stifel, 2000, 2003; Filmer and Pritchett, 2001). Such asset indices are applied to many countries to assess poverty differentially and poverty trends over time. While asset indices are often well-correlated with income, it is not clear how well they are able to reproduce poverty trends over time.

The problem of missing data is also relevant for Bolivia where there exist urban household surveys—leaving nearly half of the population uncovered—and nationally representative DHS since 1989, while comparable nationally representative household income surveys only exist since 1999. In **Essay 1**, we adjust a technique developed for poverty mapping exercises by Hentschel et al. (2000) and Elbers et al. (2003) to link urban household income surveys with DHS data to generate a nationally representative time series of household income data from 1989 to 1999. We show that our extension of the poverty mapping methodology is able to reproduce trends in differential in poverty well where we have comparable data. It also appears superior to the use of asset indices for measuring trends in poverty which might more reflect changes in preferences, prices, and non-income indicators. As such the proposed method is of considerable use for situations where nationally representative income surveys are lacking, but DHS data are available.

Essay 2 address the questions on how to judge the goodness of fit of the methodology of **Essay 1** by statistical procedures. The methodology presented in **Essay 1** was based on the data constraint of having only one nationally representative pair of different household surveys (one survey such as an LSMS having income and the other survey such as a DHS not having income in the survey), and to have some urban LSMS surveys for other years together with some national-wide DHS. Having a second pair of full surveys allows us in **Essay 2** to make a backward and forward check of the approach described, in the sense of an out-of-sample prediction that can be compared to observed data. Our technique explicitly estimates the stability of this backward extension by repeating it for two base periods with two sets of nationally representative data of LSMS and DHS (1998/9 and 2002/3) for Bolivia. Furthermore, we use and compare two different methods of modeling dynamics. What is normally applied in the literature is to neglect dynamics. However, changes in endowments and changes in returns are likely to occur over time and thus impact on income poverty and inequality.[13]

How to Investigate Multidimensional Pro-Poor Growth?

Essay 3, based on joint work with Kenneth Harttgen and Stephan Klasen, and **Essay 4**, based on joint work with Adriana Cardozo, address the question how to investigate the multidimensionality of wellbeing and poverty and their distribution and changes over time. In this context, pro-poor growth has recently become a central issue for researchers and policy makers, especially in the context of reaching the MDGs. The various proposals to measure pro-poor growth have also allowed a much more detailed assessment of progress on reducing poverty as they explicitly examine growth along the entire income distribution, rather than simply focusing on mean progress. However, current concepts and measurements of pro-poor growth are entirely focused on the income dimension of wellbeing, which neglects the multidimensionality of poverty and wellbeing. There are no corresponding measures for tracking progress on non-income dimensions of poverty.

In **Essay 3**, we propose to extend the approach of pro-poor growth measurement to non-income dimensions of poverty by applying the growth incidence

[13]This is investigated, for example, by Grimm (2004) for Cote d'Ivoire and by Bourguignon et al. (2005) in a multi country study for 4 countries in Latin America and 3 in Asia.

curve to non-income indicators. This extension allows the assessment of the linkage between progress in income and non-income dimensions of poverty. Categorizing the different and conflicting definitions, we introduce three definitions of pro-poor growth: weak absolute pro-poor growth, relative pro-poor growth, and strong absolute pro-poor growth. Pro-poor growth in the weak absolute sense means that the income growth rates are, on average, above 0 for the poor. Pro-poor growth in the relative sense means that the income growth rates of the poor are higher than the average growth rates, thus that relative inequality falls. Pro-poor growth in the strong absolute sense requires that absolute income increases of the poor are stronger than the average, thus, that absolute inequality falls. The definition of strong absolute pro-poor growth is the strictest definition of pro-poor growth and the hardest to achieve, which is also shown empirically by White and Anderson (2000). This is why most researchers concentrate, in general, on the weak absolute and relative definition. But this ignores that decreases in relative inequality might be—and often are—accompanied by increases in absolute inequality, which is seen as undesirable by many and can be an important source of social tension (Atkinson and Brandolini, 2004; Duclos and Wodon, 2004; Klasen, 2004).

We investigate the multidimensionality of pro-poor growth empirically for Bolivia between 1989 and 1998 in **Essay 3**. We find that growth was pro-poor both in the income and in the non-income dimension, but results for the non-income dimensions are less clear when the poor are ranked by income. The objective of **Essay 4** is to deepen this analysis for Colombia between 1997 and 2003. We benefit from the rich data set available to us that allow us to create indicators reflecting human and physical capital (education and assets), health status, and subjective welfare. By applying the method of **Essay 3** to the Colombian Living Standard Measurement Survey (LSMS) we discuss whether changes in assets, education, health, and subjective welfare were more beneficial to the poor than to the non-poor. For constructing indices, we select a subset of variables and apply polychoric principal component analysis (PPCA), suggested by Kolenikov and Angeles (2009) to define weights. Their methodology allows to correctly calculate the correlation matrix before applying traditional principal components analysis, diverging from the standard procedure used up to now in the literature. Results are compared to the same indicators using normatively selected weights to enrich the discussion about the weighting procedure of multidimensional indicators.

Although the time span is short and covers a turbulent economic period with a large recession, it is quite relevant because it gives an insight into how it affected non-income dimensions like education, health, assets ownership, and access to public services. We find that multiple dimensions of welfare might contradict each other in the short run, particularly when they depend on public policies. Public spending can thus play an important role for counteracting the depth of economic crisis like the one experienced in Colombia in 1999. We also find that even though infrastructure conditions and access to education improved due to reforms and higher public spending, self reported welfare perception was largely driven by available income and thus by consumption possibilities. In contrast to the available literature on Colombia, our subjective welfare indicator does not show improvements in self reported welfare of Colombians between 1997 and 2003. Results also show that while income and expenditures fluctuated according to economic growth, reflecting the effects of the 1999 economic crisis, non-income indicators proved to be more stable, less unequally distributed, and had minor improvements during the period of analysis.

The **Appendices** following Essay 4 contain additional country specific information on the data sets and results of the respective empirical analysis. The **Bibliography** for all parts is also located at the end of the book.

Essay 1

Matching Household Surveys with DHS Data to Create Nationally Representative Time Series of Poverty: An Application to Bolivia

Stell dir vor, es geht, und keiner kriegt's hin.
Wolfgang Neuß (1923–1989)

Abstract: In many developing countries, a repeated cross-section of nationally representative household budget or income surveys does not exist, while often repeated urban household surveys as well as nationally representative Demographic and Health Surveys (DHS) are available, the latter however lacking information on income. This makes an analysis of trends and determinants of poverty and inequality over a longer time period impossible. This is also the situation in Bolivia where there exist urban household surveys and nationally representative DHS since 1989, while nationally representative household income surveys only exist since 1997. In this paper, we adjust a technique developed for poverty mapping exercises to link urban household income surveys with DHS data to generate a nationally representative time series of household income data from 1989 to 1999. Our technique performs well on validation tests, is superior to proxying welfare with asset ownership in the DHS, and is able to generate new information on poverty and inequality in Bolivia.

---

based on joint work with Stephan Klasen and Julius Spatz.

1.1 Introduction

In many developing countries, it is difficult to obtain a time series of household income surveys for poverty and inequality analyses. Nationally representative surveys were often only conducted very recently (e.g., with the support of the World Bank living standard measurement survey (LSMS) program), but before that time often only regional—and frequently urban—income surveys are available. At the same time, many developing countries have participated in the program of Demographic and Health Surveys (DHS) since the late 1980s and by now often have 2–4 such surveys available. This is the situation in Bolivia, where urban household surveys and nationally representative DHS are undertaken since 1989, while nationally representative household income surveys only exist since 1997. Similar data constraints hold for most Latin American countries before the mid-1990s, for example for Colombia with 5 DHS from 1986 onwards but household income surveys only since the mid-1990s, or Peru with also 5 DHS since 1986 and national household surveys only from 1997 onwards. An even worse example is Haiti where 3 DHS and only 1 income survey of 2001 are available. This data constraint is also similar in several Sub-Saharan African countries where the 1-2-3 income surveys are typically only urban,[1] but several DHS have been undertaken.

The great advantage of the DHS is the high degree of standardization over time (and countries) as well as that they are freely available. Unfortunately, these DHS data do not contain information on household incomes or expenditures. In order to use these data nevertheless for poverty analysis, asset indices have often been created and used to assess poverty differentially and poverty trends over time (Sahn and Stifel, 2000, 2003; Filmer and Pritchett, 2001). While these asset indices are often highly correlated with income, it is not clear how well they are able to reproduce poverty trends over time but rather reflect changes in prices or preferences.

To be able to explore poverty and inequality trends at the national level and especially concerning the urban–rural divide in more depth and detail for the 1990s in Bolivia, irrespective of the above mentioned data constraints, we set up a dynamic cross-survey microsimulation methodology.[2] Our approach basically fol lows the poverty mapping literature based on Hentschel et al. (2000) and Elbers et al. (2003) who use household surveys and Census data to generate detailed poverty maps at one point in time. A more recent application is done by Stifel and Christiaensen (2007) who use a single household survey and several DHS surveys to generate poverty data over time, i.e., for several years over one decade. Different to the first two studies we develop a dynamic component rather than a static

[1] http://www.dial.prd.fr and http://www.afristat.org/.

[2] The term "dynamic" might be slightly too strong since our approach also uses "static" coefficients, however, different from being "the same" over time, see below.

poverty mapping within a single (or nearby) year. Different to the third study we explicitly model dynamics rather than assuming that there are none.

In Section 1.2, we develop the methodology and describe the data used. In Section 1.3, the empirical application for the case of Bolivia is carried out in three steps. First, we generate an inter-temporally comparable microdata set of simulated incomes for total Bolivia (i.e., national-wide and separately for departmental capitals (short: cities), other urban areas (short: towns), and rural areas) between 1989 and 1999, and check the consistency between observed and simulated incomes where the former are available. Second, we use the simulated incomes to estimate detailed national poverty profiles by place of residence and by household characteristics to track the evolution of poverty for different subgroups of the population over time.[3] Third, we evaluate the "pro-poorness" of the simulated 1989–to–1999 income changes using growth incidence curves.[4] In Section 1.4, we perform sensitivity analyses to (a) check the robustness of our results to alternative specifications and assumptions and to (b) compare our results with those derived from the asset-index approach. In Section 1.6, we discuss the results.

1.2 Approach and Data

Our methodology to create a nationally representative time series of income data out of incomplete income or consumption expenditure data (and to generate poverty profiles and growth incidence curves) builds upon the static cross-survey microsimulation methodology of Hentschel et al. (2000) and Elbers et al. (2003). Their objective is to analyze the spatial dimension of poverty in detailed poverty maps of national coverage for Ecuador.

Their problem is that the Ecuadorian LSMS did not collect consumption expenditures for all households but only for a nationally representative sample of two-stage randomly selected households. The two-stage sample design, first selecting clusters and then households within the selected clusters, generates a sample in which the households are not randomly distributed over space, but are geographically grouped. Their solution to this problem is to combine the LSMS data with concurrent unit-record Census data of all Ecuadorian households and impute consumption expenditures for those municipalities which were not included in the LSMS sample. To this end, they estimate a consumption expenditure model in the LSMS data restricting the set of covariates to those which are also available in the

[3]In a related study, Klasen et al. (2007) investigate also the effect of macroeconomic shocks and policies on poverty and inequality for a 10-years-period ahead. The authors use a dynamic computable general equilibrium model that is linked to the microdata also used in this study.

[4]For the results of the Datt and Ravallion (1992) growth-inequality decomposition of poverty changes, see Grosse et al. (2005, 2007).

Census data. Then they multiply for each household in the Census its covariates with the corresponding regression coefficient from the consumption expenditure model and add a randomly distributed error term.

We have a similar objective but face different data constraints. The pre–1997 LSMS of Bolivia are not nationally representative, but cover only cities. The 1997 LSMS is nationally representative but not comparable over time due to changes in the survey design. Moreover, the Bolivian rounds of Census are only available for 1992 and 2001. To overcome these data constraints, we extend the static cross-survey microsimulation methodology of Hentschel et al. (2000) and Elbers et al. (2003) by a dynamic component and use DHS data (of the years 1989, 1994, and 1998) instead of Census data.

Stifel and Christiaensen (2007) apply the same technique, which is also based on Hentschel et al. (2000) and Elbers et al. (2003), to Kenyan data facing similar data constraints as we do. They use a household survey—the 1997 welfare monitoring survey (WMS)—and the three DHS rounds of 1993, 1998, and 2003. The difference to our paper is that their estimation procedure, despite predicting incomes in the past and the future of the actual WMS, remains stable concerning the modeling of the regression coefficients and the error terms over time. This means that they run a log-linear regression model in the WMS of 1997, and they use the coefficients (and error terms) obtained from this model in all three DHS surveys to simulate incomes. They argue that there are some parameters that are expected to be relatively stable over time (e.g., the coefficients on consumer durables or housing characteristics) and exclude others that are expected to be instable over time (e.g., the coefficients education or employment). Testing if the parameters are stable or not, however, is not possible with their data set. Theoretical arguments on their selection strategy are scarce; instead their selection is based on stepwise regression models.

Our methodology takes dynamics explicitly into account and proceeds in three steps. First, we choose a base period t in which we have a nationally representative LSMS as well as a nationally representative DHS, and develop an empirical model of a monetary welfare indicator y (hereafter referred to as income) using the LSMS data. Similar to Stifel and Christiaensen (2007), Hentschel et al. (2000), and Elbers et al. (2003), we restrict the set of covariates X to those which are also available in the corresponding DHS in t. We choose the covariates that (a) exhibit the highest possible consistency between LSMS and DHS data and do not change too strongly over time, and (b) shows the best possible fit of the regression model. We then construct a 3×3 block diagonal structure of the covariates by interacting them with three regional dummies, and run a weighted standard log-linear OLS regression model where the indices C, T, and R stand for cities, towns, and rural areas, respectively, β are coefficient vectors, and ε is an independent error term:

$$\begin{pmatrix} \ln y_t^C \\ \ln y_t^T \\ \ln y_t^R \end{pmatrix} = \begin{pmatrix} X_t^C & 0 & 0 \\ 0 & X_t^T & 0 \\ 0 & 0 & X_t^R \end{pmatrix} \begin{pmatrix} \beta_t^C \\ \beta_t^T \\ \beta_t^R \end{pmatrix} + \begin{pmatrix} \varepsilon_t^C \\ \varepsilon_t^T \\ \varepsilon_t^R \end{pmatrix}. \tag{1.1}$$

Note that this is equivalent to running three separate regressions. We account for heteroskedasticity using the covariance matrix estimator proposed by White (1980).[5] We predict incomes within the LSMS sample to detect problems that might arise from the modeling of the error term (see below).

Second, we check the consistency between the observed incomes of the LSMS and the simulated incomes of the DHS in period t. To this end, we apply the coefficient estimates $\hat{\beta}$ from regression model (Equation 1.1) to the DHS covariates $\tilde{X}$ and generate simulated incomes $\tilde{y}$

$$\begin{pmatrix} \ln \tilde{y}_t^C \\ \ln \tilde{y}_t^T \\ \ln \tilde{y}_t^R \end{pmatrix} = \begin{pmatrix} \tilde{X}_t^C & 0 & 0 \\ 0 & \tilde{X}_t^T & 0 \\ 0 & 0 & \tilde{X}_t^R \end{pmatrix} \begin{pmatrix} \hat{\beta}_t^C \\ \hat{\beta}_t^T \\ \hat{\beta}_t^R \end{pmatrix} + \begin{pmatrix} u_t^C \\ u_t^T \\ u_t^R \end{pmatrix}. \tag{1.2}$$

Since the regression model in Equation (1.1) explains only a fraction (around 50 percent) of the variation in the data we add normally distributed random variables u^C, u^T, and u^R with mean 0 and a standard deviation equal to the standard deviation of the error term in the respective region. We repeat simulation procedure of Equation (1.2) for 200 times to simulate 200 nationally representative income samples. Letting $P(\tilde{y})$ be a poverty or inequality measure based on the simulated income distribution, we can generate the distribution of $P(\tilde{y})$, in particular, its mean point estimate and its prediction error, from the 200 samples of simulated incomes. The fit of the simulation can be evaluated by comparing the poverty and inequality measures estimated from observed incomes of the LSMS, $P(y)$, with those from simulated incomes of the DHS, $P(\tilde{y})$.

Third, we choose an earlier period $t-1$ in which the LSMS covers only cities and partially re-run our regression model

$$y_{t-1}^C = X_{t-1}^C \cdot \beta_{t-1}^C + \varepsilon_{t-1}^C \tag{1.3}$$

to obtain the coefficient estimates and the standard deviation of the error term for cities in period $t-1$. Concerning the modeling of dynamics, we assume that the

[5]Unfortunately, the primary sample units (or clusters) of the pre–1997 LSMS are not available in Bolivia so that we cannot split the error term into a spatial and an idiosyncratic component as in Elbers et al. (2003) and Stifel and Christiaensen (2007).

absolute differences[6] in the regression coefficients between cities and towns and between cities and rural areas remain constant over time. We therefore calculate the coefficient estimates for towns and rural areas, respectively, in period $t-1$ in the following way:

$$\beta_{t-1}^{T} = \beta_{t-1}^{C} + (\beta_{t}^{T} - \beta_{t}^{C}) \quad \text{and} \quad \beta_{t-1}^{R} = \beta_{t-1}^{C} + (\beta_{t}^{R} - \beta_{t}^{C}). \tag{1.4}$$

We check the robustness of our results to alternative assumptions on the evolution of the regression coefficients between period $t-1$ and t in Section 1.4.2. The results are compared with the "static" case of $\beta_{t-1} = \beta_t$ in **Essay 2**.

In a similar vein, we assume that the relative change in the standard deviations of the error terms between period $t-1$ and t is identical for all three regions. We calculate the standard deviations of the error terms for towns and rural areas, respectively, in period $t-1$ in the following way:

$$\sigma(\varepsilon_{t-1}^{T}) = \sigma(\varepsilon_{t-1}^{C}) \cdot \frac{\sigma(\varepsilon_{t}^{T})}{\sigma(\varepsilon_{t}^{C})} \quad \text{and} \quad \sigma(\varepsilon_{t-1}^{R}) = \sigma(\varepsilon_{t-1}^{C}) \cdot \frac{\sigma(\varepsilon_{t}^{R})}{\sigma(\varepsilon_{t}^{C})}. \tag{1.5}$$

Repeating the simulation exercise of Equation (1.2) with the estimated coefficients from Equations (1.3)–(1.5) and the DHS data in period $t-1$, we can create 200 nationally representative samples of simulated incomes in period $t-1$. Again, we can compare the poverty and inequality measures between the two household surveys. However, this is only possible for cities where also observed incomes in the LSMS are available, but not for towns and rural areas. After this consistency check, we use the simulated incomes to construct inter-temporally comparable poverty profiles of national coverage for Bolivia and to evaluate the "pro-poorness" of changes of simulated incomes over time using growth incidence curves.

Our data set of LSMS consists of three multi-purpose household surveys conducted by the Instituto Nacional de Estadisticas de Bolivia (National Statistical Office of Bolivia, INE): the 2nd round (Nov. 1989) and the 7th round (July to Dec. 1994) of the Encuesta Integrada de Hogares (EIH), and the 1st round (Nov. 1999) of the Encuesta Continua de Hogares (ECH). The EIH cover only cities of Bolivia, while the ECH are nationally representative. Two-stage sampling techniques were used in selecting the sample of households, and sampling was done in a way to ensure self-weighting. The purpose of the LSMS is to collect individual, household, and community level data to measure the welfare level of the sampled population and its changes over time. In addition to income and/or expenditure data, the LSMS provide information on demographics, asset ownership, education, employment, and health.

[6] Note that we use the term "absolute" not in the mathematical meaning of $|-1| = 1$, but to contrast it to "relative", i.e., percentage changes.

In order to be able to compare our results with earlier empirical studies, we use household members as the unit of analysis. As welfare indicator, we use monthly consumption expenditures (including own consumption, but excluding annualized costs for durable consumer goods) for rural areas, and monthly labor income (excluding fringe benefits)[7] plus monthly capital income for urban areas. The choice of the mixed welfare indicator can be justified by that (a) it is common for Bolivia (INE-UDAPE, 2002), (b) an all-expenditure specification is not possible since the EIHs collected only income but no expenditure data, and (c) an all-income specification is not preferable since incomes only poorly reflect the long-term welfare in rural areas due to large seasonal income fluctuations and a high degree of own consumption in agricultural households (Deaton and Zaidi, 2002).[8] In order to account for non-declaration of incomes, we apply a statistical matching approach similar to Hernany (1999).[9] By contrast, we do not adjust for sub-declaration (under-reporting) of incomes (i.e., we do not scale up the mean income and mean consumption expenditures in the LSMS to those in the national accounts) in our baseline scenario because (a) it is a priori not clear whether national account data or LSMS data are more accurate,[10] and (b) Bolivia does not report separate national account data for cities, towns, and rural areas.[11]

To identify the poor, we use the two sets of poverty lines provided by the Unidad de Analisis de Politicas Sociales y Economicas (UDAPE) (Appendix Table B.1). The extreme poverty lines are given by the costs of food baskets which reflect the nutritional requirements of adults and the local eating habits of the middle quintile of the income distribution. The moderate poverty lines additionally include the costs of non-nutritional basic needs and are obtained by multiplying the extreme poverty lines by the inverse of local Engel coefficients. Since no rural poverty lines are available for 1989 and 1994, we extrapolate the difference between the rural poverty line and the weighted-average urban poverty line of 1999.

[7]Only if we exclude fringe benefits the measurement unit is inter-temporally comparable between 1989 and 1999. This is because the EIHs collected, if at all, only the incidence and type of fringe benefits but not their value. As a consequence, our poverty estimates for 1999 are somewhat higher than the official figures provided by INE (various issues).

[8]For simplicity, we will use only the term "income" for this mixed welfare indicator.

[9]We apply a rather simple cell matching approach, replacing missing incomes with mean incomes based on characteristics such as region, area, language, gender, type and sector of occupation, education, labor market participation, etc. of the nearest cells or neighbors.

[10]For a description and evaluation of, and an analysis of the sensitivity of poverty measures to, different adjustment methods, see Székely et al. (2000).

[11]In Section 1.4, we change this assumption and compare our results with the ones derived from an upscaling exercise using national account data which is available at the departmental level combined with sectoral employment data.

Our set of DHS consists of the first three Bolivian rounds which were conducted in 1989, 1994, and 1998.[12] Two-stage sampling techniques were used to select nationally representative samples of women aged between 15 and 49 who serve as eligible respondents of the DHS, i.e., women of reproductive age. The main objective of the DHS is to collect demographic data on health and fertility trends. Additionally, it includes some questions on the educational attainment and the employment situation of the respondent and her partner and on the asset ownership of the household.

The covariates taken from the two data sources and their sample means are listed in Appendix Tables B.2 and B.3. They can be grouped into five categories: information on (a) demographics of the household, (b) asset ownership of the household, (c) educational attainment of adult men and women, (d) employment situation of adult men and women, and (e) health situation of children. By choosing suitable variables and dummy categories, we obtained a high degree of consistency both across surveys and over time.

We build our methodology around the base period 1998/9 and then apply it to the earlier periods 1989 and 1994. Additional data constraints impede our empirical analysis in three respects. First, to create inter-temporally comparable samples of simulated incomes for Bolivia it would be ideal to use a set of covariates which is available in all three pairs of concurrent surveys of 1989, 1994, and 1998/9. At the same time, however, the availability of covariates in the LSMS and the DHS changes over time due to changes in their questionnaires. In order to avoid a too small set of covariates we, thus, decided to use different sets of covariates for each period, i.e., different X enter for each of the three points in time t, to (a) check the consistency between the LSMS and the DHS data in 1999, (b) to create 200 samples of simulated incomes in the DHS 1989 data, and (c) to create 200 samples of simulated incomes in the DHS 1994 data.[13]

Second, since no Bolivian DHS round was conducted in 1999, we have to use the DHS 1998 data for our consistency check. That is, we compare the poverty and inequality measures based on observed incomes of the LSMS 1999 with those based on simulated incomes of the DHS 1998, assuming that the distribution of the covariates (and also of the returns to covariates) remained reasonably constant in between.[14] By contrast, for 1989 and 1994 we have concurrent rounds of LSMS

[12]The fourth Bolivian DHS round, which was conducted in 2003, is used in **Essay 2** for sensitivity analyses on the robustness of results using other models and error-specifications in the microsimulation, also focussing on the stability of the estimated results.

[13]To put it more formally, we only require that the set of covariates is identical for the LSMS and the DHS in period $t-1$ as well as for the LSMS in period t. In **Essay 2**, a smaller set of common covariates is used for the analysis from 1989 to 2002.

[14]Note that for Ecuador, Hentschel et al. (2000) and Elbers et al. (2003) use the LSMS from 1994 and the Census from 1990, so 4 years of distance of surveys, and assume that distance to

and DHS. Third, due to its focus on health and fertility trends, the DHS data only include households with at least one woman of reproductive age (i.e., eligible women are those aged between 15 and 49). We, thus, have to replicate this implicit sample selection in the LSMS data.[15]

1.3 Empirical Results

1.3.1 Estimation Properties

Before comparing poverty and inequality indices based on observed, predicted (i.e., within-LSMS), and simulated (i.e., over-to-DHS) incomes, we present some details on the regression results (Table 1.1) as well as on the properties of the predicted incomes (Tables 1.2 and 1.3). Table 1.1 presents the regression results (β coefficients and P-values) of regressing $\ln y$ on the selected variables, run separately for the three regions (city, town, rural) in 1999. One major concern might be that the simple log-linear OLS regression model is too simple or that the log-normality assumption of incomes does not hold,[16] but we take the above described estimation as a baseline estimation model.[17] Also note that we leave questions of insignificance of coefficients and multicollinearity aside, but include all variables

be "reasonably" small. The same holds for Stifel and Christiaensen (2007), who face a 1 year difference for the base year. They also apply the same coefficients, similar as Hentschel et al. (2000) and Elbers et al. (2003), for predictions 4 years back and forth in time.

[15]For 1994 and 1998, but not for 1989, the DHS provide an additional data module on, and responded by, male adults. We opted against using this data module for two reasons: (a) the information was only collected for the husbands and partners of all women included in the main module (but not for men in households with no woman in reproductive age) so that we also would have had to reduce the sample size and possibly would have introduced another sample-selection bias, and (b) our microdata set of simulated incomes would no longer be inter-temporally comparable over the whole observation period.

[16]The visual inspection of the error terms in the three regions show no further signs of heteroskedasticity after using the White (1980) estimator. However, we have tried weighted least squares estimations as well, but the results are very similar, presented in Grosse et al. (2007). Kernel estimates and qqplots show that, besides the extremes, the log-normality assumption seems to hold.

[17]We find a slight tendency of overprediction of incomes in the DHS, see below. Problems might arise if there were some coefficients that drive the results—i.e., have a high regression coefficient strongly impacting the estimation—but which are insignificant. However, this is not the case. Of the 201 coefficients entering the estimation 120 are insignificant. Despite this being a high number, first of all, of the total 201 coefficients only 5 have a share of more than 10 percent of the total discrepancy of the mean of observed and simulated log income in the LSMS compared to the DHS and only 6 coefficients have a share of more than 5 percent. Additionally, of the 120 insignificant coefficients, not a single one has a share of more than 10 or 5 percent of the total discrepancy. Overall, the by far highest coefficients, i.e., share of explanatory power, have the regional dummies for cities, towns, and rural areas (Table 1.1).

for the prediction. Overall, the relatively high adjusted R^2 makes us confident that the simple baseline model is a good starting point.

Table 1.2 shows observed incomes and the logs (y and $\ln y$) compared to within-LSMS predicted incomes and the logs ($\hat{y}$ and $\ln\hat{y}$) using the regression coefficients of the LSMS data of 1999. Figure 1.1 shows the cumulative distribution function and the kernel density estimator for the different income sets, for Bolivia at the national level (short: total Bolivia). What becomes clear from Table 1.2 is that the prediction of income without adding an error term gives too low values for $\hat{y}$ but not for $\ln\hat{y}$ compared with observed values (y and $\ln y$). This result is due to the log-linear relation between y and $\ln y$, i.e., that $E(y) \neq e^{E(\ln y)}$. By construction, the mean of $\ln y$ and $\ln\hat{y}$ is the same, even after adding an error term that is normally distributed and has mean 0. However, transforming $\ln\hat{y}$ to $\hat{y}$ by taking the anti-log gives exponentially higher values to $\hat{y}$ the higher $\ln\hat{y}$ was, so without error terms there are less larger values as in the observed case. This can be seen in Table 1.2 for total Bolivia, where the mean of the logarithm for observed $\ln y$, predicted without error $\ln\hat{y}$, and average $\ln\hat{y}$ are nearly exactly the same (columns 6–8), but the means of income for observed y, predicted without error $\hat{y}$, and average $\hat{y}$ are different.

The mean of observed income for total Bolivia is at 344 Bolivianos compared to 292 for the predicted value without adding an error term. The within-LSMS prediction renders a different picture than the observed income because the prediction does not capture all the variation in the data set. Looking at the average of these 200 repetitions (first taking the anti-log and then averaging) reveals that the mean (of 351 Bolivianos) comes very close to the observed mean y. However, the variation (SD) of the average of the predicted mean y is lower than the observed, because averaging partly eliminates the variation that had been added with the error terms. Rather, when looking at the fourth column "one expl." (which shows the summary statistics of one example, i.e., of the first predicted $\hat{y}$) we see the similarity between observed and predicted incomes, thus comparisons should be done between observed values and values for "one example".[18] In Table 1.3, all results are based on one prediction run (within the LSMS) and one simulation run (over to the DHS data set), but not on the average of the 200 replications. For cities, the prediction of the mean is better in 1989 and in 1994[19] than in 1998/9.

For all regions, there is a tendency of overprediction of the mean, being higher for the simulated data in the DHS compared to the observed and predicted data in the LSMS. The reason for this overprediction on the national level as well as in each region is the different endowment of the two data sets, i.e., on average higher

[18]The finding similarly holds for specific percentiles such as median (P50) or at the extremes of the distribution such as such as of the 5th percentile (P5) or the 95th percentile (P95).

[19]Even P5 and P95 as well as minima and maxima are relatively well reproduced when taking into account that they are most prone to being outliers or measurement error.

Table 1.1: Regression Results, Log-Linear OLS, 1999

	City		Town		Rural	
	β	P	β	P	β	P
La Paz	0.09	0.39	0.13	0.81	0.19	0.04
Cochabamba	0.28	0.01	0.62	0.22	0.28	0.01
Oruro	0.04	0.75	-0.26	0.65	0.31	0.03
Potosi	0.10	0.45	0.14	0.78	0.04	0.65
Tarija	0.59	0.00	0.37	0.49	0.64	0.00
Santa Cruz	0.68	0.00	0.47	0.35	0.74	0.00
Beni & Pando	0.70	0.00	0.17	0.75	0.81	0.00
# elderly	-0.08	0.60	0.09	0.73	-0.08	0.34
# males	-0.07	0.02	0.10	0.22	-0.10	0.02
# females	-0.12	0.00	-0.10	0.09	-0.17	0.00
# youngsters	-0.03	0.62	-0.08	0.23	-0.01	0.79
# children	-0.11	0.16	-0.18	0.05	-0.08	0.10
# of working age / # all	1.02	0.01	0.22	0.66	0.74	0.01
gender hh head	0.03	0.73	0.25	0.15	-0.02	0.84
language of hh head	-0.01	0.86	-0.12	0.30	-0.06	0.32
hh head age $\leq$ 24	-0.21	0.31	0.01	0.98	0.01	0.98
hh head age 25–34	-0.25	0.22	0.03	0.94	0.05	0.74
hh head age 35–44	-0.39	0.05	0.01	0.99	0.08	0.62
hh head age 45–54	-0.45	0.03	0.13	0.77	-0.04	0.80
hh head age 55–65	-0.34	0.09	0.03	0.94	0.03	0.84
has house	0.07	0.20	-0.07	0.51	0.08	0.25
floor (cement)	0.17	0.21	0.03	0.86	0.24	0.00
floor (brick)	0.30	0.05	0.17	0.33	0.00	1.00
floor (other floor)	0.38	0.01	0.10	0.61	0.24	0.02
2-3 sleeping rooms	0.21	0.00	-0.18	0.11	0.07	0.24
$\geq$ 4 sleeping rooms	0.22	0.04	0.09	0.73	0.30	0.14
access to public water	-0.18	0.11	0.06	0.63	-0.07	0.22
has no toilet	-0.02	0.86	-0.22	0.10	-0.08	0.11
has electricity	-0.32	0.03	-0.19	0.46	0.13	0.05
cooking material	-0.26	0.02	-0.02	0.91	0.30	0.00
has phone	0.24	0.00	0.38	0.00	0.30	0.01
has radio	0.02	0.79	-0.11	0.29	0.10	0.07
has television	0.18	0.10	0.10	0.54	0.23	0.01
has fridge	0.23	0.00	0.03	0.77	-0.02	0.85
no partner in household	0.31	0.15	0.52	0.15	0.38	0.01
com. basic edu. (m.)	-0.12	0.35	-0.01	0.96	0.02	0.78
incom. secondary edu. (m.)	0.04	0.70	-0.20	0.25	-0.04	0.56
com. secondary edu. (m.)	-0.04	0.67	0.11	0.48	-0.02	0.83
tertiary edu. (m.)	0.24	0.03	-0.10	0.66	0.15	0.49
com. basic edu. (w.)	-0.02	0.89	0.04	0.81	0.20	0.00
incom. secondary edu. (w.)	0.05	0.64	0.12	0.41	0.27	0.00
com. secondary edu. (w.)	0.06	0.54	0.11	0.50	0.18	0.08
tertiary edu. (w.)	0.26	0.03	0.27	0.19	0.28	0.17

continued on next page

Table 1.1 continued

	City		Town		Rural	
	β	P	β	P	β	P
high skilled white collar (m.)	0.68	0.00	1.09	0.01	0.60	0.00
med. skilled white collar (m.)	0.41	0.03	1.02	0.01	0.45	0.00
skilled manual (m.)	0.44	0.02	0.69	0.07	0.54	0.00
unskilled manual (m.)	0.37	0.08	0.45	0.21	0.45	0.00
agr. employed (m.)	-0.19	0.60	0.47	0.28	0.48	0.00
agr. self-employed (m.)	0.88	0.01	0.07	0.88	0.31	0.01
sales and services (m.)	0.51	0.01	0.94	0.02	0.47	0.00
high skilled white collar (w.)	0.35	0.01	0.51	0.02	0.04	0.90
med. skilled white collar (w.)	0.24	0.01	0.77	0.00	0.26	0.07
skilled manual (w.)	0.03	0.78	0.37	0.02	-0.09	0.35
unskilled manual (w.)	0.32	0.00	0.61	0.00	-0.08	0.51
agr. employed (w.)	1.20	0.02	-0.81	0.17	0.07	0.45
agr. self-employed (w.)	0.53	0.00	-0.32	0.33	0.03	0.64
sales and services (w.)	0.30	0.00	0.67	0.00	0.20	0.06
has social security	0.09	0.09	0.08	0.48	0.16	0.05
birth in last 12 month	0.08	0.71	-0.32	0.30	-0.05	0.51
attended by doctor	-0.09	0.72	0.63	0.09	0.11	0.32
delivered in hospital	-0.08	0.64	-0.20	0.37	0.12	0.31
child under 4 years	0.02	0.86	0.14	0.57	0.13	0.29
has first polio vaccination	0.05	0.69	-0.04	0.84	-0.20	0.10
has triple dpt vaccination	0.06	0.61	-0.02	0.91	0.01	0.85
has had diarrhea	-0.14	0.14	0.04	0.79	0.03	0.60
has head cough/fever	0.03	0.67	0.08	0.54	0.02	0.71
c/t/r dummy/constant	4.57	0.00	3.95	0.00	3.53	0.00
# of observations	1037		332		922	
R^2	51.40		44.16		53.80	

Notes: β: regression coefficient; P: P-value. For details on the regression, see text. For details on the variables, see text and notes of Appendix Tables B.2 and B.3.
Source: Own calculations based on ECH.

endowment in the DHS with the covariates that have higher returns to income and lower endowment with those that have lower returns (compare Appendix Tables B.2 and B.3). In addition, the overprediction for the entire country comes from the different geographical allocation of the population (city, town, rural) with the DHS having more people living in cities and fewer living in towns and rural areas. When we combine this with the regression coefficient being very high for cities compared to other regression coefficients, we can explain the main part of the difference. Whether or not we over-, well-, or underpredict poverty mea-

Table 1.2: LSMS: Observed and Predicted Income and Log Income, 1999

	y				$\ln y$			
	Obs.	within-LSMS-Prediction			Obs.	within-LSMS-Prediction		
		no error	aver.	one expl.		no error	aver.	one expl.
				Total Bolivia				
Mean	345	292	351	351	5.33	5.33	5.33	5.34
Min	1	16	20	10	0.04	2.75	2.82	2.34
Max	9,515	2,727	3,306	8,218	9.16	7.91	7.92	9.01
P5	40	59	66	41	3.68	4.07	4.07	3.72
P25	105	111	130	100	4.65	4.71	4.70	4.61
P50	206	199	238	206	5.33	5.29	5.30	5.33
P75	399	374	448	412	5.99	5.92	5.93	6.02
P95	1,167	851	1,026	1,186	7.06	6.75	6.74	7.08
SD	460	274	335	465	1.01	0.82	0.82	1.01
SK	5	3	3	5	-0.07	0.17	0.18	0.15
KUR	55	14	14	44	3.49	2.46	2.45	2.80
				City				
Mean	490	409	497	497	5.78	5.78	5.78	5.79
Min	1	52	64	22	0.04	3.96	3.99	3.10
Max	9,515	2,727	3,306	8,218	9.16	7.91	7.92	9.01
P5	86	115	137	84	4.45	4.74	4.74	4.43
P25	173	190	230	172	5.15	5.25	5.25	5.15
P50	320	311	376	317	5.77	5.74	5.74	5.76
P75	575	540	654	585	6.35	6.29	6.29	6.37
P95	1,425	966	1,162	1,677	7.26	6.87	6.88	7.42
SD	573	314	384	572	0.92	0.68	0.68	0.90
SK	5	2	2	4	-0.29	0.22	0.22	0.17
KUR	41	11	11	33	5.04	2.48	2.48	2.89
				Town				
Mean	334	285	348	357	5.42	5.42	5.43	5.47
Min	2	16	20	10	0.87	2.75	2.82	2.34
Max	3,500	1,242	1,599	3,767	8.16	7.12	7.19	8.23
P5	50	70	87	40	3.92	4.25	4.27	3.70
P25	140	142	171	142	4.94	4.95	4.95	4.96
P50	217	230	279	245	5.38	5.44	5.46	5.50
P75	417	355	428	430	6.03	5.87	5.86	6.06
P95	938	724	906	1,071	6.84	6.58	6.60	6.98
SD	346	209	258	376	0.93	0.69	0.69	0.94
SK	3	2	2	3	-0.60	-0.18	-0.17	-0.37
KUR	21	7	7	21	4.82	3.44	3.41	3.61

continued on next page

Table 1.2 continued

	y				$\ln y$			
	Obs.	within-LSMS-Prediction			Obs.	within-LSMS-Prediction		
		no error	aver.	one expl.		no error	aver.	one expl.
				Rural Areas				
Mean	146	130	149	145	4.67	4.67	4.67	4.66
Min	10	29	34	13	2.34	3.36	3.41	2.57
Max	1,801	997	1,081	1,408	7.50	6.90	6.87	7.25
P5	31	47	53	34	3.44	3.85	3.84	3.51
P25	61	70	79	61	4.10	4.25	4.23	4.11
P50	105	96	110	101	4.65	4.56	4.58	4.61
P75	182	154	175	174	5.20	5.04	5.04	5.16
P95	384	340	389	399	5.95	5.83	5.82	5.99
SD	140	103	118	142	0.78	0.59	0.59	0.77
SK	4	3	3	3	0.05	0.72	0.73	0.30
KUR	35	15	14	18	2.94	3.37	3.37	2.96

Notes: P: percentile; SD: standard deviation; SK: skewness; KUR: kurtosis; y: nominal income; Obs.: observed (i.e., "true"); aver.: average over 200 y; one expl.: one example of simulated y. Comparisons between the columns "Obs" showing observed values and "one expl." showing values for one example reveal how well the simulation procedure reproduces the observed trends. *Source:* Own calculations based on ECH.

sures mainly depends on the income level of the poverty line, as can be seen in Figure 1.1.[20]

In Table 1.4, we provide moderate poverty estimates: (a) point estimates from observed incomes of all households in the LSMS (column All HH), (b) point estimates from observed incomes of households with at least one woman of reproductive age in the LSMS (column Sample), (c) mean point estimates and standard deviation from 200 samples of predicted incomes in the LSMS (column Pred.), and (d) mean point estimates and standard deviation from 200 samples of simulated incomes in the DHS (column Sim.). Results for extreme poverty and for inequality are shown in Appendix Tables B.4 and B.5.[21]

[20]Interesting to note is that the study of Stifel and Christiaensen (2007) also finds an underestimation of the poverty headcount (i.e., overprediction of income) in the DHS 1998 data of 1–2 percentage points which they do not investigate further. Instead, they adjust the poverty line in 1998 in the DHS to match the observed 1997 WMS levels and apply this poverty line back and forth in time.

[21]Note that, different from above, mean point estimates denote that we estimate the poverty and inequality indicators based on the 200 examples of predicted and simulated incomes and over them calculate the average of 200 poverty and inequality estimates. That is, poverty or inequality measures are not calculated using the mean income of the 200 prediction or simulation examples. To put it differently, we calculate the mean of poverty/inequality and not the poverty/inequality of the mean.

Standard deviations for poverty estimates are very low and for inequality estimates even lower. This translates into ranges of about ±2 percentage points for the poverty headcount (P0), ±1 for the poverty gap (P1), and even less for the squared poverty gap (P2). Similar results hold for inequality measures.

Taking differences between these columns enables us to decompose the overall difference between observed and simulated poverty and inequality measures into three components related to (a–b) the implicit sample selection of only households with at least one women in reproductive age (thus, replicating the sample selection of the DHS), (b–c) the specification of the error term in the underlying regression model, and (c–d) differences in the distribution of the covariates between LSMS and DHS.

For 1989 and 1994, for which the consistency check is limited to cities, the results are very encouraging, as they had also been for the income properties in Table 1.3. For 1999, the situation is somewhat less favorable. Restricting the sample to households with at least one eligible woman does not induce a serious bias in estimating poverty and inequality measures. Poverty indices are slightly higher and inequality indices slightly lower when comparing the first with the second column. Adding a normally distributed error term to create 200 samples of predicted incomes in the LSMS only slightly understates P0 and slightly overstates P1 and P2. It also only slightly understates income inequality as evidenced by lower values of the Gini coefficient and the Atkinson indices in 1989 and 1994 and slightly overstates them in 1998.

Figure 1.1: Cumulative Distribution Functions and Kernel Densities, 1998/9

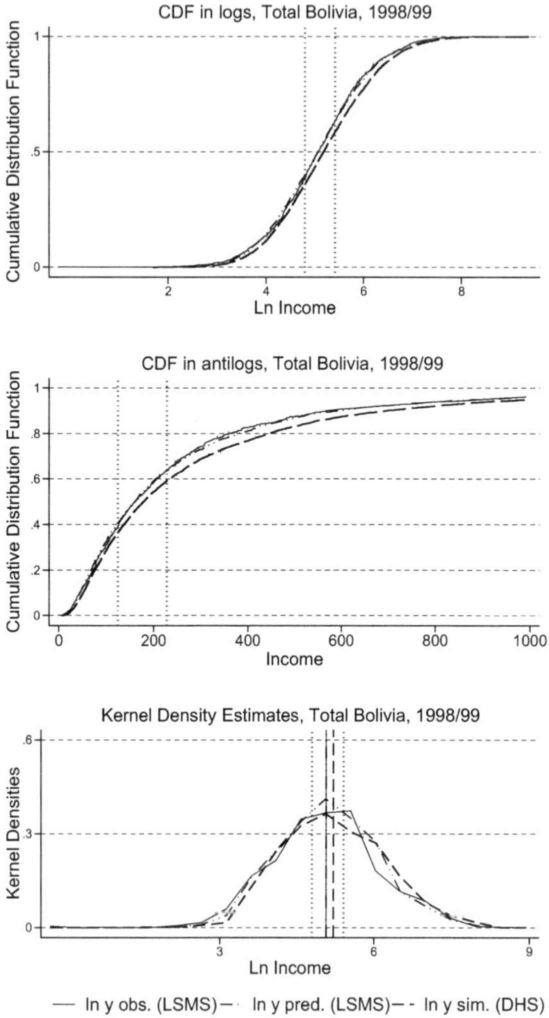

Notes: The dotted vertical lines mark the weighted poverty lines and the other vertical lines the means for the respective data set.
Source: Own calculations based on ECH and DHS.

Table 1.3: Descriptive Statistics of the LSMS and DHS, 1989, 1994, 1998/9

	LSMS 1989		DHS 1989	LSMS 1994		DHS 1994	LSMS 1999		DHS 1998
	Observed	Predicted	Simulated	Observed	Predicted	Simulated	Observed	Predicted	Simulated
					Total Bolivia				
Mean Ln y	n.a.	n.a.	4.09	n.a.	n.a.	4.47	5.33	5.34	5.47
Mean y	n.a.	n.a.	103	n.a.	n.a.	189	345	351	402
Min y	n.a.	n.a.	2	n.a.	n.a.	1	1	10	7
Max y	n.a.	n.a.	1,793	n.a.	n.a.	4,264	9,515	8,218	15,610
P5 y	n.a.	n.a.	12	n.a.	n.a.	7	40	41	48
P50 y	n.a.	n.a.	57	n.a.	n.a.	110	206	206	231
P95 y	n.a.	n.a.	348	n.a.	n.a.	626	1,167	1,186	1,324
SD y	n.a.	n.a.	139	n.a.	n.a.	266	460	465	530
					City				
Mean Ln y	4.56	4.56	4.59	5.29	5.29	5.33	5.78	5.79	5.88
Mean y	151	147	150	296	290	289	490	497	553
Min y	2	5	5	4	15	19	1	22	19
Max y	3,885	3,276	1,793	7,035	4,708	4,264	9,515	8,218	15,610
P5 y	23	23	23	56	55	57	86	84	81
P50 y	92	92	98	189	187	199	320	317	353
P95 y	448	451	451	874	863	794	1,425	1,677	1,693
SD y	216	183	170	370	325	292	573	572	634

continued on next page

Table 1.3 continued

	LSMS 1989		DHS 1989	LSMS 1994		DHS 1994	LSMS 1999		DHS 1998
	Observed	Predicted	Simulated	Observed	Predicted	Simulated	Observed	Predicted	Simulated
					Town				
Mean Ln y	n.a.	n.a.	4.00	n.a.	n.a.	4.71	5.42	5.47	5.41
Mean y	n.a.	n.a.	95	n.a.	n.a.	212	334	357	359
Min y	n.a.	n.a.	2	n.a.	n.a.	2	2	10	7
Max y	n.a.	n.a.	1,385	n.a.	n.a.	4,129	3,500	3,767	4,733
P5 y	n.a.	n.a.	9	n.a.	n.a.	14	50	40	41
P50 y	n.a.	n.a.	51	n.a.	n.a.	121	217	245	226
P95 y	n.a.	n.a.	285	n.a.	n.a.	691	938	1,071	1,052
SD y	n.a.	n.a.	131	n.a.	n.a.	349	346	376	432
					Rural Areas				
Mean Ln y	n.a.	n.a.	3.54	n.a.	n.a.	3.37	4.67	4.66	4.82
Mean y	n.a.	n.a.	52	n.a.	n.a.	62	146	145	171
Min y	n.a.	n.a.	2	n.a.	n.a.	1	10	13	12
Max y	n.a.	n.a.	756	n.a.	n.a.	1,334	1,801	1,408	1,942
P5 y	n.a.	n.a.	9	n.a.	n.a.	4	31	34	36
P50 y	n.a.	n.a.	33	n.a.	n.a.	27	105	101	120
P95 y	n.a.	n.a.	165	n.a.	n.a.	247	384	399	486
SD y	n.a.	n.a.	63	n.a.	n.a.	97	140	142	173

Notes: P: percentile; SD: standard deviation; y: nominal income. Simulated and Predicted is one example of simulated y.
Source: Own calculations based on ECH and DHS.

The transition from LSMS data to DHS data does, as mentioned, reduce poverty measures and increase inequality measures, due to the better endowment in the DHS compared to the LSMS data sets, especially in 1998/9. In total, the underestimation of the poverty headcount is about 5 percentage points (65.18 in LSMS, column Sample, compared to 60.33 in DHS). Most of the underprediction is driven by rural areas (with the headcount being 5 percentage points lower) but also for cities and towns with the headcount also being 2 to 3 percentage points lower. For the extreme poverty line, the underprediction is less severe for cities and towns, but even worse for rural areas. In total, an additional problem is that the share of people living in (richer) cities is higher in DHS surveys (Appendix Tables B.2 and B.3). The underlying economic reason of the underprediction is most probably the lack of consistency with respect to the collection period of the two underlying household surveys. The DHS 1998 data, the covariates of which were used to create the simulated incomes, were collected during an economic boom. By contrast, the observed incomes of the LSMS 1999 were collected after a sharp economic downturn when Bolivia experienced negative growth in GDP per capita.

These slight inconsistencies notwithstanding, we are confident that the conditions for applying our dynamic cross-survey microsimulation methodology are fulfilled for the case of Bolivia. First, the simulations can accurately reproduce the observed poverty trends in cities, where we have observed incomes for comparison. The differences between observed and simulated poverty measures are small compared to their changes over time. Second, the DHS 1998 data, which are least consistent to those of the corresponding LSMS, are not used in the subsequent poverty and inequality analysis. Only the poverty profiles and growth incidence curves for 1989 and 1994 draw on simulated incomes of the DHS. Those for 1999 are based on observed incomes of the LSMS.

Table 1.4: Moderate Poverty Indices Based on Observed, Predicted, and Simulated Incomes, 1989, 1994, 1998/9

	1989				1994				1998/9			
	LSMS			DHS	LSMS			DHS	LSMS			DHS
	All HH	Sample	Pred.	Sim.	All HH	Sample	Pred.	Sim.	All HH	Sample	Pred.	Sim.
	Total Bolivia											
P0	n.a.	n.a.	n.a.	76.10	n.a.	n.a.	n.a.	72.44	63.52	65.18	65.08	60.33
				(0.53)				(0.42)			(0.93)	(0.46)
P1	n.a.	n.a.	n.a.	44.45	n.a.	n.a.	n.a.	45.28	31.53	32.45	33.63	30.04
				(0.35)				(0.22)			(0.57)	(0.24)
P2	n.a.	n.a.	n.a.	30.48	n.a.	n.a.	n.a.	33.95	19.48	20.11	21.19	18.50
				(0.31)				(0.19)			(0.46)	(0.18)
	City											
P0	65.92	67.07	65.08	64.84	58.09	59.56	58.06	57.36	48.39	50.97	50.67	47.99
			(0.80)	(0.91)			(0.59)	(0.73)			(1.60)	(0.72)
P1	31.96	32.64	32.79	32.92	25.15	25.87	25.89	25.26	19.75	20.90	22.47	21.22
			(0.48)	(0.53)			(0.33)	(0.39)			(0.86)	(0.37)
P2	19.18	19.64	20.35	20.55	13.91	14.31	14.65	14.17	10.80	11.46	12.82	12.12
			(0.38)	(0.41)			(0.24)	(0.29)			(0.62)	(0.27)

continued on next page

Table 1.4 continued

	1989				1994				1998/9			
	LSMS			DHS	LSMS			DHS	LSMS			DHS
	All HH	Sample	Pred.	Sim.	All HH	Sample	Pred.	Sim.	All HH	Sample	Pred.	Sim.
						Town						
P0	n.a.	n.a.	n.a.	80.21	n.a.	n.a.	n.a.	73.42	66.60	69.03	67.49	64.26
				(1.26)				(1.16)			(2.48)	(1.18)
P1	n.a.	n.a.	n.a.	49.66	n.a.	n.a.	n.a.	43.40	32.99	34.58	34.90	33.67
				(0.87)				(0.64)			(1.48)	(0.66)
P2	n.a.	n.a.	n.a.	35.58	n.a.	n.a.	n.a.	30.66	19.94	20.97	22.21	21.76
				(0.79)				(0.55)			(1.22)	(0.53)
						Rural Areas						
P0	n.a.	n.a.	n.a.	87.96	n.a.	n.a.	n.a.	90.23	81.64	83.37	84.24	79.11
				(0.70)				(0.43)			(1.02)	(0.63)
P1	n.a.	n.a.	n.a.	56.35	n.a.	n.a.	n.a.	69.86	46.02	47.71	48.74	43.11
				(0.53)				(0.28)			(0.90)	(0.40)
P2	n.a.	n.a.	n.a.	40.54	n.a.	n.a.	n.a.	58.66	30.39	31.85	32.48	27.66
				(0.50)				(0.28)			(0.82)	(0.34)

Notes: Poverty indices are calculated using the moderate poverty line and are based on income data for cities and towns, expenditure data for rural areas, and mixed income-expenditure data for total Bolivia. Standard deviations in brackets. Results for the extreme poverty line are shown in Appendix Table B.4.
Source: Own calculations based on ECH, EIH, and DHS.

1.3.2 Poverty and Inequality Trends

To extend our illustration, we provide different analyses of poverty trends between 1989 and 1999.[22] We start our empirical analysis with a disaggregation of the poverty headcount by place of residence and household characteristics in Table 1.5. Between 1989 and 1999, total Bolivia experienced a significant decrease in the incidence of poverty. Moderate poverty decreased from three-quarters to two-thirds of the population. The reduction in extreme poverty was even more spectacular; it decreased from 55 to less than 40 percent.[23]

As expected, rural households were more likely to be poor than those in cities and towns even after controlling for local cost-of-living differences. What is more of concern is that rural households did not fully participate in the reduction of moderate poverty between 1989 and 1999. Cities and towns could reduce the incidence of moderate poverty by 16 and 11 percentage points, respectively. In rural areas, this reduction was only 4 percentage points—despite starting from a higher level of poverty.[24] Furthermore, poverty in rural areas increased between 1989 and 1994 contrary to the trends in cities and towns.[25] Taken together, the poverty trends suggest that rural areas were quite detached from improvements and deteriorations in the overall economic environment.

Lower incomes and thus higher poverty in rural areas is driven by either endowment or return-to-covariate effects. Thus, over time, rural areas could catch up either if the endowments of rural people increased for those variables contributing positively to income (e.g., more education), or if national-wide the coefficients changed in favor of those abundant in rural areas (e.g., belonging to an indigenous group). In Section 1.2, we assumed that the absolute difference in the regression coefficients between cities and towns and between cities and rural areas remained constant between 1989 and 1999. If this assumption does not hold the small decline in poverty would either be understated or (which would be even more worrisome) overstated. For example, if the coefficients in rural areas deteriorated relative to those in urban areas (thus the absolute difference became wider, e.g., the returns to tertiary education increased more for urban than for rural areas), the decline in poverty in rural areas shown in the subsequent analysis would be

[22]For results on pro-poor growth using in addition the 4th round (Nov. 2002) of the Encuesta Continua de Hogares (ECH), see Grosse et al. (2007).

[23]In the late 1990s, the poverty trend reversed and the incidence of moderate and extreme poverty in total Bolivia started to increase again (Grosse et al., 2007).

[24]That is, in relative terms, the performance of rural areas was even worse. Concerning extreme poverty, rural areas also experienced the lowest absolute (!) reduction of the poverty headcount index between 1989 and 1999.

[25]By contrast, households in cities were most affected by the economic downturn in the late 1990s, leading to an increase of moderate and extreme poverty in total Bolivia between 1999 and 2002 (Grosse et al., 2007).

Table 1.5: Poverty Profiles, by Income, 1989, 1994, 1998/9

	Moderate Poverty			Extreme Poverty		
	1989	1994	1998/9	1989	1994	1998/9
Total	76.10	72.44	65.21	54.92	51.99	38.35
	(0.53)	(0.42)		(0.62)	(0.40)	
By Region						
City	67.07	59.56	51.05	39.11	28.90	24.22
Town	80.21	73.42	69.09	59.43	50.97	34.31
	(1.26)	(1.16)		(1.44)	(1.14)	
Rural	87.96	90.23	83.37	71.87	80.85	59.98
	(0.70)	(0.43)		(0.92)	(0.47)	
By Department						
Chuquisaca	87.41	85.87	84.15	71.76	73.31	64.34
	(0.97)	(0.97)		(1.28)	(1.06)	
La Paz	77.73	69.96	68.55	55.90	48.59	46.33
	(1.07)	(0.82)		(1.22)	(0.89)	
Cochabamba	73.21	75.50	64.69	50.64	53.69	31.70
	(1.19)	(1.10)		(1.48)	(1.20)	
Oruro	82.13	81.35	68.64	63.33	65.46	47.63
	(1.16)	(1.19)		(1.41)	(1.27)	
Potosi	91.44	87.90	84.66	82.05	79.62	63.01
	(0.85)	(0.91)		(1.14)	(0.99)	
Tarija	81.26	81.49	61.68	60.00	58.95	26.39
	(1.18)	(1.12)		(1.46)	(1.19)	
Santa Cruz	60.30	57.20	50.59	33.28	30.79	21.66
	(1.22)	(1.10)		(1.38)	(0.90)	
Beni & Pando	78.43	77.95	53.00	54.83	55.49	14.73
	(1.16)	(1.32)		(1.48)	(1.59)	
By age of household head						
≤ 34	78.25	73.77	67.29	56.64	51.22	39.02
	(0.88)	(0.70)		(1.05)	(0.81)	
35–49	76.07	73.23	66.97	55.44	53.75	40.43
	(0.84)	(0.64)		(0.95)	(0.60)	
50–65	74.01	68.18	57.86	52.33	48.91	31.56
	(1.18)	(1.09)		(1.32)	(0.97)	
≥ 66	70.73	70.80	63.66	49.79	54.38	39.13
	(2.25)	(1.85)		(2.26)	(1.70)	
By household size						
≤ 3	70.94	62.24	47.35	46.99	40.02	22.02
	(1.29)	(0.95)		(1.55)	(0.86)	
4–6	73.46	71.62	61.01	51.45	50.64	34.28
	(0.79)	(0.63)		(0.86)	(0.58)	
≥ 7	84.54	83.51	80.35	66.77	65.85	52.61
	(0.82)	(0.75)		(1.03)	(0.85)	

continued on next page

Table 1.5 continued

	Moderate Poverty			Extreme Poverty		
	1989	1994	1998/9	1989	1994	1998/9
By percent of household members between 15 and 65 years						
≤ 50	82.31	81.52	74.93	63.00	62.00	48.79
	(0.65)	(0.54)		(0.80)	(0.56)	
> 50	67.59	60.90	53.64	43.86	39.27	25.91
	(0.82)	(0.64)		(0.95)	(0.56)	
By language of household head						
Spanish	70.10	63.34	51.27	46.16	38.08	22.27
	(0.67)	(0.55)		(0.71)	(0.53)	
Indigenous	93.27	93.72	79.75	80.01	84.51	55.11
	(0.71)	(0.49)		(1.12)	(0.65)	
By gender of household head						
Male	76.67	73.14	65.64	55.89	53.06	38.82
	(0.56)	(0.47)		(0.67)	(0.45)	
Female	73.17	69.07	62.82	49.98	46.83	35.73
	(1.49)	(1.11)		(1.63)	(1.10)	
By average years of schooling of adults						
≤ 5	89.70	89.20	86.04	72.49	75.63	61.53
	(0.60)	(0.51)		(0.92)	(0.60)	
6–12	68.50	67.56	63.14	42.10	40.78	32.01
	(0.97)	(0.70)		(1.01)	(0.68)	
≥ 13	33.82	28.92	20.11	13.41	10.19	4.65
	(1.94)	(1.47)		(1.45)	(1.03)	
By profession of principal wage earner						
White-Collar	49.47	37.30	33.84	26.49	16.18	14.82
Worker	(1.48)	(1.25)		(1.32)	(0.97)	
Blue-Collar	78.15	74.04	69.23	53.41	46.40	30.80
Worker	(1.03)	(0.85)		(1.22)	(0.97)	
Agriculture	92.53	94.15	88.11	79.45	87.69	65.56
	(0.68)	(0.38)		(1.07)	(0.50)	
Sales and	68.63	63.43	53.30	42.42	34.37	29.74
Services	(1.43)	(1.30)		(1.57)	(1.19)	
Not	80.61	72.86	53.82	58.31	46.66	32.02
Employed	(1.42)	(1.66)		(1.77)	(1.66)	
By percent of adult women in employment						
> 0	59.22	70.36	63.95	34.95	51.90	37.27
	(1.08)	(0.50)		(1.09)	(0.47)	
0	83.33	76.80	67.95	63.48	52.18	40.69
	(0.55)	(0.68)		(0.73)	(0.88)	

Notes: Poverty indices are calculated using mixed income-expenditure data. Standard deviations (calculated using the 200 samples of predicted income values applying Equations 1.1 to 1.5) in brackets. For the category schooling: Adult women aged between 15 and 49 and their husbands and partners. For the category wage earner: In the case of DHS, husband or partner of the oldest woman aged between 15 and 49. If she is single, this women herself. In case of LSMS, household head. For the category female employment: Women aged between 15 and 49.
Source: Own calculations based on ECH, EIH, and DHS.

overstated. We address this potential bias in Section 1.4. Another factor that may contribute to overstating the decline in poverty—albeit in this case not limited to rural areas—is that the degree of underreporting, which is common to all income and expenditure surveys, may have fallen over time due to improvements in the questionnaire design.[26] Taken together, we, thus, treat the reduction in poverty as an upper bound, particularly so in rural areas.[27]

There are also substantial differences in the incidence of poverty across the nine departments of Bolivia (Table 1.5). The moderate poverty headcount in 1989 ranged from 60 percent in Santa Cruz to 91 percent in Potosi. The corresponding figures for the extreme poverty headcount were 33 percent and 82 percent, respectively. The departmental distribution of the poverty headcount was also very stable in Bolivia. While Santa Cruz, which is a major host of commercial agriculture and food-processing industry, had the lowest incidence of poverty throughout the entire observation period, it was highest in Potosi, followed by Chuquisaca, which are particularly dependent on subsistence agriculture.

When looking at household characteristics, one of the mayor determinants of poverty is household size with poverty increasing in line with increasing numbers of family members. The higher the share of working-aged members to overall members is, the lower is poverty. The relation of the age of the household head and poverty follows a u-shaped trend with the cohort of 50–65 years olds being the ones with the lowest poverty incidence. Clearly to be seen is that indigenous households are much poorer than Spanish-speaking ones. As observed in several studies for Latin American countries (Marcoux, 1998), households with a female head seem to be less poor than those with a male head. Increasing education has a very strong poverty-decreasing effect. The same holds for the sector of employment of the principal wage earner where high-skilled professionals have a much lower poverty incidence than other groups. Working in agriculture is correlated with the highest poverty incidence. Female participation in the labor force reduces poverty.

1.3.3 Pro-Poor Growth

To evaluate whether the simulated income changes over time were "pro-poor" in the sense that the poor benefited more from economic growth than the rich, we apply the methodology of growth incidence curves (GIC) developed by Ravallion

[26]Of course, and that is what the evidence mainly suggests, the degree of underreporting might have risen over time. Taking our data for Bolivia, underreporting seems to have fallen from 1989 to 1999, see Chapter 1.4.1 and especially Table 1.7 where the ratio of household survey to national accounts mean increases from 0.7 to 0.8 (LSMS) or even 0.9 (DHS) over time.

[27]For a literature overview of other studies on poverty in Bolivia, see Spatz (2006).

and Chen (2003).[28] Comparing two periods, $t-1$ and t, the growth incidence curve plots the cumulative share of the population (depicted on the x-axis) against the income growth rate of the pth quantile (depicted on the y-axis) when the population quantiles are ranked in ascending order of their income. It is given by

$$GIC := g_t(p) = \frac{y_t(p)}{y_{t-1}(p)} - 1 = \frac{\mu_t}{\mu_{t-1}} \cdot \frac{L_t'(p)}{L_{t-1}'(p)} - 1, \tag{1.6}$$

where $L'(p)$ is the slope of the Lorenz curve at the pth quantile, and μ is the mean income. It can be shown that the area under the GIC up to the poverty headcount H gives (minus one times) the rate of change of the Watts index over time

$$-\frac{dW_t}{dt} = \int_0^{H_t} \frac{d\log y_t(p)}{dt} \cdot dp = \int_0^{H_t} g_t(p) \cdot dp. \tag{1.7}$$

The desirable axiomatic properties of the Watts index motivate us to evaluate the "pro-poorness" of economic growth by comparing the growth rate in mean income (GRIM) with the mean of the income growth rates of the poor which Ravallion and Chen (2003) coined the "pro-poor growth rate" (PPGR) which is evaluated at the headcount of the first year, thus evaluated at H_{t-1}:

$$PPGR := \frac{1}{H_t} \cdot \int_0^{H_t} g_t(p) \cdot dp. \tag{1.8}$$

The comparison of the growth rates is shown in Table 1.6. Between 1989 and 1999, economic growth in Bolivia can be classified as pro-poor following the baseline scenario (first column labeled "base"). For both poverty lines and for all three regions, the PPGR exceeded the GRIM suggesting that economic growth was accompanied by falling inequality. For all regions, the income distribution of 1999 first-order dominates the income distribution of 1989 as shown by the GIC which lies above 0 for all p (Figure 1.2).[29] For rural areas, this condition is met at least for all poor. Abstracting from individual income mobility across quantiles, the welfare of all citizens in cities and of all poor citizens in the rest of the country improved during the 1990s.[30]

Taken together, economic growth in Bolivia has been pro-poor since 1989, also so in rural areas. This result seems to be at odds with Table 1.5 which shows

[28] An overview over alternative approaches of measuring pro-poor growth can be found in Klasen (2004) and Son (2003).

[29] For some regions only the first percentile shows a negative growth rate. This, however, is mainly a problem of measurement error at the tails of the distribution since the results are sensitive to outliers which are likely to be found at the tails of the distribution.

[30] For results on pro-poor growth between 1999 and 2002, see Grosse et al. (2007).

only slowly falling poverty rates in rural areas since 1989. However, this puzzle resolves when taking into account that the depth of poverty in rural areas is so large that even substantial pro-poor growth did not lift the poor above the poverty line.[31] Hence, the prime concern is not that economic growth in the 1990s was anti-poor, but that it was so low and that the initial income inequality was so high that the poor remained poor despite some welfare improvements. For Bolivia with these unfavorable initial conditions it would take another decade of the given economic growth rate to make serious inroads into poverty.

Table 1.6: Annual Average Income Growth per Capita, 1989–1999

	1989–1998/9						
	base	a.dum	a.na	con01	div01	con05	div05
	Total Bolivia						
GRIM	2.16	1.61	0.80	2.01	1.92	2.10	1.65
PPGR mod.	2.91	1.86	1.14	2.65	2.12	3.76	1.09
PPGR extr.	3.05	1.85	1.19	2.79	2.10	4.25	0.82
	City						
GRIM	2.01	2.01	1.89	2.01	2.01	2.01	2.01
PPGR mod.	2.53	2.53	2.56	2.53	2.53	2.53	2.53
PPGR extr.	2.48	2.47	2.51	2.48	2.47	2.48	2.48
	Town						
GRIM	2.85	2.34	1.12	2.74	2.54	2.87	1.86
PPGR mod.	5.25	4.61	2.47	5.39	4.45	7.40	2.68
PPGR extr.	5.87	5.19	2.85	6.09	4.95	8.55	2.87
	Rural						
GRIM	0.46	-1.43	-1.26	-0.26	-0.56	0.09	-1.42
PPGR mod.	1.86	-0.05	0.10	1.51	0.53	3.56	-1.31
PPGR extr.	1.95	0.01	0.30	1.64	0.55	3.99	-1.48

Notes: Annual average income growth rates are calculated using income data for cities and towns, expenditure data for rural areas, and mixed income-expenditure data for total Bolivia. For 1989, only the data for cities can be taken from the LSMS. All other growth rates are calculated using the DHS of 1989. GRIM: growth rate in mean; PPGR (mod. and extr.): (moderate and extreme) pro-poor growth rate; base: baseline scenario. The different adjustment procedures are explained in Chapter 1.4. The abbreviations stand for: a.dum: adjustment of regional dummies; a.na: adjustment to national accounts; con01 (con05): convergence scenario with range of $\phi = 1 \pm 0.1(0.5)$; div01 (div05): divergence scenario(s) with range of $\phi = 1 \pm 0.1(0.5)$.
Source: Own calculations based on ECH, EIH, and DHS.

[31] But it did reduce the poverty gap in rural areas, results not shown here.

Figure 1.2: Growth Incidence Curves, 1989–1999

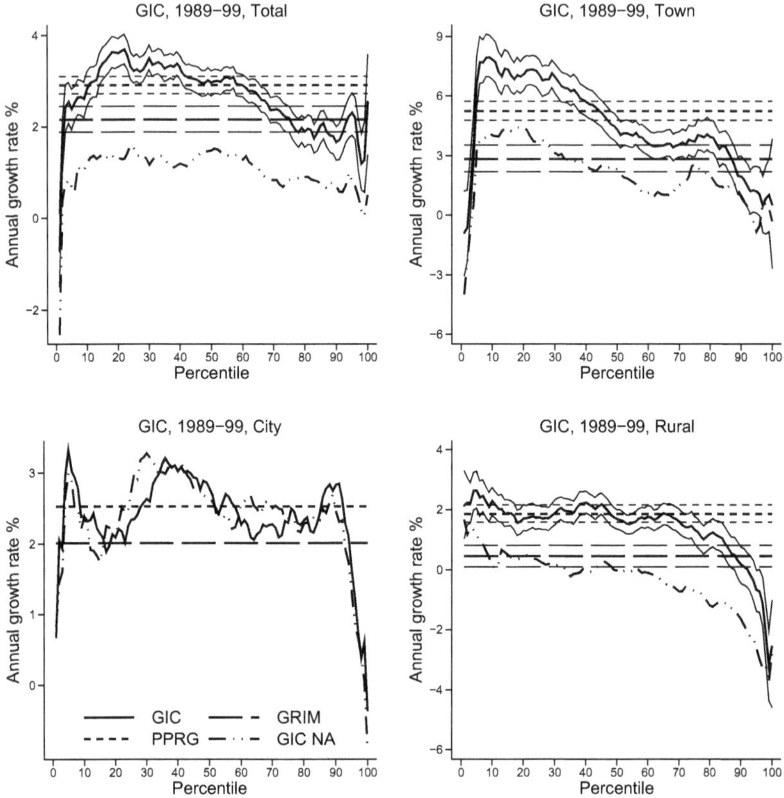

Notes: The 90% "confidence intervals" for GIC, GRIM, and PPGR are calculated using the 200 simulation runs. Thus, they are based on the variances resulting from repeating Equation 1.2 and especially Equation 1.5 for 200 times for the two years (1989 and 1999), calculating based on these 200 sets of income 200 values for GIC, GRIM, and PPGR, respectively. For these 200 values of GIC, GRIM, and PPGR, the 90% CIs are calculated using the standard formulas for confidence intervals. GIC: growth incidence curve; GRIM: growth rate in mean; PPGR: pro-poor growth rate (moderate poverty line); GIC NA: based on the adjustment to departmental national accounts as described in Section 1.4.1. For GIC NA, no CI are shown for better visuality of the graphs. For cities, no CIs are necessary since they are based on observed data from EIH and ECH.
Source: Own calculations based on ECH, EIH, and DHS.

1.4 Sensitivity Analyses

1.4.1 Disaggregated Data on GDP

One basic problem with the simulated data is that there are hardly any possibilities to cross-check the results with any other data source. National accounts are one option but, as mentioned before, not available for the urban–rural divide. The only data available is GDP per capita at the departmental level. To get an idea about the plausibility of our results, we compare national account data with the results from the LSMS and DHS household surveys. Furthermore, we try to impute national account information for cities, towns, and rural areas separately (Section 1.4.2).

The national account series available to us is compared to the original LSMS data and simulated DHS data in the upper part of Table 1.7 ("original data").[32] As mentioned above, it is not a priory clear if household survey data is inferior in quality compared to national account data.[33] What becomes clear from the table is that, as expected, household survey data shows lower values compared to national account data. What also becomes obvious is that this difference is not stable over time and that it is not the same for all departments. For total Bolivia, the relation between DHS and national account data is 0.72 in 1989, goes down to 0.68 in 1994, and increases to 0.94 in 1998. Especially the latter value is pretty high, also compared to the value of 0.81 for the LSMS of 1999.

For the departments, the relation is between 0.42 up to values close to 1. For the DHS, some values are even above 1. Obviously, there seem to be some differences between the three data sources. This becomes especially clear when looking at the ranking of departments and the difference of this ranking between household surveys and national accounts. There are 2 or 3 departments for which our simulated and observed data differ strongly from the national account data. First, La Paz appears to be richer when looking at household surveys compared to national accounts. The difference in ranking is very high, for example in 1994, La Paz is the third poorest department looking at national accounts but the second richest looking at DHS data. Another extreme case is Oruro, which is throughout the whole decade the second or third richest department on national account data but the third poorest on household survey data. Furthermore, the different dynamics of Beni and Pando cannot be taken into account correctly since their values cannot be separated in the household surveys. Pando seems to be richer and also more dynamic than Beni. However, both departments account for only less than

[32]Note that the household surveys are not meant to be representative at this level, but for a first check, it generates some intuition for possible problems of the household survey data.

[33]For example, national accounts are standardized and include imputed rents, while surveys better capture activities in the informal sector. There is a whole strand of literature dealing with this issue, see, for example, Ravallion (2003) or Deaton (2005).

Table 1.7: Subnational Income from NA, LSMS, and DHS, 1989–1999

	1989		1994		1998/9		
	NA	DHS	NA	DHS	NA	DHS	LSMS
				Original data			
Total Bolivia	306	219	309	209	330	302	266
City		312		323		411	379
Town		197		210		273	259
Rural		117		72		134	112
Chuquisaca	281	134	252	125	300	187	145
La Paz	268	201	289	224	280	253	256
Cochabamba	318	241	329	195	360	319	262
Oruro	346	161	339	143	418	231	195
Potosi	196	102	165	90	192	162	127
Tarija	322	193	316	161	382	390	254
Santa Cruz	401	348	394	310	399	442	377
Beni	316	214	311	185	329	320	338
Pando	346	214	375	185	501	320	338
				Adjusted data			
Total Bolivia		299		308		331	328
City	385	421	419	463	443	453	461
Town	326	279	352	361	359	290	316
Rural	217	165	240	106	273	144	147
Chuquisaca		270		240		293	300
La Paz		257		285		274	280
Cochabamba		315		337		357	360
Oruro		344		352		427	418
Potosi		198		171		186	192
Tarija		317		339		376	382
Santa Cruz		408		384		423	399
Beni		336		295		347	329
Pando		336		295		347	329

Notes: Monthly per capita income, in constant Bolivianos (1995). Beni and Pando are not separated in the LSMS and DHS questionnaires, so the values hold for both departments. National accounts (NA) are not imputed for city/town/rural for the 1998 data, instead values of 1999 are shown.
Source: Own calculations based on ECH, EIH, DHS, and NA.

1 percent (Pando) and 4.5 percent (Beni) of the total population. For the other departments, our simulation is pretty close to the national accounts concerning the ranking. Another general difference is, as mentioned above, that the DHS simulation for 1998 is higher in nearly all departments compared to the LSMS data

of 1999 (except for Beni). The only strong difference between LSMS and DHS in ranking of departments is Tarija for which the DHS shows the second highest value and for the LSMS only the sixth. When looking at national accounts and DHS from earlier years, the lower rank seems to be more plausible, i.e., in the middle of the distribution rather than one of the richest departments. The overall poorest department according to all three data sets and showing hardly any growth is Potosi.

For a first sensitivity analysis, we adjust the LSMS and DHS data to the national accounts, however done at the level of the departments rather than at the national income level (as often done in the literature). Adjusting to the departmental level might be slightly less problematic than to overall national accounts because it takes some region-specific income dynamics and differences into account, but doubts remain about the correspondence of national accounts and participation of private households in GDP (Stifel and Christiaensen, 2007). This is also true at the departmental level, but maybe to a lesser extent. Results on pro-poor growth of this exercise can be found in Table 1.6, column "a.na" (third column, the abbreviation stands for adjustment to national accounts) as well as in Figure 1.2. Growth remains pro-poor, however the growth rates are becoming smaller because the distance of household surveys to national accounts was wider in the earlier years, so closing this distance automatically decreases growth rates.[34]

1.4.2 Regional Differentials in Sectoral Participation

The differences in our results compared to national accounts motivate us to conduct one further sensitivity analyses with this data at hand since we want to focus somewhat more strongly on the urban–rural divide. For this, we use sectoral GDP and employment shares in sectors to break down the national account data to the urban–rural divide.

We have made a rather simple calculation to break down the data to the urban–rural divide, illustrated in Table 1.8. The data for the 3 points in time available is (i) total sectoral GDP $Y_{s_1,s_2,\ldots s_n}$ (from the national accounts), (ii) population shares in cities, towns, and rural areas $p_{c,t,r}$ (from the three DHS rounds and from the 1999 LSMS) from which the total population per area $P_{c,t,r}$ can be obtained by simply multiplying the shares with the total population of Bolivia (from Census or WDI data), and (iii) employment shares by sector of the population for all three regions $e_{s_{c,t,r}}$ (from the LSMS data, only available for 1999) from which the total

[34]For the time period from 1999 to 2002, household surveys underestimated incomes compared to the national accounts even more, so that the negative growth during this time span would turn positive using the adjustment to national accounts (results not shown in the table).

number of people working in sector and area $E_{s_{c,t,r}}$ can be calculated by simply multiplying e with P for sector and region.

Table 1.8: Illustration of Income Imputation Using Sectoral Participation

	Population share p	Empl. in sector 1 e_{s1}	Empl. in sector 2 e_{s2}
City c	0.5	0.03	0.97
Town t	0.1	0.12	0.88
Rural r	0.4	0.83	0.17
	Population	GDP in sector 1	GDP in sector 1
Total	7,000	300,000	2,700,000

Notes: The illustration is not representing Bolivian data.
Source: Own compilation.

So if we impute the per capita income in, for example, cities, $y_c = (\sum_s Y_c)/(P_c)$, we derive this from $Y_c = \sum_s P_{s_c} \cdot y_s$, where y_s is the per capita income per sector $y_s = (P_{s_{c,t,r}})/(Y_s)$. In the simple illustration in Table 1.8, this means that the per capita income in cities, y_c = 587, can be derived from knowing the number of people living in cities P_c = 3,500 and knowing how many people of those work in the two sectors (Sector 1, say agriculture, E_{s1} = 105 and Sector 2, say industry, E_{s2} = 3,395) and deriving the per capita income that can be earned in each sector $y_{s1} = 119$ and $y_{s2} = 601$.

Table 1.7, lower part "adjusted data", shows that the relation of national account data to household survey data is higher in cities (around 0.8) than in towns (between 0.6 and 0.7) and way higher than in rural areas (between 0.3 and 0.5) when comparing the original data in the upper part of Table 1.7 with the adjusted data for national accounts in the lower part. The finding of lower household survey mean compared to national account mean holds for LSMS as well as DHS data. One of the basic assumptions of our dynamic cross-survey microsimulation methodology is that the absolute difference in the regression coefficients between cities and towns and cities and rural areas remained constant between 1989 and 1999. We present two additional methods to model relative changes in returns to covariates in which the constancy assumption is relaxed, the first using urban-rural growth differential from national account data.[35]

The first very simple method does the following: The constancy-of-differences assumption of the basic model implies that the widening of the urban–rural divide between 1989 and 1999 is, thus, entirely attributed (a) to changes in the endowment of covariates favoring urban areas, and (b) to nationwide changes in the

[35]Explicitly testing these modeling exercises is only possible using data from the DHS 2003 so that out of sample predictions become possible. This is done in **Essay 2**.

return to covariates favoring those covariates which are relatively abundant in urban areas. If this assumption does not hold, i.e., if additionally (c) the returns to covariates in rural areas deteriorated relative to those in urban areas, the widening of the urban–rural divide would be understated. To get an idea of the possible size of this bias we have to simulate the opposite scenario where we assume that the widening of the urban–rural divide between 1989 and 1999 is entirely due to deteriorating returns to covariates in rural areas relative to those in urban areas. Adjusting Equation (1.4) leads to:

$$\beta_{t-1}^{R} = \beta_{t-1}^{C} + (\beta_t^R - \beta_t^C) + Ad_{growth} \tag{1.9}$$

where Ad_{growth} stands for the adjustment of the growth differential. Since it is a priori not clear which covariates are affected and to what extent, we take a rather simple approach and attribute the regional growth differentials in GDP per capita to growth differentials in the regression coefficients of the regional dummies, so only the regional dummies ($\beta_0^{T,R}$) are adjusted.

This sensitivity analysis proceeds in three steps. First, we impute the 1989–to–1994 and the 1994–to–1999 cumulative growth differentials in GDP per capita between cities on the one hand and towns and rural areas on the other hand.[36] We find that the economic growth performance was nearly identical across the three regions in the first half of observation period, but differed substantially thereafter.

Between 1989 and 1994, citics (cumulatively) grew by only 0.1 and 0.2 percent faster than towns and rural areas, respectively. The corresponding figures for the period from 1994 to 1999 are about 2 and 9 percent, respectively. Second, we sterilize the growth differentials in GDP per capita by adding for towns and for rural areas the 1994–to–1999 growth differential in GDP per capita (relative to cities) to the 1994 regression coefficient of the corresponding regional dummy, and sum of the 1989–to–1994 and the 1994–to–1999 growth differential in GDP per capita (relative to cities) to the 1989 regression coefficient of the corresponding regional dummy. Third, we partially re-run our simulation with the adjusted coefficients to generate an adjusted spatial disaggregation of pro-poor growth in Bolivia (Table 1.6, second column "a.dum", which stands for adjustment via dummy correction).

Comparing the results (column "a.dum") with the corresponding entries of the baseline scenario in Table 1.6 (column "base") reveals that the bias of neglecting

[36]We impute, as explained above, the separate growth rates of GDP per capita for cities, towns, and rural areas by multiplying for each economic sector the average annual growth rate of value added per capita over the respective period (taken from the national accounts) by the employment shares of those sectors in cities, towns, and rural areas, respectively (estimated from the LSMS 1999). Note that this is a constancy assumption as well. Here, employment shares do not change over time.

a possible deterioration of the returns to covariates in rural areas relative to those in urban areas is evident when applying this simple method of modeling changes in relative returns. Including the regional growth differentials in GDP per capita decreases income in rural areas and less so in towns in 1989 compared to the baseline estimation, so that the GRIM and PPGR are lower. Due to lower growth in rural areas and towns, (mean) growth in total Bolivia is now smaller between 1989 and 1999, and the growth is also less pro-poor as the rate of growth in rural areas, whose population predominates among the poor, is now estimated to have been lower. But the qualitative results from above do not change: We find that growth and pro-poor growth are somewhat smaller in total Bolivia and more significantly so in rural areas which even experienced negative mean income growth between 1989 and 1999; but the PPGR remain higher, however very small, suggesting that the poor were able to make only few gains over the period.

1.4.3 Mobility Assumption

In the second sensitivity analysis for relaxing the assumption of constancy of the distance between urban and non-urban areas we do not make a priory assumptions about the changes in relative returns to covariates, but we generate a "mobility" scenario around the baseline scenario.[37] We again recall the constancy assumption in Equation (1.4) and rearrange it in the following way:

$$\beta_{t-1}^R = \beta_{t-1}^C + (\beta_t^R - \beta_t^C) \implies (\beta_{t-1}^R - \beta_{t-1}^C) = \phi(\beta_t^R - \beta_t^C) \qquad (1.10)$$

where ϕ is the "mobility" parameter. In our baseline scenario, ϕ is equal to 1, thus absolute changes of the coefficients remain constant between the regions, here exemplarily only for cities versus rural areas.

As an illustration, let us assume that we observe a coefficient β_E for tertiary education of $\beta_{E,t}^R = 0.4$ and $\beta_{E,t}^C = 0.9$, which leads to an absolute difference of –0.5 in t, and that we observe $\beta_{E,t-1}^C = 0.8$ for $t-1$. What we have done in the baseline regression was to assume "no mobility" in the sense that the absolute difference stays constant over time which would be fulfilled for a coefficient of $\beta_{E,t-1}^R = 0.3$. If we assume that the difference decreases over time (which would for example be fulfilled for $\beta_{E,t-1}^R = 0.2$), we think of this as "mobility" in the sense of converging or becoming more similar over time. This leads to a greater absolute difference of –0.6 in $t-1$, and the mobility parameter takes a value $\phi = 1.2 > 1$. If we assume the opposite in the sense of divergence or dissimilarity the absolute difference has to increase, from for example –0.2 in $t-1$ for $\beta_{E,t-1}^R = 0.6$ which leads to $\phi = 0.4 < 1$.

[37] We thank Martin Ravallion for this suggestion.

As mentioned above, there is no way to know the exact structure of change of relative returns over time, especially because this change will be different of magnitude and even sign for each coefficient.[38] We present two different assumptions, one of a weak mobility scenario of $\phi = 1 \pm 0.1$ and of a strong mobility scenario of $\phi = 1 \pm 0.5$. The results on moderate poverty of this exercise are shown in Table 1.9 (for extreme poverty and inequality, see Appendix Tables B.6 and B.7). It is only relevant for towns and rural areas in 1989 and 1994 (and also for the aggregate data for total Bolivia), so for comparison, the baseline scenario (no mobility) is copied from Table 1.4 (and Appendix Tables B.4 and B.5).

Overall the results for poverty and inequality are pretty stable. The weak scenario generates a mobility band around the point estimate of about 1 percentage point or even less for all poverty measures. This holds for both poverty lines and for both years. Of course, the strong mobility scenario results in a broader band, and differences get larger in 1994, especially for P1 and P2. The deviations are not symmetric which is caused by the above explained non-linear relation between y and $\ln y$. Looking at inequality, the results are similar. Again, for the weak mobility scenario, the inequality indicators assuming no mobility do not differ too much from the mobility results. However, results are more sensitive to the strong assumption and also to the more sensitive Atkinson indices, especially to A(2.0). In summary, the results are stable and convincing, because even with the stronger assumption of $\phi = 1 \pm 0.5$ and the more sensitive indicators (P2 and A(2.0)), the trends in poverty and inequality remain. The same holds for the results on pro-poor growth. In Table 1.6, the columns labeled "con01–div05" show the results. As expected the "convergence" scenarios give stronger evidence of pro-poor growth and the "divergence" scenarios give lower growth rates compared to the baseline assumptions.

[38] See **Essay 2** for results on ϕ over time.

Table 1.9: Moderate Poverty: Mobility Assumptions, 1989 and 1994

	1989					1994				
	Convergence		Divergence		No mobility	Convergence		Divergence		No mobility
	ϕ=1.1	ϕ=1.5	ϕ=0.9	ϕ=0.5	ϕ=1.0	ϕ=1.1	ϕ=1.5	ϕ=0.9	ϕ=0.5	ϕ=1.0
					Total Bolivia					
P0	75.35	75.63	75.08	73.98	76.10	72.24	72.40	72.07	71.28	72.44
	(0.47)	(0.47)	(0.47)	(0.49)	(0.53)	(0.43)	(0.42)	(0.43)	(0.45)	(0.42)
P1	43.68	45.75	42.49	39.81	44.45	46.22	48.37	44.75	40.57	45.28
	(0.33)	(0.32)	(0.34)	(0.35)	(0.35)	(0.24)	(0.24)	(0.25)	(0.26)	(0.22)
P2	29.80	32.39	28.42	25.60	30.48	35.25	38.41	33.18	27.75	33.95
	(0.29)	(0.29)	(0.30)	(0.30)	(0.31)	(0.19)	(0.19)	(0.20)	(0.21)	(0.19)
					Town					
P0	79.74	80.44	79.17	77.17	80.21	73.44	73.60	73.20	71.91	73.42
	(1.24)	(1.19)	(1.32)	(1.40)	(1.26)	(1.28)	(1.18)	(1.35)	(1.42)	(1.16)
P1	49.72	53.12	47.81	43.53	49.66	44.27	47.34	42.47	38.19	43.40
	(0.92)	(0.86)	(0.95)	(0.99)	(0.87)	(0.79)	(0.75)	(0.81)	(0.83)	(0.64)
P2	35.85	40.02	33.63	29.06	35.58	31.78	35.71	29.58	24.69	30.66
	(0.82)	(0.79)	(0.83)	(0.84)	(0.79)	(0.63)	(0.61)	(0.63)	(0.64)	(0.55)
					Rural Areas					
P0	86.49	86.96	85.97	83.86	87.96	90.34	90.68	90.00	88.40	90.23
	(0.62)	(0.57)	(0.65)	(0.79)	(0.70)	(0.44)	(0.39)	(0.48)	(0.54)	(0.43)
P1	54.90	59.01	52.54	47.22	56.35	71.35	75.82	68.21	59.06	69.86
	(0.51)	(0.46)	(0.53)	(0.58)	(0.53)	(0.26)	(0.23)	(0.28)	(0.34)	(0.28)
P2	39.31	44.45	36.57	30.96	40.54	60.82	67.53	56.30	44.18	58.66
	(0.51)	(0.48)	(0.52)	(0.52)	(0.50)	(0.25)	(0.22)	(0.27)	(0.31)	(0.28)

Notes: The mobility parameter comes from $(\beta^R_{t-1} - \beta^C_{t-1}) = \phi(\beta^R_t - \beta^C_t)$. See Chapter 1.4.3 for explanation. Standard deviations in brackets. Results for the extreme poverty line are shown in the Appendix Table B.6 and for inequality in Appendix Table B.7.
Source: Own calculations based on ECH, EIH, and DHS.

1.5 The Asset Index Approach

The asset-index approach to construct national time series of basic poverty measures goes back to Filmer and Pritchett (2001) and Sahn and Stifel (2000, 2003). To proxy welfare in the absence of income or expenditure data, they assume that the asset ownership of households closely reflects their living standard. Using DHS data, we define a set of assets[39] and construct a metric asset index

$$AI_j = \frac{s_1(a_{j1} - \overline{a}_1)}{\sigma_1} + \ldots + \frac{s_k(a_{jk} - \overline{a}_k)}{\sigma_k} \tag{1.11}$$

where s_k is the "scoring factor" or the weight of the asset k, a_{jk} takes the value of 1 if household j owns asset k and 0 otherwise, $\overline{a}_k$ is the mean value of a_{jk} over all households, and σ_k is its standard deviation.

Following Filmer and Pritchett (2001), we use the principal component analysis (rather than the closely related factor analysis as in Sahn and Stifel (2000, 2003)) to determine the asset weights s_k. The underlying idea is to find a linear combination of the variables—the principal component or the asset index—which contains most of the common information of the variables and can be interpreted as a background variable contained in all of them.[40] Hence, the asset-index approach is valid if welfare is indeed the main determinant of asset variability among households. We apply the asset-index approach to track the evolution of poverty between period $t-1$ and t. Since the mean value of the asset index is zero by construction, we do not estimate Equation (1.11) for each period separately but over a pooled sample of the periods $t-1$ and t.

In contrast to our dynamic cross-survey microsimulation methodology, the creation of national poverty profiles on the basis of the asset index requires a common set of assets for all observation years.[41] Unfortunately, there was a change in the DHS questionnaire design: the DHS 1994 and 1998 collected information on more and other assets than the DHS 1989.[42] The set of common assets over all Bolivian DHS rounds would have been very small so that we decided to restrict

[39]Our asset definition is rather broad and includes not only real estate and financial assets, but also consumer durables and the household's endowment with human capital.

[40]A more recent method to construct asset indices using polychoric principal component analysis is proposed by Kolenikov and Angeles (2009) and applied in **Essay 4** for Colombia. The innovation is that it is possible to include ordinal variables rather than only dummy variables. For example, in **Essay 4**, we include several ordered categories for wall and floor material rather than just a dummy for good and bad material.

[41]The asset index requires a joint set over time. Furthermore, we have a much smaller set of variables in the asset index, comparing Table 1.10 for the asset index with Table 1.1 for the microsimulation methodology.

[42]The lack of consistency applies especially to consumer durables (Appendix Table B.3).

our empirical analysis to the years 1994–1998. The derivation of the asset index and the summary statistics of the assets included therein are shown in Table 1.10. We use 25 assets—17 tangible assets and 8 human capital variables—to capture the welfare of households.[43] The eigenvalues of the principal component analysis suggest that the asset index is indeed an important determinant for the asset distribution among households. The first principal component explains about 22 percent of total asset variability.

Since all tangible assets are dummy variables, their scoring factors have a simple interpretation. Moving from "non-ownership" to "ownership" of one asset changes the asset index by s_k/σ_k. For example, having private telephone connection increases the asset index by 0.83 in 1994 and 0.59 in 1998.[44] In the case of the human capital variables, s_k/σ_k gives the change in the asset index if the average education of adult household members switches from the reference state "less than complete basic schooling or unknown" to the respective schooling category.

As expected, consumer durables, such as telephone, radio, television, and fridge, have high scoring factors suggesting that they are highly correlated with welfare. By contrast, owning a house or of a plot of agricultural land indicates poverty which can mainly be explained by the widespread subsistence agriculture in rural areas of Bolivia.[45] The quality of the dwelling also reflects the welfare of households. Access to public utilities, high-quality cooking materials, high quality toilet facilities, high-quality floor materials, and a large number of sleeping rooms all increase the asset index. The scoring factors of the human capital variables are more difficult to reconcile. We find negative returns to schooling up to lower secondary schooling (9 years of schooling)[46] which we attribute to that (a) our reference state includes "unknown" and that (b) the returns to basic and secondary schooling are indeed very small in Bolivia.

The asset-index value of the individual household is obtained by multiplying the deviation of the household's asset endowment from the mean asset endowment with the vector of normalized scoring factors according to Equation (1.11). Aggregating the asset-index values over all households, we find the mean asset index increasing from -0.37 in 1994 to 0.38 in 1998, suggesting a favorable trend of the living standard in Bolivia during the observation period. Based on the estimates

[43]To check the robustness of our empirical results, we also estimated the asset index without human capital variables. The empirical results (not shown here) do not change qualitatively.

[44]The reduction in the asset weight reflects the fact that private telephone connection has become more affordable and, thus, more widespread in Bolivia (Appendix Table B.3).

[45]This might sound surprising, but it has to take the reference categories into account. This would be for example being able to rent a flat in cities (as opposed to a small house) or working outside agriculture (as opposed to working on an own piece of land).

[46]Comparing the results with the results for 1994–2003, we find a switching sign for lower secondary schooling for women which is negative for the period 1994–1998 but turned positive for the period including 2003 (results not shown here).

Table 1.10: The Derivation of the Asset Index, 1994 and 1998

	pooled	1994			1998		
	s_k	$\bar{a}_k$	σ_k	s_k/σ_k	$\bar{a}_k$	σ_k	s_k/σ_k
Tangible Assets							
Telephone	0.28	0.11	0.31	0.90	0.25	0.43	0.64
Radio	0.16	0.85	0.36	0.45	0.88	0.32	0.50
Television	0.36	0.58	0.49	0.73	0.68	0.46	0.77
Fridge	0.30	0.30	0.46	0.65	0.38	0.48	0.61
Family Land	-0.29	0.28	0.45	-0.64	0.21	0.41	-0.70
Electricity	0.35	0.68	0.47	0.75	0.76	0.43	0.82
Public Water	0.31	0.56	0.50	0.62	0.70	0.46	0.67
Other Water Source	-0.10	0.14	0.35	-0.29	0.11	0.31	-0.32
Cooking Material	0.35	0.64	0.48	0.72	0.72	0.45	0.77
Shared Toilet	0.08	0.36	0.48	0.16	0.19	0.40	0.19
Private Toilet	0.18	0.24	0.43	0.43	0.48	0.50	0.37
Cement Floor	0.10	0.33	0.47	0.22	0.38	0.48	0.22
Brick Floor	0.04	0.12	0.32	0.13	0.08	0.26	0.15
Other Floor	0.20	0.18	0.38	0.52	0.26	0.44	0.46
2-3 Sleeping Rooms	0.10	0.41	0.49	0.20	0.35	0.48	0.21
$\geq$ 4 Sleeping Rooms	0.12	0.06	0.23	0.50	0.06	0.24	0.48
Human Capital							
% of Men with							
Complete Basic	-0.10	0.12	0.32	-0.31	0.09	0.29	-0.35
Lower Secondary	-0.02	0.14	0.34	-0.07	0.12	0.32	-0.07
Higher Secondary	0.10	0.24	0.43	0.24	0.24	0.42	0.24
Tertiary Education	0.19	0.11	0.31	0.62	0.16	0.36	0.53
% of Women with							
Complete Basic	-0.08	0.12	0.31	-0.25	0.10	0.29	-0.27
Lower Secondary	0.02	0.14	0.33	0.07	0.13	0.32	0.07
Higher Secondary	0.18	0.25	0.41	0.44	0.30	0.43	0.42
Tertiary Education	0.19	0.08	0.25	0.76	0.14	0.32	0.59
Asset Index		-0.41	2.26		0.30	2.32	

Notes: For the explanation of the variables, see Appendix Table B.2. The left-out categories are: open water source, no toilet, earth floor, 0–1 sleeping rooms, no or incomplete basic schooling. The two data sets are joined and the principal component analysis is done over the pooled sample.
Source: Own calculations based on DHS.

of the asset-index values at the household level, we can check the consistency of poverty trends between our dynamic cross-survey microsimulation methodology and the asset-index approach.[47] We construct poverty profiles based on asset-

[47] When we rank the households according to (a) their simulated incomes and (b) their asset-index values and calculate the Spearman rank correlation coefficient between the two welfare

index values and compare them to those in Section 1.3.2. To this end, we rank the households according to their asset-index values and calibrate the thresholds (i.e., poverty lines) between extremely poor, moderately poor, and non-poor so as to ensure that the incidence of poverty at the aggregated national level (i.e., in the first row of the poverty profile) in 1994 coincides with the one of the dynamic cross-survey microsimulation methodology, which is shown in Table 1.5.[48] We keep this threshold level for the asset-index poverty line of 1994 constant and apply it also to the 1998 data. The spatial poverty profile based on asset-index values is shown in Table 1.11.

Although the direction of change and determinants are qualitatively similar to our findings using the microsimulation methodology, there are some differences. The most striking difference between the asset index and the microsimulation methodology is that overall poverty reduction from 1994 to 1998 appears much stronger using the asset index. Keeping the threshold of 1994 constant yields a 5 percentage points higher poverty reduction using the moderate poverty line (from 72 to 65 percent for the income-based approach and to 60 for the asset-based approach) and 2 percentage points using the extreme poverty line compared to the results shown in Table 1.5. We suspect that this sharper reduction in poverty using the asset index is due to a combination of changes in preferences favoring some assets (e.g., televisions), relative price reductions of some assets (e.g., telephones), and public investment in infrastructure or education which have not (yet) translated into income gains. Thus, the sharper poverty reduction using the asset index says more about developments in preferences and in non-income dimensions of well-being than being the most reliable proxy for the income dimension.

Furthermore, taking the corresponding results of the microsimulation methodology in Table 1.5 as reference point, we find that the asset-index approach strongly underpredicts poverty in cities and towns and strongly overpredicts poverty in rural areas. In doing so, the results of the asset-index approach are closer to those of the unsatisfied-basic-needs approach[49] than those of the microsimulation methodology. Additionally, not only the level but also the change in the incidence of poverty is more unevenly distributed across the three areas. While according to the microsimulation methodology rural areas participated—albeit less

indicators we find a close relationship between the simulated incomes and the asset-index values. The Spearman rank correlation coefficient is about 0.8.

[48]The distribution of the assets among extremely poor, moderately poor, and non-poor is given in Appendix Table B.8.

[49]The unsatisfied-basic-needs approach is very similar to the asset-index approach. It generates a weighted average of welfare indicators (e.g., educational attainment, housing quality, access to public utilities, and access to basic health services, in the case of Bolivia) and classifies households as poor if their weighted average indicator value is below a certain threshold. In contrast to the asset-index approach, the indicator weights are set arbitrarily. For a more detailed description of the unsatisfied-basic-needs approach and its application to Bolivia, see Hernany (1999).

than proportionately—in the overall poverty reduction, they experienced nearly no progress in reducing poverty according to the asset-index approach. These dif-

Table 1.11: Poverty Profiles, by Asset Index, 1994 and 1998

	Moderate Poverty		Extreme Poverty	
	1994	1998	1994	1998
Total	72.57	60.07	50.45	36.92
By Region				
City	52.20	38.59	19.91	9.54
Town	70.03	57.25	35.27	23.59
Rural	97.76	97.14	91.66	88.55
By Department				
Chuquisaca	79.42	70.54	69.39	57.82
La Paz	71.45	60.97	47.43	33.62
Cochabamba	75.78	56.71	57.21	37.91
Oruro	72.65	60.55	41.30	29.66
Potosi	84.57	76.77	68.01	55.75
Tarija	67.88	54.86	45.48	35.02
Santa Cruz	63.60	50.88	37.71	26.38
Beni & Pando	81.82	69.41	62.86	50.06
By age of household head				
≤ 34	77.19	70.99	52.64	40.42
35–49	72.42	57.47	50.64	36.43
50–65	65.92	49.59	46.46	32.18
≥ 66	61.65	47.29	46.17	34.43
By household size				
≤ 3	73.32	63.01	49.48	35.70
4–6	69.29	56.44	46.71	33.97
≥ 7	79.22	66.10	59.69	45.31
By percent of household members between 15 and 65 years				
≤ 50	79.49	71.52	58.25	47.72
> 50	63.77	47.53	40.54	25.07
By language of household head				
Spanish	61.37	49.93	33.18	23.21
Indigenous	98.74	97.01	90.82	86.83
By gender of household head				
Male	73.09	61.04	51.42	38.22
Female	70.05	55.49	45.77	30.74
By average years of schooling of adults				
≤ 5	97.27	93.82	83.87	73.45
6–12	64.62	50.85	32.10	21.58
≥ 13	9.60	9.37	1.58	1.96

continued on next page

Table 1.11 continued

	Moderate Poverty		Extreme Poverty	
	1994	1998	1994	1998
By profession of principal wage earner				
White-collar admin.	27.57	18.39	10.90	6.82
Blue-collar admin.	80.65	68.47	46.27	29.28
Agriculture	98.89	96.75	94.52	91.20
Sales and services	64.27	48.85	29.66	15.92
Not employed / DK	54.01	44.13	26.93	19.94

Notes: For the category schooling: Adult women aged between 15 and 49 and their husbands and partners. For the category wage earner: Husband or partner of the oldest woman aged between 15 and 49. If she is single, this women herself. For the category female employment: Women aged between 15 and 49.
Source: Own calculations based on DHS.

ferences are partly due to that only the microsimulation methodology accounts for differences in the local price levels (Table B.1); they also show that progress in improving the asset base in rural areas have been much slower in the 1990s.[50]

By contrast, Table 1.11 shows less variation in the incidence of poverty across departments. The 1994 moderate poverty headcount index ranges only from 66 percent in Santa Cruz and Tarija to 84 percent in Potosi. For comparison, the corresponding figures of the microsimulation methodology were 58 percent and 88 percent, respectively. Concerning the departmental poverty ranking, we find greater consistency between the two approaches.[51] Santa Cruz is the richest department and Potosi and Chuquisaca are the poorest departments. The notable exception is Oruro which is relatively poor according to the microsimulation methodology but relatively rich according to the asset-index approach. Another exception are Beni and Pando which are relatively rich according to the microsimulation but relatively poor according to the asset index.[52]

Concerning household characteristics, some differences are observed compared to the income poverty profiles. For example, medium-sized households are the richest compared to smaller or bigger ones. Furthermore, also the "oldest" households are the richest. However, this might be due to the fact that older households accumulate assets over time which constantly lose value but remain as an

[50]Alternatively, one could estimate the asset index separately for urban and rural ares to better capture the differences.

[51]This result becomes even more obvious when we compare the departmental disaggregation of the poverty headcount by quintiles rather than only at the thresholds between extremely poor, moderately poor, and non-poor (results are not reported here).

[52]For more detailed poverty maps also at regional levels, see Spatz (2006).

item in the household, irrespective of their value. Some characteristics using the asset index are even more strongly indicating poverty, such as ethnicity, gender, schooling, or employment sector.

1.6 Discussion

In this paper, we developed a new methodology to create a national income time series out of incomplete income or expenditure data, and applied it to the case of Bolivia between 1989 and 1999. We show that our extension of the poverty mapping methodology is able to well reproduce trends in poverty where we have comparable data. As such it is of considerable use for situations where nationally representative income surveys are lacking, but urban income surveys are available and can be combined DHS data. With this method it should be possible to generate longer time series of poverty and inequality than is currently possible for most Latin American and many African countries.

The methodology also appears superior to the use of asset indices for measuring trends in poverty which might more reflect changes in preferences, prices, and non-income indicators. Furthermore, standard asset indices, for example using principal component analysis, attach weights that are "relative in a double sense": First, the weights are relative to mean ownership ($\overline{a}$), thus the more scarce an asset is, the higher is the weight for a household owning it. This can be justified, even if the difference in weights can be very high.[53] Second, the weighting factor ($1/\sigma$) gives larger weights to assets that are *either* very scarce *or* very common, compared to relatively lower weights to assets that half of the population owns.[54] This is much harder to be justified and it is not a priory clear why this should be the case.[55]

Further research should address the questions on how to judge the goodness of fit of the methodology by statistical procedures. The methodology presented here is based on the data constraint of having only one nationally representative pair of different household surveys (one having and the other not having income in the survey), and to have some urban income surveys for other years together with some national-wide other survey. Having a second pair of full surveys allows

[53]Consider the scenario A when 90 percent of the population own an asset i, with $\overline{a}_{i(A)} = 0.9$, and scenario B when 10 percent own the asset $\overline{a}_{i(B)} = 0.1$. In both cases, $\sigma = 0.3$. Under scenario A, a household j owning the asset i is 9 times as rich than under scenario B, since $(a_{ji} - \overline{a}_{i(A)})/\sigma_i = 0.1/0.3$ compared to $(a_{ji} - \overline{a}_{i(B)})/\sigma_i = 0.9/0.3$.

[54]For example, for both the scarce case $\overline{a} = 0.01$ and common $\overline{a} = 0.99$ case, the weighting is $1/\sigma = 10$ compared to the medium case of $\overline{a} = 0.5$ with the weighting of $1/\sigma = 2$.

[55]An alternative is to set weights in a more normative way, shown in **Essay 4** for Colombia.

a backward and forward check of the approach described, in the sense of an out-of-sample prediction that can be compared to observed data.[56]

Our methodology is based on the idea that changes over time should be explicitly modeled. Of course, our proposed methods of modeling dynamics are based on arbitrary assumptions regarding the time series in the regression coefficients. However, what is normally applied in the literature is to totally neglect dynamics. For example, the study of Stifel and Christiaensen (2007) uses a static prediction procedure for the regression coefficients and also tries to use variables that are "likely to remain stable over time", i.e., that are not sensitive to "economic or polity change" (Stifel and Christiaensen (2007), p. 323). However, this makes poverty trends over time somewhat slow: if regression coefficients are constant and variables are chosen to be nearly constant then changes are hardly to be observed. In this regard, such results hardly reflect income poverty dynamics but are closer to looking at asset poverty.

[56]As done in **Essay 2** for Bolivia using LSMS data from 2002 and DHS data from 2003, or in Mathiassen (2008) using several income surveys for Uganda.

Essay 2

Estimating the Stability of Poverty Analysis: Out-of-Sample Predictions in Dynamic Poverty Mapping

Truth emerges more readily from error than from confusion.
Francis Bacon (1561–1626)

Abstract: In Bolivia, as in many other developing countries, a sufficiently long time series of nationally representative income surveys does not exist which makes it difficult to analyze trends and determinants of poverty and inequality over a longer time period. However, in many countries, there are urban household surveys, and there are nationally representative Demographic and Health Surveys (DHS) which lack information on income. For the case of Bolivia, we have two urban household surveys and four nationally representative DHS available since 1989, while comparable nationally representative household income surveys only exist since 1999. In this paper, we modify a technique developed for (static) poverty mapping exercises by combining urban household income surveys with DHS data to (dynamically) extend the time series of household income data back in time until 1989 and 1994, starting from the base period (1998/9). Our technique explicitly estimates the robustness of this backward extension by repeating it for a second base periods with two sets of nationally representative household surveys and DHS (2002/3). Furthermore, we use and compare two different methods of modeling dynamics. In doing so, we are able to gain insights about the stability and reliability of dynamic poverty mapping analysis.

---

based on joint work with Boris Branisa.

2.1 Introduction

In the mid-1980s, Bolivia experienced a dramatic macroeconomic crisis, with an annual inflation rate that peaked at 25.000 percent and great social unrest (Sachs and Morales, 1988). According to some authors, the crisis was a consequence of the government's growing fiscal deficit and of the public companies that had been financed with external debt during the 1970s (Morales, 1994). This funding was used to support a model where the government played a major role in the economy. The debt crisis in Latin America made it very difficult for Bolivia to obtain new external funding, and the government was forced to finance the fiscal deficit with monetary emission. As the government was unable to solve the crisis, President Siles Suazo resigned and called for general elections. In 1985, the newly elected government of President Paz Estenssoro started a stabilization program which included a tax reform, a sharp reduction in government spending, and liberalization of the economy. The program was successful to combat hyperinflation and to transform the economy into a more market-oriented one. It was the beginning of a reform process that continued during the 1990s (Morales, 2001).[1] The impact of these reforms on the levels of income poverty and inequality is, however, subject of debate. As nationally representative household income surveys have been only conducted since 1999, the trends of income poverty and inequality in Bolivia since the late 1980s are still an open empirical question.

Since a sufficiently long time series of nationally representative income surveys does not exist it is difficult to analyze the determinants and trends of poverty and inequality over a longer time period. A method used in the literature to overcome this difficulty is modifying or extending poverty mapping models. The basic idea of poverty mapping is to use one specific micro-data survey which contains all relevant information for poverty analysis, and to combine this information with another survey which typically contains only part of the necessary information. The classical application is to use a household survey such as a Living Standard Measurement Survey (LSMS)[2] which contains the relevant information on income and income determinants for a representative subsample of the population and to apply this information structure to a Census that does not contain all parts of the information, i.e., missing information on income, but providing some other information for the whole population of a country, such as asset ownership, education, or demographics. The logic is to establish a statistical correlation structure between various covariates and income, for example with an OLS regression, in the first survey (LSMS) that can be applied to the second survey (Census) to predict

[1]The market-oriented approach continued until the year 2005 when President Evo Morales was elected and initiated the return to more government-led development.

[2]For simplicity, we call all kinds of household income surveys LSMS even if they belong to a different kind of income survey family.

incomes. Proposed by Hentschel et al. (2000) and Elbers et al. (2003) for Ecuador, the method has been applied to many countries and different kinds of surveys. Applying this method makes it possible to calculate detailed poverty maps, e.g., at the municipality level to, for example, target public spending policies in the most effective way.

Besides the geographic use of this method, there have also been attempts to apply poverty mapping back and forth in time. Klasen et al. (2007), Grosse et al. (2009),[3] and Stifel and Christiaensen (2007) have used LSMS and Demographic and Health Surveys (DHS) for their temporal analysis. The difference between the attempts basically lies the assumption about dynamics when modeling the correlation structure. Whereas Stifel and Christiaensen (2007) assume no dynamics in the regression model, the other studies propose several ways of modeling dynamics.

Explicitly judging or verifying the results whether the estimation is correct (with other data) is hardly possible. In fact, poverty mapping was invented *because* no other data is available, so there is hardly any way to check the predictive power of these models. One exemption is Mathiassen (2008) who uses several LSMS for Uganda and explicitly tests how well a regression model of one point in time can predict incomes for other points in time. The author has all necessary information at hand to explicitly test the predictive power of poverty maps using static coefficients over time. Demombynes et al. (2004) also show how well their Census predictions coincide with the LSMS estimates for three countries.

This paper draws heavily from the previous study on poverty mapping in Bolivia by Grosse et al. (2009). Since national household income surveys exist only since 1999 and only urban surveys for earlier years, analysis would leave more than half of the population living in non-urban areas uncovered by data. There are several nationally representative DHS which, however, lack information on incomes. In this paper, we use four nationally representative DHS (1989, 1994, 1998, and 2003), two nationally representative household income surveys (1999 and 2002), and two urban household surveys (1989 and 1994). We modify the technique developed for (static) poverty mapping exercises of Hentschel et al. (2000) and Elbers et al. (2003) by combining urban household income surveys with DHS data to (dynamically) extend the time series of household income data back in time until 1989 and 1994 following Grosse et al. (2009).

Our technique explicitly estimates the robustness of this backward extension to 1989 and 1994 by repeating it for two base periods with two sets of nationally representative data sets of LSMS and DHS (1998/9 and 2002/3). We additionally take a look at the robustness of the estimations by focussing on two years for which we have complete data and perform out-of-sample predictions for poverty

[3]Note that Grosse et al. (2009) is equivalent to **Essay 1**.

and inequality assuming that the LSMS of 1999 had also been only urban (using 2002 as base year) and vice versa. Furthermore, we compare the results of the assumptions of Grosse et al. (2009) with, for example, the ones used by Stifel and Christiaensen (2007). In doing so, we are able to gain insights in the reliability of poverty mapping analysis over time.

2.2 Approach and Data

The basic idea of this paper applies the approach of Hentschel et al. (2000) and Elbers et al. (2003). The authors use Ecuadorian LSMS data which contains information on income and income determinants and extend their poverty analysis spatially to the whole country using Census data. To be able to do so, they run an expenditure model in the LSMS data using only covariates that are also available in the Census data. Simulating income in the Census data is achieved by simply multiplying the covariates of the Census with the regression coefficients obtained from the LSMS survey (plus adding an error term). With this simulated data, they are able to generate detailed poverty maps of national coverage at the municipality level.[4]

Only very few papers explicitly test how well it works to simulate incomes using the described cross-survey matching. Demombynes et al. (2004) replicate the exercise of Hentschel et al. (2000) and Elbers et al. (2003) for Ecuador and two more countries, Madagascar and South Africa, and compare their results for the strata where both observed expenditures from LSMS data and simulated expenditures from Census are available. For most strata, but not for all, they find that the observed poverty levels are similar in LSMS and Census data.[5] Stifel and Christiaensen (2007) use the same methodology, but apply the coefficients obtained from Kenyan LSMS data (of 1997) to several DHS surveys (instead of Census), and they do so back and forth in time (1993 and 2003) instead of across space. In doing so, they assume that the returns to covariates remain constant over time. For the DHS of 1998, which is closest in time, they find a persistent underestimation of poverty when applying the regression coefficients of 1997 to the 1998 data. They correct for it by shifting the poverty line until the simulated headcount in the DHS matches the observed one of the LSMS.

[4]The second main contribution of Elbers et al. (2003) was to investigate how to correctly estimate standard errors by splitting the error term into a spatial and an idiosyncratic component. We cannot do this since the primary sample units (or clusters) of the pre–1999 LSMS are not available for the Bolivian data sets.

[5]For Ecuador, 2 out of 8 strata show different results for P0. For Madagascar, all estimates are inside each others' confidence intervals, however, due to very high standard errors causing a range for point estimates of up to 13 percentage points. The same holds for South Africa with ranges up to 6 percentage points.

In a study of Mathiassen (2008), the author uses a series of Ugandan LSMS data sets and tests the predictive power of models from one LSMS survey for the other surveys and compares observed poverty with simulated poverty for all years and all surveys. She finds that for 2 of the 7 surveys, the simulations are working very badly. She assumes the reason to be either an unexpected large change of poverty or the distance of time between the surveys. In addition, the adequacy of applying the models is much worse for rural areas where nearly half of the simulated poverty levels are statistically different from observed poverty levels.

We draw strongly on previous work by Grosse et al. (2009). It is similar to Stifel and Christiaensen (2007), in that we also use LSMS and DHS data. Differently to Stifel and Christiaensen (2007), we explicitly model dynamics of changes in the regression coefficients instead of assuming that the coefficients stay constant over time. We test the ways of taking dynamics into account (or not) and are able to check which model comes closer to observed values. This is only possible as soon as two full sets of nationally representative surveys are available. In this respect, our paper is more similar to Mathiassen (2008). We start presenting the model that follows Grosse et al. (2009).

We construct a 3×3 block diagonal structure of the covariates by interacting them with three regional dummies, and run a weighted standard log-linear OLS regression model where the indices C, T, and R stand for cities, towns, and rural areas, respectively, β are coefficient vectors, and ε is an independent error term:

$$\begin{pmatrix} \ln y_t^C \\ \ln y_t^T \\ \ln y_t^R \end{pmatrix} = \begin{pmatrix} X_t^C & 0 & 0 \\ 0 & X_t^T & 0 \\ 0 & 0 & X_t^R \end{pmatrix} \begin{pmatrix} \beta_t^C \\ \beta_t^T \\ \beta_t^R \end{pmatrix} + \begin{pmatrix} \varepsilon_t^C \\ \varepsilon_t^T \\ \varepsilon_t^R \end{pmatrix}. \tag{2.1}$$

Concerning the modeling of dynamics, we test the following assumptions proposed in the literature. Our baseline assumption for earlier periods $t-1$, in which the LSMS covers only cities, is that the absolute differences[6] in the regression coefficients between cities and non-urban areas remain constant between period $t-1$ and t:

$$\beta_{t-1}^T = \beta_{t-1}^C + (\beta_t^T - \beta_t^C) \quad \text{and} \quad \beta_{t-1}^R = \beta_{t-1}^C + (\beta_t^R - \beta_t^C). \tag{2.2}$$

[6]Note that we use the term "absolute" not in the mathematical meaning of $|-1| = 1$, but to contrast it to "relative", i.e., percentage changes.

The second proposed way of capturing "dynamics" in the literature is to assume that there are none, as done in Stifel and Christiaensen (2007)[7] and tested in Mathiassen (2008):[8]

$$\beta_{t-1}^{C} = \beta_t^{C} \quad \text{and} \quad \beta_{t-1}^{T} = \beta_t^{T} \quad \text{and} \quad \beta_{t-1}^{R} = \beta_t^{R}. \tag{2.3}$$

As the predicted income is obtained from a regression, its variance is too small as compared to observed income. To compensate for this the simulation is run 200 times, where a random variable is added each time to the predicted values. The random variable is assumed to be normally distributed with mean zero and with the estimated variance of the error term. For computing the estimated variance of the error term for non-urban areas, we assume for (i) the dynamic case the constancy of relative changes

$$\sigma(\varepsilon_{t-1}^{T}) = \sigma(\varepsilon_{t-1}^{C}) \cdot \frac{\sigma(\varepsilon_t^{T})}{\sigma(\varepsilon_t^{C})} \quad \text{and} \quad \sigma(\varepsilon_{t-1}^{R}) = \sigma(\varepsilon_{t-1}^{C}) \cdot \frac{\sigma(\varepsilon_t^{R})}{\sigma(\varepsilon_t^{C})}, \tag{2.4}$$

and for (ii) the no-dynamics case we assume no changes over time:

$$\sigma(\varepsilon_{t-1}^{C}) = \sigma(\varepsilon_t^{C}) \quad \text{and} \quad \sigma(\varepsilon_{t-1}^{T}) = \sigma(\varepsilon_t^{T}) \quad \text{and} \quad \sigma(\varepsilon_{t-1}^{R}) = \sigma(\varepsilon_t^{R}). \tag{2.5}$$

Different from the studies applying the poverty mapping approach cited above, there is a whole literature addressing the question of changing endowments, changing coefficients, and changing unobservables over time. In a multi-country study, edited by Bourguignon et al. (2005), the authors investigate this question of changes and the resulting impacts on inequality (and partly also on poverty and income) for 7 countries.[9] The authors apply generalized Oaxaca-Blinder decomposition methods to investigate how different groups (such as the urban versus rural population) are affected by changes in the distribution of endowments (called population or endowment effect), changes in the returns to these endowments (called price effects), and changes in decisions how to use the endowments such as behavior on the labor market (called occupational effects). They point out, that these factors are not independent from each other, and that, in addition, they are likely to be affected by external shocks (e.g., international prices) or internal shocks (e.g., government policies). Furthermore, they highlight that both shocks as well

[7]It must be noted that Stifel and Christiaensen (2007) use in their study assets whose parameters are expected to remain stable over time, and that unlike the case in our paper, Stifel and Christiaensen (2007) use different regressions for the regions they consider. We are forced to use the same regressors for all regions to be able to calculate Equation (2.2).

[8]Mathiassen (2008) suggests to "update" coefficients in order to take dynamics or "outlier years" into account by averaging coefficients over different years.

[9]Argentina, Brazil, Colombia, Indonesia, Malaysia, Mexico, Taiwan.

as changes are likely to be different for subgroups (such as the urban-rural divide) of the population.

Only three studies of Bourguignon et al. (2005) address the specific questions on urban versus rural trends. The chapter on Colombia suggests that there are substantial differences between urban and rural areas. For example, the first time period of observation showed increasing inequality in rural areas and stagnating in urban areas whereas the second period showed exactly the opposite pattern. Especially the effect of increased schooling differed: More and more equally distributed years of schooling in urban areas caused higher inequality, whereas more years of schooling in rural areas cause an inequality decline, due to lower marginal returns in rural areas. Indonesia showed a massive increase in income and a massive reduction in poverty, combined with a increase in inequality. Concerning differences in price effects, returns to education went down in urban areas and caused decreasing inequality, whereas they went up in rural areas and caused increasing inequality. Also other regional differences played a role (such as living on Java or elsewhere). Indonesia experienced in addition a massive urbanization, causing increasing self-employment in urban areas: There was selective migration of the mainly landless poorer wage-workers from rural to urban areas which was in turn profitable for the migrants. For Mexico, the authors find growing negative returns to living in rural areas. Similar to Indonesia, there was a strong rural-to-urban migration as well as from poorer-to-richer-regions migration which lead to increasing inequality. In Mexico, also urban-rural differentials in education increased.[10]

The model which is used similarly in all studies is very different from our model, which is driven by the data Bourguignon et al. (2005) use. The DHS, which we use, has hardly any employment questions, except for the few variables listed in Appendix Table B.3, so that their approach goes beyond of what we could do with our data. In our study, apart from testing the assumptions on different dynamics for urban versus rural areas, we change the original estimation procedure of Grosse et al. (2009) in some ways. As a first test for stability of income, poverty, and inequality estimates, we rerun the Grosse et al. (2009) regression using only covariates that are available in all four DHS and LSMS surveys. To reduce the number of covariates in a more meaningful way, we first statistically test for the equality of means of covariates X of the LSMS of 1999 and the DHS of 1998.

[10]The study from Grimm (2004) for Cote d'Ivoire also takes urban-rural differentials into account and separates the model into three different models: for urban men, rural men, and women. Also here, price effects can go into different directions, can be of different sign, and can be of different magnitude for the three models. Grimm (2004) points out the relevance of external and internal factors such as rising world market prices for the main cash crops, freezing of public wages, devaluation of the exchange rate, adjustment policies. Overall, the author finds an urbanization of poverty (combined with decreasing between-region and increasing within-region inequality.).

This improves the original method since the equality of means is desirable for being able to apply the β coefficients of one survey to the data of the other survey (Stifel and Christiaensen, 2007). Second, we continue to reduce the number of regressors to avoid a large number of insignificant coefficients by redefining covariates, from a disaggregation into many dummy categories to a simpler categorization.[11]

The data set we use consists of four LSMS: the 2nd round (1989) and the 7th round (1994) of the Encuesta Integrada de Hogares (EIH), both only covering urban areas, and the 1st round (1999) and the 4th round (2002) of the Encuesta Continua de Hogares (ECH), both being nationally representative. The purpose of the LSMS is to collect individual, household, and community level data to measure the welfare level of the sampled population. In addition to income and/or expenditure data, the LSMS provide information on demographics, asset ownership, education, employment, and health.[12]

Our set of DHS consists of the first four Bolivian rounds which were conducted in 1989, 1994, 1998, and 2003. Two-stage sampling techniques were used to select nationally representative samples of women aged between 15 and 49 who serve as eligible respondents of the DHS, i.e., women in reproductive age. The main objective of the DHS is to collect demographic data on health and fertility trends. Additionally, it includes some questions on the educational attainment and the employment situation of adults and on the asset ownership of the household.

2.3 Results of Out-of-Sample Predictions

2.3.1 Regression

A first test for the stability of estimation results arises when we change the regression model itself. The idea for the estimation in Grosse et al. (2009) was to use the model with the largest number of possible regressors with the data at hand.[13] The

[11] With the remaining coefficients, we believe to have found a model that is stable. We opted against running stepwise regressions or an alternative data-driven approach as we want to choose the variables to be included based on theory and findings from the literature. It must be noted that some of the variables where equality of means is not given are nevertheless included as dummies since they are meaningful category that cannot be left out (e.g., some of the departments or education categories).

[12] Note that our monetary variable is mixed: We use income for cities and towns and expenditures for rural areas, see Grosse et al. (2009) for details.

[13] In his master thesis, Branisa (2006) reproduces the calculations for poverty and inequality for 1989 and 1994 based on Grosse et al. (2005) (which is an earlier version of the Grosse et al. (2009) paper on which the pre-test was based), but with 2002 as the base year instead of 1999, and with the largest number of possible regressors. His point estimates for the poverty measures, compared to the results presented in Chapter 2.3.4, are systematically below those computed by

estimation model should transfer the largest possible correlation structure from the LSMS to the DHS data. Since the authors did not want to explain causalities or establish an expenditure or income model (as it is the purpose of standard income regressions), insignificance of coefficients and multicollinearity were left aside. For each year, the largest possible model was used, i.e., with different coefficients for the different years, since the questionnaire designs have changed over time.

We start by comparing the results of the models using all possible variables, i.e., different ones at different points in time, with the results using only the common model. The impact on the regression is presented in Table 2.1 showing the β coefficients and P-values. As expected, the explanatory power of the common model is lower (shown by a lower adjusted R^2). Most coefficients keep the sign, especially the significant ones.[14] The models of 1989 and 1994 for cities perform way better than for 1999 and 2002 when looking at significance levels. The number of insignificant variables increases for example from 16 in 1989 (12 in 1994) to 30 in 1999 and 28 in 2002 for cities, out of a total of 51 variables. The regressions are weak for rural areas both in 1999 and 2002 and even weaker for towns, and the latter are based on the smallest number of observations.

The final regression model is shown in Table 2.2. Besides reducing the number of regressors to common variables, the main changes are in the variables showing household composition (which are reduced from 6 to 3 variables), for household headship (from 5 to 2 variables), for employment (from 14 to 8 variables), and for child health (from 6 to 3 variables). For department dummies, education, gender, and access to infrastructure, the variables remained the same.[15]

Grosse et al. (2005) for both years. Apparently, the change of the base period has in this case an impact on the level of the estimates. If one looks at the evolution of inequality between 1989 and 1999, a similar pattern is observed: estimates by Grosse et al. (2005) suggest a decrease in inequality, while estimates by Branisa (2006) suggest hardly any changes.

[14]Concerning signs and the significance level, the evolution over time is shown in Appendix Table C.1.

[15]Results and some discussion on other dynamics represented by ϕ in Equation (2.6) are found in Chapter 2.4.

Table 2.1: Regression Results, Log-Linear OLS, Full Model versus Common Model, 1999

	City				Town				Rural			
	all		common		all		common		all		common	
	β	P	β	P	β	P	β	P	β	P	β	P
La Paz	0.09	0.39	-0.02	0.88	0.13	0.81	0.11	0.81	0.19	0.04	0.25	0.00
Cochabamba	0.28	0.01	0.27	0.02	0.62	0.22	0.65	0.17	0.28	0.01	0.40	0.00
Oruro	0.04	0.75	-0.06	0.66	-0.26	0.65	-0.27	0.61	0.31	0.03	0.27	0.08
Potosi	0.10	0.45	-0.02	0.89	0.14	0.78	0.16	0.74	0.04	0.65	0.06	0.57
Tarija	0.59	0.00	0.53	0.00	0.37	0.49	0.47	0.33	0.64	0.00	0.63	0.00
Santa Cruz	0.68	0.00	0.70	0.00	0.47	0.35	0.52	0.27	0.74	0.00	0.67	0.00
Beni & Pando	0.70	0.00	0.63	0.00	0.17	0.75	0.18	0.72	0.81	0.00	0.71	0.00
# elderly	-0.08	0.60	0.11	0.41	0.09	0.73	0.09	0.73	-0.08	0.34	-0.11	0.27
# males	-0.07	0.02	-0.07	0.03	0.10	0.22	0.08	0.33	-0.10	0.02	-0.08	0.05
# females	-0.12	0.00	-0.12	0.00	-0.10	0.09	-0.11	0.07	-0.17	0.00	-0.15	0.00
# youngsters	-0.03	0.62	-0.01	0.76	-0.08	0.23	-0.08	0.16	-0.01	0.79	-0.02	0.55
# children	-0.11	0.16	-0.10	0.21	-0.18	0.05	-0.20	0.02	-0.08	0.10	-0.10	0.05
# of working age / hh size	1.02	0.01	1.13	0.00	0.22	0.66	0.14	0.80	0.74	0.01	0.60	0.04
gender hh head	0.03	0.73	0.00	0.97	0.25	0.15	0.27	0.12	-0.02	0.84	0.05	0.57
language of hh head	-0.01	0.86			-0.12	0.30			-0.06	0.32		
hh head age <= 24	-0.21	0.31	-0.41	0.05	0.01	0.98	0.04	0.91	0.01	0.98	0.04	0.83
hh head age 25 - 34	-0.25	0.22	-0.27	0.19	0.03	0.94	0.05	0.90	0.05	0.74	0.06	0.73
hh head age 35 - 44	-0.39	0.05	-0.29	0.14	0.01	0.99	0.04	0.92	0.08	0.62	0.12	0.48
hh head age 45 - 54	-0.45	0.03	-0.34	0.09	0.13	0.77	0.14	0.72	-0.04	0.80	-0.06	0.72
hh head age 55 - 65	-0.34	0.09	-0.21	0.31	0.03	0.94	0.04	0.92	0.03	0.84	0.05	0.78
has house	0.07	0.20			-0.07	0.51			0.08	0.25		
floor (cement)	0.17	0.21			0.03	0.86			0.24	0.00		
floor (brick)	0.30	0.05			0.17	0.33			0.00	1.00		
floor (other floor)	0.38	0.01			0.10	0.61			0.24	0.02		

continued on next page

Table 2.1 continued

	City				Town				Rural			
	all		common		all		common		all		common	
	β	P	β	P	β	P	β	P	β	P	β	
2-3 sleeping rooms	0.21	0.00			-0.18	0.11			0.07	0.24		
>=4 sleeping rooms	0.22	0.04			0.09	0.73			0.30	0.14		
access to public water	-0.18	0.11	-0.07	0.52	0.06	0.63	0.02	0.91	-0.07	0.22	0.02	0.73
has no toilet	-0.02	0.86	-0.05	0.59	-0.22	0.10	-0.28	0.05	-0.08	0.11	-0.22	0.00
has electricity	-0.32	0.03			-0.19	0.46			0.13	0.05		
cooking material	-0.26	0.02			-0.02	0.91			0.30	0.00		
has phone	0.24	0.00			0.38	0.00			0.30	0.01		
has radio	0.02	0.79			-0.11	0.29			0.10	0.07		
has television	0.18	0.10			0.10	0.54			0.23	0.01		
has fridge	0.23	0.00			0.03	0.77			-0.02	0.85		
no partner in household	0.31	0.15	0.11	0.64	0.52	0.15	0.47	0.17	0.38	0.01	0.41	0.03
com. basic edu. (m.)	-0.12	0.35	-0.16	0.21	-0.01	0.96	0.01	0.96	0.02	0.78	-0.05	0.55
incom. secondary edu. (m.)	0.04	0.70	-0.03	0.78	-0.20	0.25	-0.14	0.44	-0.04	0.56	-0.05	0.47
com. secondary edu. (m.)	-0.04	0.67	-0.06	0.52	0.11	0.48	0.26	0.10	-0.02	0.83	0.03	0.77
tertiary edu. (m.)	0.24	0.03	0.35	0.00	-0.10	0.66	0.01	0.97	0.15	0.49	0.56	0.01
com. basic edu. (w.)	-0.02	0.89	0.10	0.44	0.04	0.81	0.07	0.70	0.20	0.00	0.27	0.00
incom. secondary edu. (w.)	0.05	0.64	0.14	0.17	0.12	0.41	0.16	0.23	0.27	0.00	0.28	0.00
com. secondary edu. (w.)	0.06	0.54	0.26	0.01	0.11	0.50	0.18	0.20	0.18	0.08	0.43	0.00
tertiary edu. (w.)	0.26	0.03	0.53	0.00	0.27	0.19	0.48	0.01	0.28	0.17	0.59	0.02
high skilled white collar (m.)	0.68	0.00	0.74	0.00	1.09	0.01	1.07	0.00	0.60	0.00	0.99	0.00
med. skilled white collar (m.)	0.41	0.03	0.37	0.09	1.02	0.01	0.95	0.01	0.45	0.00	0.64	0.00
skilled manual (m.)	0.44	0.02	0.24	0.25	0.69	0.07	0.55	0.13	0.54	0.00	0.73	0.00
unskilled manual (m.)	0.37	0.08	0.22	0.35	0.45	0.21	0.35	0.34	0.45	0.00	0.54	0.00
agr. employed (m.)	-0.19	0.60	-0.32	0.48	0.47	0.28	0.46	0.25	0.48	0.00	0.57	0.00

continued on next page

Table 2.1 continued

	City				Town				Rural			
	all		common		all		common		all		common	
	β	P	β	P	β	P	β	P	β	P	β	
agr. self-employed (m.)	0.88	0.01	0.27	0.29	0.07	0.88	-0.09	0.82	0.31	0.01	0.31	0.06
sales and services (m.)	0.51	0.01	0.34	0.12	0.94	0.02	0.86	0.02	0.47	0.00	0.72	0.00
high skilled white collar (w.)	0.35	0.01	0.40	0.01	0.51	0.02	0.65	0.00	0.04	0.90	-0.06	0.83
med. skilled white collar (w.)	0.24	0.01	0.32	0.00	0.77	0.00	0.84	0.00	0.26	0.07	0.17	0.27
skilled manual (w.)	0.03	0.78	-0.07	0.53	0.37	0.02	0.44	0.00	-0.09	0.35	-0.11	0.29
unskilled manual (w.)	0.32	0.00	0.31	0.00	0.61	0.00	0.63	0.00	-0.08	0.51	-0.03	0.85
agr. employed (w.)	1.20	0.02	0.93	0.11	-0.81	0.17	-1.02	0.06	0.07	0.45	-0.04	0.66
agr. self-employed (w.)	0.53	0.00	0.51	0.01	-0.32	0.33	-0.24	0.46	0.03	0.64	-0.05	0.47
sales and services (w.)	0.30	0.00	0.28	0.00	0.67	0.00	0.73	0.00	0.20	0.06	0.31	0.00
has social security	0.09	0.09			0.08	0.48			0.16	0.05		
birth in last 12 month	0.08	0.71	0.18	0.39	-0.32	0.30	-0.25	0.36	-0.05	0.51	-0.08	0.27
attended by doctor	-0.09	0.72	-0.16	0.51	0.63	0.09	0.61	0.07	0.11	0.32	0.21	0.07
delivered in hospital	-0.08	0.64	-0.09	0.57	-0.20	0.37	-0.25	0.25	0.12	0.31	0.10	0.45
child under 4 years	0.02	0.86	0.07	0.48	0.14	0.57	0.12	0.48	0.13	0.29	-0.04	0.65
has first polio vaccination	0.05	0.69			-0.04	0.84			-0.20	0.10		
has triple dpt vaccination	0.06	0.61			-0.02	0.91			0.01	0.85		
has had diarrhea	-0.14	0.14	-0.18	0.07	0.04	0.79	0.00	0.98	0.03	0.60	0.02	0.74
has head cough/fever	0.03	0.67	-0.02	0.85	0.08	0.54	0.06	0.65	0.02	0.71	0.01	0.87
c/t/r dummy/constant	4.57	0.00	4.63	0.00	3.95	0.00	3.82	0.00	3.53	0.00	3.88	0.00
# of observations	1037		1037		332		332		922		922	
R^2	51.40		43.26		44.16		43.48		53.80		45.96	

Notes: For details on the regression and variables, see text and notes of Table 2.2. β: regression coefficient; P: P-value; all: all possible covariates; common: covariates common over all 4 years.
Source: Own calculations based on ECH and EIH.

Table 2.2: Regression Results, Log-Linear OLS, Reduced Model, 1989–2002

	City								Town				Rural			
	1989		1994		1999		2002		1999		2002		1999		2002	
	β	P	β	P	β	P	β	P	β	P	β	P	β	P	β	P
La Paz	0.01	0.77	0.15	0.00	-0.04	0.70	-0.03	0.75	0.16	0.75	0.18	0.26	0.25	0.00	0.26	0.00
Cochabamba	0.16	0.00	0.13	0.00	0.24	0.03	0.17	0.06	0.75	0.14	0.17	0.26	0.39	0.00	0.16	0.04
Oruro	-0.17	0.00	-0.20	0.00	-0.06	0.65	-0.23	0.04	-0.18	0.74	-0.11	0.56	0.35	0.01	0.23	0.01
Potosi	-0.26	0.00	-0.21	0.00	-0.07	0.63	-0.08	0.41	0.18	0.72	-0.09	0.62	0.05	0.62	-0.08	0.38
Tarija	-0.03	0.52	0.03	0.53	0.50	0.00	0.16	0.13	0.57	0.27	0.40	0.01	0.71	0.00	0.56	0.00
Santa Cruz	0.43	0.00	0.43	0.00	0.70	0.00	0.44	0.00	0.58	0.25	0.11	0.47	0.71	0.00	0.46	0.00
Beni & Pando	0.44	0.00	0.28	0.00	0.62	0.00	0.31	0.00	0.29	0.57	0.25	0.10	0.74	0.00	0.59	0.00
elderly dependency ratio	-0.23	0.00	-0.28	0.00	-0.20	0.00	-0.32	0.00	-0.18	0.01	-0.24	0.00	-0.03	0.28	-0.08	0.01
child dependency ratio	0.08	0.42	-0.08	0.41	0.17	0.51	0.00	1.00	0.55	0.13	-0.01	0.95	-0.12	0.41	0.05	0.60
hh size	-0.07	0.00	-0.05	0.00	-0.08	0.00	-0.05	0.00	-0.06	0.01	-0.05	0.01	-0.09	0.00	-0.10	0.00
hh head age	0.03	0.00	0.01	0.18	0.00	0.75	0.02	0.14	0.01	0.39	0.01	0.54	0.02	0.18	0.03	0.00
hh head age squared	0.00	0.01	0.00	0.69	0.00	0.91	0.00	0.21	0.00	0.33	0.00	0.66	0.00	0.14	0.00	0.00
gender hh head	-0.12	0.05	-0.12	0.01	-0.05	0.59	0.03	0.73	0.22	0.19	0.06	0.54	-0.01	0.87	-0.12	0.24
access to public water	0.15	0.00	0.03	0.20	-0.08	0.51	-0.05	0.48	0.05	0.70	0.06	0.49	0.00	0.99	0.13	0.00
has no toilet	-0.20	0.00	-0.21	0.00	-0.03	0.77	-0.04	0.58	-0.27	0.06	0.06	0.52	-0.23	0.00	-0.15	0.00
no partner in household	0.35	0.00	0.58	0.00	0.21	0.37	0.34	0.03	0.47	0.15	0.25	0.24	0.39	0.03	0.06	0.77
com. basic edu. (m.)	0.02	0.72	0.03	0.51	-0.16	0.23	-0.04	0.68	-0.02	0.89	0.05	0.65	-0.02	0.79	0.15	0.01
incom. secondary edu. (m.)	0.02	0.65	0.05	0.17	-0.01	0.95	-0.11	0.36	-0.17	0.37	0.07	0.47	-0.01	0.87	0.11	0.04
com. secondary edu. (m.)	0.10	0.03	0.10	0.01	-0.05	0.63	0.06	0.51	0.29	0.07	0.07	0.44	0.05	0.57	0.19	0.01
tertiary edu. (m.)	0.52	0.00	0.40	0.00	0.39	0.00	0.43	0.00	-0.02	0.93	0.29	0.02	0.44	0.06	0.27	0.07
com. basic edu. (w.)	0.00	0.95	0.07	0.07	0.12	0.33	-0.07	0.57	-0.01	0.96	-0.01	0.96	0.26	0.00	0.22	0.00
incom. secondary edu. (w.)	0.14	0.01	0.01	0.74	0.10	0.34	0.01	0.88	0.11	0.41	0.05	0.60	0.27	0.00	0.26	0.00
com. secondary edu. (w.)	0.17	0.00	0.06	0.06	0.24	0.02	0.02	0.77	0.12	0.40	0.31	0.00	0.44	0.00	0.33	0.00
tertiary edu. (w.)	0.39	0.00	0.40	0.00	0.53	0.00	0.44	0.00	0.45	0.01	0.58	0.00	0.75	0.01	0.64	0.00

continued on next page

Table 2.2 continued

	City								Town				Rural			
	1989		1994		1999		2002		1999		2002		1999		2002	
	β	P	β	P	β	P	β	P	β	P	β	P	β	P	β	P
high & med. skilled white collar (m.)	0.45	0.00	0.79	0.00	0.53	0.01	0.62	0.00	1.03	0.00	0.61	0.00	0.67	0.00	0.21	0.27
skilled & unskilled manual (m.)	0.37	0.00	0.47	0.00	0.23	0.27	0.23	0.05	0.57	0.09	0.41	0.01	0.60	0.00	0.04	0.80
agriculture (m.)	0.42	0.00	0.51	0.00	-0.21	0.61	0.21	0.22	0.19	0.59	0.30	0.14	0.25	0.12	-0.05	0.75
sales and services (m.)	0.42	0.00	0.57	0.00	0.34	0.12	0.53	0.00	0.87	0.01	0.62	0.00	0.67	0.00	0.26	0.15
high & med. skilled white collar (w.)	0.45	0.00	0.46	0.00	0.38	0.00	0.55	0.00	0.73	0.00	0.72	0.00	0.13	0.41	0.43	0.00
skilled & unskilled manual (w.)	0.22	0.00	0.28	0.00	0.14	0.07	0.19	0.01	0.51	0.00	0.17	0.03	-0.12	0.19	0.05	0.54
agriculture (w.)	0.52	0.01	0.10	0.57	0.64	0.04	-0.14	0.61	-0.24	0.49	-0.54	0.00	-0.05	0.42	-0.08	0.19
sales and services (w.)	0.34	0.00	0.30	0.00	0.31	0.00	0.23	0.00	0.71	0.00	0.35	0.00	0.36	0.00	0.25	0.00
birth in last 12 month	-0.13	0.03	-0.13	0.01	0.20	0.23	-0.06	0.64	-0.29	0.36	-0.17	0.26	-0.12	0.09	-0.03	0.71
attended by doctor	0.07	0.45	0.04	0.62	-0.22	0.28	-0.02	0.89	0.68	0.05	0.10	0.55	0.20	0.10	0.02	0.86
delivered in hospital	0.03	0.74	0.00	0.98	-0.10	0.49	-0.26	0.14	-0.38	0.06	0.12	0.37	0.08	0.56	0.15	0.26
c/t/r dummy/constant	4.31	0.00	4.66	0.00	5.05	0.00	4.80	0.00	3.84	0.00	4.41	0.00	4.09	0.00	4.23	0.00
# of observations	4607		5131		1037		1506		332		1120		922		1709	
R^2	40.44		46.01		41.35		40.39		43.46		40.28		44.17		38.24	

Notes: β: regression coefficient, P: P-value. The variables are defined as follows: Of the nine departments, Beni and Pando are grouped into one single variable (left-out category: Chuquisaca). The elderly (child) dependency ratio is number of elderly (children) divided by number of men and women in working age, and the total number of household members is additionally included (hh size). We include age and age squared of the household head as well as gender of the household head. For infrastructure, due to changes in questionnaire design, we are only able to include access to public water and having a toilet. For education, we include (for men (m.) and women (w.) separately) the categories complete (com.) basic, incomplete (incom.) secondary, complete secondary, and tertiary education (left-out category: no or incomplete basic eduction). For employment, we we include (for men (m.) and women (w.) separately) the categories high and medium skilled white collar, skilled and unskilled manual, employed and self-employed in agriculture (agr.), and sales and services (left-out category: unknown or unemployed). For health, we include only the variables on how the last birth took place (attended by doctor and/or in hospital). Further, the constants for the three regions (city, town, rural) are included (c/t/r).
Source: Own calculations based on ECH and EIH.

2.3.2 Method

We consider the following three poverty measures: the headcount ratio (P0), the poverty gap ratio (P1), and the squared poverty gap ratio (P2). These three measures are special cases of the general P(α) family of poverty measures proposed by Foster et al. (1984). The parameter α is an indicator of the degree to which inequality among the poor is considered relevant in assessing poverty. For inequality we consider the Gini coefficient and the Atkinson family of inequality indices (Atkinson, 1970) with a constant inequality aversion parameter γ that allows giving more or less emphasis to redistributions that take place at the lower end of the income distribution. We compute inequality using 0.5 and 2.0 for γ. A higher value of this parameter will give more importance to income transfers that make income differences smaller at the bottom of the distribution relative to those at the top of it. Jenkins (1991) states that the Atkinson measure becomes very bottom-sensitive if γ is larger than 1.0.

As we are mainly concerned with the stability and reliability of the evolution of poverty and inequality in Bolivia in the period 1989–2002, we do not only need point estimates for the relevant figures, but also proper confidence intervals. In Grosse et al. (2009) standard errors were computed for the measures corresponding to predicted income which were based on 200 simulations where an error term was added to the predicted values from the regression. We construct 95 percent confidence intervals as follows.

Concerning poverty and inequality measures using observed income, confidence intervals are constructed based on the asymptotic distribution of the measures.[16] Kakwani (1993b) proposes a general method for deriving the distribution of poverty indices and provides formulas for the estimated standard errors of the FGT poverty measures. It is interesting to highlight that Kakwani (1993b) finds that the precise estimation of a poverty measure depends on how sensitive the measure is to income transfers among the very poor. For FGT measures, this is reflected in the parameter α. The precision of the poverty measure is a monotonically decreasing function of this parameter. In other words, a higher α translates larger standard errors for a given sample size.

The standard errors that Kakwani (1993b) proposed are valid under the assumption that the sample was collected under a simple random design. We follow Jolliffe and Semykina (1999) who extend this approach and provide estimated standard errors for the FGT poverty measures which are robust to complex survey design, such as stratification and multiple stages.

[16] An alternative would have been to use bootstrap methods for computing the confidence intervals (Biewen, 2002). The accuracy of asymptotic and bootstrap methods for poverty and inequality measures is discussed by Davidson and Flachaire (2007).

Inequality measures are usually nonlinear functions of the observations, and for complex surveys their variances are hard to estimate. Approximate variance estimation techniques have been proposed which rely on linearization methods such as a Taylor series approximation. For the Gini coefficient, we use the approximate standard error estimation technique proposed by Kovacevic and Binder (1997) which is based on the theory of estimating equations (Binder and Patak, 1994). They show that for complex survey design the estimated variance of the Gini coefficient can be estimated based on the variance of the estimated population totals.

For the Atkinson measures, we apply the linearization method proposed by Biewen and Jenkins (2006) who draw on an approximation of the variance suggested by Woodruff (1971). Starting from the fact that Atkinson inequality indices can be written in terms of population totals of the variable of interest, they derive an expression for the sampling variance that can handle complex survey design aspects.

With respect to measures based on predicted and simulated income, confidence intervals are also based on the asymptotic distribution of theses measures. We assume that predicted income is similar (in its statistical properties) to observed income and apply the techniques for poverty and inequality confidence intervals as described above. As predicted income is based on information from two surveys, we acknowledge that the confidence intervals are too narrow as they do not explicitly consider sampling error. One main difference between the approach pioneered by Hentschel et al. (2000) and Elbers et al. (2003) and the dynamic extension suggested by Grosse et al. (2009) and Stifel and Christiaensen (2007) is that the former studies combine a Census with a household survey, while the latter combine two surveys with the obvious implication that in the latter case sampling error is an issue.[17]

2.3.3 Income

Taking a first look at the properties of observed, predicted (i.e., within the LSMS data), and simulated (i.e., over to the DHS data) incomes for the years from 1989 to 2002 reveals that different estimation assumptions, different data sets, and different base years deliver different results for Bolivia. For the four years, we present several different values, depending on the base year and the dynamics of regression coefficients assumed (Table 2.3). For 1989, the first column shows the observed values as calculated from the LSMS. The next three columns show

[17]One could think of using bootstrap methods to account for the sampling error. We have decided not to follow this approach for practical reasons. The computations needed for this paper are already very time consuming taking around half a day to run, and considering doing at least 100 replications seems unfeasible for the time being.

the within-LSMS predictions. The abbreviation GKS stands for the assumptions of Grosse et al. (2009) following Equations (2.2) and (2.4) and the abbreviation SC for Stifel and Christiaensen (2007) following Equations (2.3) and (2.5). The number stands for the base year. For example, the column "SC99" refers to the estimation using the Stifel and Christiaensen (2007) method and the base year 1999, i.e., the coefficients of 1999. For the GKS case, the predictions for cities in the LSMS data set is the same independently of the base year because the method always uses the observed coefficients for cities of the respective years instead of the ones from the base year, that is why the column is labeled only "GKS" without number.

For the years 1989 and 1994, the comparison of observed incomes with predicted incomes in the LSMS is limited to cities.[18] Of course, when comparing the poverty and inequality measures based on observed and simulated incomes for cities, the purpose is not to verify implicitly whether the two assumptions (about the dynamics of regression coefficients and the variances of the error terms in the model) seem to work, as these assumptions are only used with the other two regions (town and rural). The second column "GKS" shows how well within-LSMS-sample prediction works using the "true" 1989 coefficients for cities. It slightly underestimates the income mean and overestimates P50. Using the coefficients from 1999 (third column "SC99") more strongly overestimates mean income, and when using the coefficients from 2002 mean income is relatively close to observed values (fourth column "SC02"). Simulating incomes in the DHS surveys overestimates incomes (mean and P50) for both assumptions and for both base years, but worse so for SC case. In nearly all cases, the standard deviation is too low compared to observed values.

[18]The comparison of the summary statistics shown is based on one example, i.e., on one prediction and simulation run. It is not based on the average income of the 200 repetitions. It would be slightly more accurate to present the average of each of the summary statistics, for example the average of all P50 instead of P50 of one income set.

Table 2.3: Descriptive Statistics of the LSMS and DHS, 1989–2002

	1989								1994							
	LSMS				DHS				LSMS				DHS			
	obs.	predicted			simulated				obs.	predicted			simulated			
		GKS	SC99	SC02	GKS99	GKS02	SC99	SC02		GKS	SC99	SC02	GKS99	GKS02	SC99	SC02
	Total Bolivia															
Mean *y*					215	215	239	232					231	241	266	255
P5 *y*					27	30	30	30					24	38	32	32
P50 *y*					126	128	135	130					142	160	154	143
P95 *y*					714	701	814	761					738	714	857	819
SD *y*					290	285	326	346					281	270	349	369
	City															
Mean *y*	310	296	323	305	311	311	350	337	326	316	339	341	337	337	382	370
P5 *y*	48	45	50	40	47	47	51	42	61	56	59	41	57	57	58	43
P50 *y*	190	196	214	186	200	200	217	198	208	214	227	199	236	236	250	228
P95 *y*	922	891	977	990	943	943	1,066	1,061	963	910	977	1,071	922	922	1,124	1,153
SD *y*	444	318	355	371	366	366	414	454	408	335	382	472	338	338	430	477
	Town															
Mean *y*					184	206	208	218					219	222	263	238
P5 *y*					21	41	26	41					26	53	31	42
P50 *y*					108	144	128	150					138	169	158	162
P95 *y*					696	576	688	626					709	568	871	713
SD *y*					235	192	246	224					245	186	326	257
	Rural Areas															
Mean *y*					112	106	119	115					107	132	129	123
P5 *y*					23	23	25	26					17	31	26	27
P50 *y*					79	75	85	84					71	99	90	88
P95 *y*					301	293	326	304					308	332	368	349
SD *y*					113	104	121	108					112	110	127	117

continued on next page

Table 2.3 continued

	1999							2002						
	LSMS				DHS			LSMS				DHS		
	obs.	predicted			simulated			obs.	predicted			simulated		
		GKSSC99	GKS02	SC02	GKSSC99	GKS02	SC02		GKSSC02	GKS99	SC99	GKSSC02	GKS99	SC99
	Total Bolivia													
Mean y	266	278	297	267	303	320	294	256	263	258	278	304	301	314
P5 y	31	32	44	29	36	43	36	31	30	20	31	36	24	35
P50 y	159	157	184	146	180	204	165	142	140	128	150	168	152	176
P95 y	901	923	921	902	948	957	971	784	866	898	878	975	1,033	1,013
SD y	355	410	405	418	385	377	412	421	416	428	401	500	514	459
	City													
Mean y	378	404	404	393	412	412	402	361	377	377	393	441	441	454
P5 y	66	57	57	45	63	63	50	51	41	41	52	50	50	62
P50 y	247	247	247	236	270	270	239	207	213	213	233	255	255	285
P95 y	1,100	1,188	1,188	1,204	1,208	1,208	1,248	1,267	1,298	1,298	1,233	1,379	1,379	1,362
SD y	442	525	525	548	450	450	504	546	539	539	500	675	675	600
	Town													
Mean y	258	248	272	229	289	314	274	244	248	261	285	281	295	297
P5 y	39	46	56	44	30	54	44	42	48	22	38	44	21	32
P50 y	167	164	209	160	182	219	180	169	164	143	174	183	159	181
P95 y	724	716	730	626	863	929	832	713	764	812	872	791	1,035	977
SD y	267	255	241	210	357	306	310	268	261	352	336	347	408	344
	Rural Areas													
Mean y	112	114	158	108	129	169	124	115	109	91	115	141	124	142
P5 y	24	24	35	23	27	31	27	24	24	13	23	28	17	27
P50 y	81	78	119	79	89	120	90	84	84	59	83	98	77	97
P95 y	297	301	412	272	353	485	331	301	284	271	310	394	388	418
SD y	108	112	134	99	129	168	120	126	104	105	110	144	154	154

Notes: See Chapter 2.3.3 for explanation.
Source: Own calculations based on ECH, EIH, and DHS.

Nearly the same holds for 1994, where the within-LSMS-survey predictions using the GKS assumption comes relatively close to observed values (tenth column) whereas the SC assumption of no dynamics overestimates mean income (eleventh and twelfth column). P50 is overestimated for the 1999 coefficients and underestimated for the 2002 coefficients. The trend from 1989 to 1994 is, in general, nearly always the same: an increase in mean income in all regions for all specifications except in one case. The income level for each of the assumptions, however, is different. For example, the observed income in cities increases from 310 to 326, whereas for the two predictions using the SC assumption, the increase would be from 323 to 339 ("SC99") or 305 to 341 ("SC02").

For the later years 1999 and 2002 (second part of Table 2.3), more comparisons are possible. First, there are observed incomes in all three regions. In cities and towns, observed income goes down whereas it goes slightly up in rural areas between 1999 and 2002. Overall, this leads to a decrease of income at the national level. The column "GKSSC99" shows the within-survey prediction for the year 1999, i.e., applying the "true" coefficients to the same data and predicting incomes, which is the same for both methods.

Stronger differences arise if 2002 is taken as a base year, and different assumptions are used to estimate the 1999 value. "GKS02" presents the results of out-of-sample predictions in "pretending" that the LSMS survey was only urban, and applying Equation (2.2) (to both LSMS and DHS) whereas "SC02" applies Equation (2.3), i.e., the coefficients from 2002 (also to both LSMS and DHS). Even within the LSMS data set, there is a tendency for overestimation of incomes, especially for cities. In addition, using the GKS assumption and 2002 as a base year, the overestimation becomes stronger in rural areas. Going to the DHS the results are even less encouraging. Both assumptions and both base years overestimate incomes in all regions. Yet, the trends in the DHS data from 1994 to 1999 remain similar: again we find increasing mean incomes, but to a different level. For 2002, the income results resemble the ones of 1999. However, within-LSMS results are slightly better, and also the ones using the GKS assumption and 1999 as the base year (comparing "obs." with "GKS99" in the LSMS columns). Here, the assumption of no dynamics of SC delivers the worst results for within-LSMS predictions. But again, going to the DHS data also renders an overestimation of incomes, independently of the assumption and base year. Worst results for simulations over to DHS are also achieved using "SC99".[19]

Besides the question of how close estimates come to observed values, the within-country differences become clear. Mean income in rural areas is only about one-third of the value of cities. Towns show also lower values than cities and are

[19]For a discussion on the possible explanations for these out-of-sample prediction errors, see Section 2.4.

most of the time close to the national average. These relations remain over time, leading to the alarming question on how to avoid that rural areas become more and more detached from overall growth.

2.3.4 Evolution of Poverty and Inequality

We discuss in this section the detailed results on poverty and inequality using a graphical presentation. In the next section, the results and performance of the two methods are compared systematically in an overview table. Figures 2.1 to 2.8 show moderate poverty for P0, P1, and P2, and inequality for Gini and two Atkinson indices (with the inequality-aversion parameter γ of 0.5 and 2.0). The results for extreme poverty are shown in Appendix Figures C.1 to C.4. For the test of the different assumptions on dynamics, we focus on the three regions and on the two years for which we have complete data (1999 or 2002) so that we can compare the measures based on simulated income, for both GKS and SC, with the measures based on observed income. When we refer to simulated values in a given year, we mean that the other year has been used as the base year for the model in both GKS and SC, with numbers after the abbreviation showing the base year. For the base year, and by construction, GKS and SC yield the same results.

The figures for total Bolivia show that results differ depending on the method and base year chosen. Moderate poverty (Figure 2.1) declines from 1989 to 1999, independently of the method and base year used. The level and dynamics, however, differ substantially depending on both base year and method. For example, using 1999 as base year, the SC assumption gives significantly lower values than the GKS assumption. The trend of poverty in the crisis-driven years between 1999 and 2002 is not clear. P0 clearly increases when looking at observed values, whereas P1 and P2 stagnate (P1 with a slightly increasing trend, P2 with a slightly decreasing trend). The SC method delivers a steady downward trend for all measures, whereas GKS is able to reproduce the increase in P0 slightly better. Worth noting furthermore is the level difference in the base year between LSMS and DHS data. The P0 estimation is 5 percentage points below the observed values for 1999 and even 7 for 2002, without overlapping confidence intervals.[20]

Inequality results (Figure 2.2) also depend considerably on base year and method. For 1989, results are nearly the same independently of year and method. For 1994, the same holds for base year 1999. In this case, inequality seems to have remained constant in the 1990s and only increased from 1999 onwards. But for 2002 as base year, differences become stronger, since the GKS assumption shows

[20]The picture for extreme poverty (Appendix Figure C.1) is very similar, however with a less strong increase in P0 and a clearer downward trend of P1 and P2.

a decrease until 1994 followed by an increase in the next observation years. Overall, GKS better reflects observed trends.

Looking at cities reveals, first, how well the cross-survey-matching method works. Here, the GKS method uses the actual regression coefficients in the LSMS data to simulate incomes in the DHS data. The SC method uses either 1999 (left part of Figure 2.3) or 2002 (right part). For P0, the GKS assumption delivers lower point estimates, sometimes not with overlapping confidence intervals. Results for SC are worse, with significantly lower levels for 1999 and mixed results for 2002. For P1 and P2, results of GKS are very close to observed values, whereas SC significantly underestimates P1 and P2 with 1999 as the base year and significantly overestimates P1 and P2 with 2002 as the base year. This result supports the doubts about the accuracy of using regression coefficients of one year for estimations of other years back and forth in time, as SC does, without taking dynamics into account.

Taking a closer look at the end of the observation period reveals that the three poverty measures based on observed income seem to have increased between 1999 and 2002. With 1999 as the base year, this trend is not well replicated using SC, which suggests a decline in poverty. GKS suggests relative little changes between both years. With 2002 as the base year, results are similar. If we focus on levels, it is clear that the estimates based on GKS are closer to the results based on observed values than the estimates based on SC. This is not surprising, as SC implies that the results from the regression of the base year are used for the other year, while GKS uses the results from the regression of the corresponding year to simulated values for cities. It is nevertheless surprising that for P0 (moderate poverty) the point estimate of GKS for 2002 is below the lower bound of the 95 percent confidence interval of poverty computed with observed income, and that both confidence intervals, the one for observed income and the one for simulated income, do not overlap. The situation is better for P1 and P2, as the confidence intervals overlap. The simulated result come closer to observed values when using GKS for the year 1999.[21]

Turning to inequality, Figure (2.4) reveals that the corresponding coefficients are able to reproduce the inequality trend (GKS), first decreasing than increasing (even if the levels tend to be smaller than the observed ones), whereas the constant coefficients (SC) deliver a constant picture on inequality with hardly any change. This again calls for some no-constancy modeling to take dynamics into account. As for cities data for all 4 years are available, observed income sug-

[21] For extreme poverty (Appendix Figure C.2), the differences using 1999 as base year are smaller using GKS for all poverty measures, but SC fails to reproduce the increase in poverty from 1999 to 2002. The results for base year 2002 using GKS deliver better simulations within the same year (observed and simulated confidence intervals overlap) compared to moderate poverty, and again SC overestimates poverty significantly.

Figure 2.1: Moderate Poverty, Total Bolivia, 1989–2002

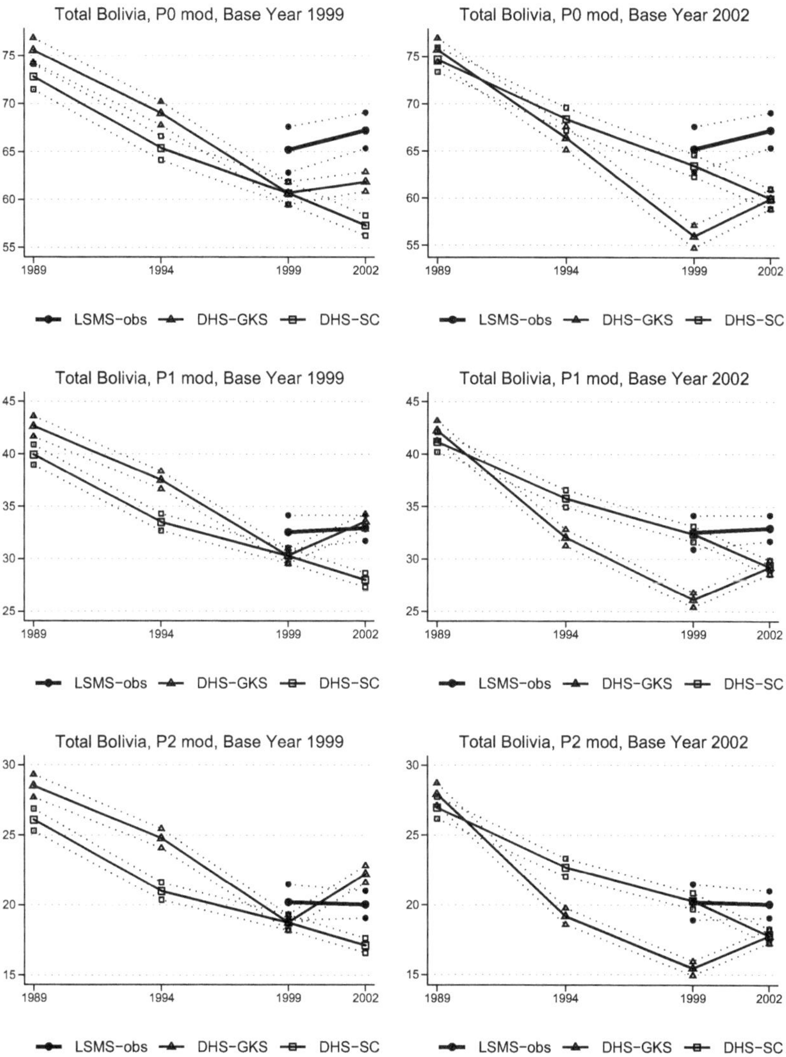

Notes: LSMS–obs: Data from LSMS using observed income; DHS–GKS: Data from DHS using GKS assumptions on dynamics; DHS–SC: Data from DHS using SC assumptions on dynamics. The basic idea of constructing confidence intervals, see Figure 1.2. Furthermore, the values are calculated using advanced techniques described in Section 2.3.2. See text for details.
Source: Own calculations based on ECH, EIH, and DHS.

Figure 2.2: Inequality, Total Bolivia, 1989–2002

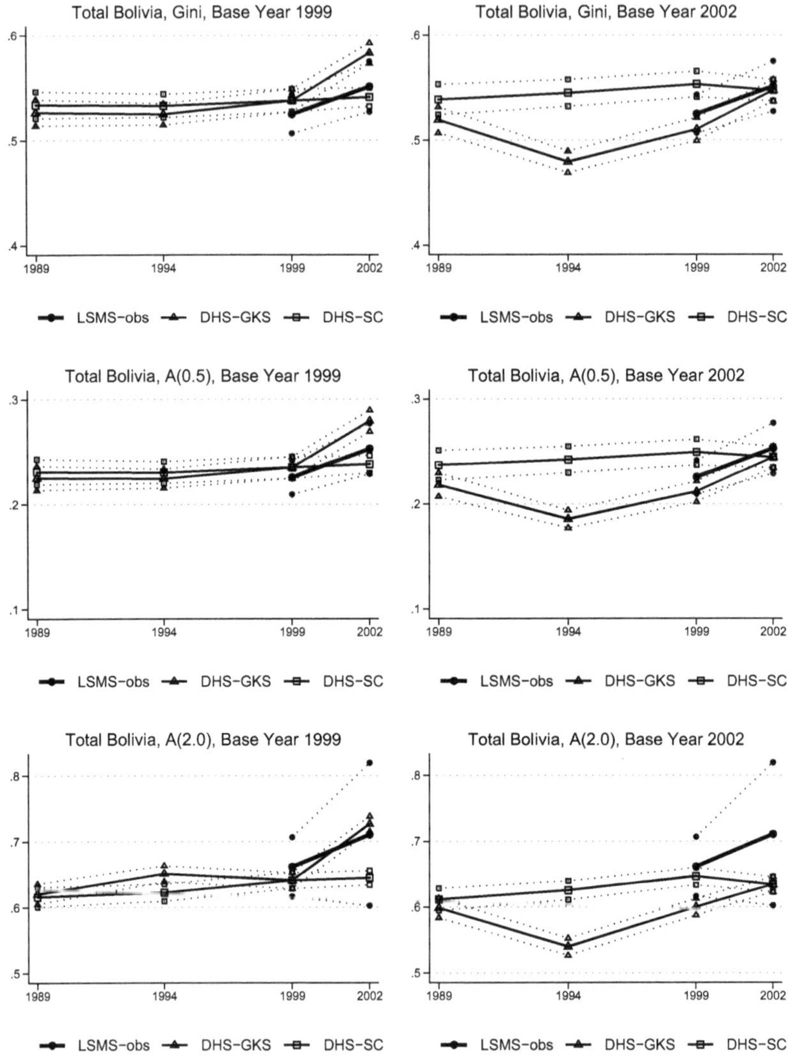

Notes: LSMS–obs: Data from LSMS using observed income; DHS–GKS: Data from DHS using GKS assumptions on dynamics; DHS–SC: Data from DHS using SC assumptions on dynamics. See notes to Figure 2.1 for details.
Source: Own calculations based on ECH, EIH, and DHS.

gests that inequality as measured by Gini and A(0.5) decreased between 1989 and 1994, remained stable until 1999 and then had an important increase until 2002. This is consistent with the fact that Bolivia experienced a macroeconomic crisis in 1999 which was related to a pronounced deterioration of terms of trade and with the Brazilian devaluation. For A(2.0) inequality increased already from 1994 onwards.

Concerning moderate poverty in towns (Figure 2.5), observed income points to a small decrease in poverty between 1999 and 2002. With 1999 as the base year, GKS shows a slight increase for P0, and a more important increase for P1 and P2. SC follows better the trend of poverty computed with observed values. Similar results are found when using 2002 as the base year. If one looks at levels, the point estimates for P0 in 2002 based on simulated income using GKS is closer to the result based on observed income than SC, but the situation is reversed when looking at P1 and P2. With 2002 as the base year, and focusing on 1999, SC is closer to the figure based on observed income than GKS for P0, P1, and P2.[22]

For inequality in towns (Figure 2.6), we focus again on the years 1999 and 2002. Gini and A(0.5) based on observed income show very little change between these two years, while A(2.0) suggests a decrease. It must be noted that the confidence intervals are especially large for A(2.0).[23] As for the case of cities, SC shows estimates that are almost unchanged between 1999 and 2002, irrespective of the base year used. GKS, on the other hand, shows a sharp increase in inequality for all mcasures if 1999 is used as the base year. With 2002 as the base year, GKS suggests a small increase in inequality. For towns, the overall level difference between the two base years is again most pronounced.

Moderate poverty in rural areas (Figure 2.7) shows an interesting picture. The levels of poverty are quite different for observed income and simulated income. Observed income suggests that P0 in 2002 has remained very close to its value in 1999. With 1999 as the base year, GKS also shows little changes, but SC suggests an important decrease in P0. For P1, while observed income points to a decrease, GKS suggests an important increase, while SC shows a trend more in line with observed income. Results with 2002 as the base year are different. For P0, GKS now suggests a sharp increase in poverty, while SC shows an important decrease.

---

[22]Extreme poverty (Appendix Figure C.3) shows one interesting difference. The headcount increases which is only replicated by the GKS method. Striking are also the overall level differences for the earlier years of 5 to 10 percentage points lower when using 2002 as base year which is even more relevant for extreme poverty.

[23]Beyond the relatively small sample for towns, this could have something to do with nonlinearities of the measure. As mentioned before, Atkinson (1970) inequality measures explicitly consider a constant inequality aversion parameter, which allows giving more or less emphasis to redistributions that take place at the lower end of the income distribution. A parameter value such as 2.0 gives much more importance to income transfers that make income differences smaller at the bottom of the distribution relative to those at the top of it (Jenkins, 1991).

Figure 2.3: Moderate Poverty, Cities, 1989–2002

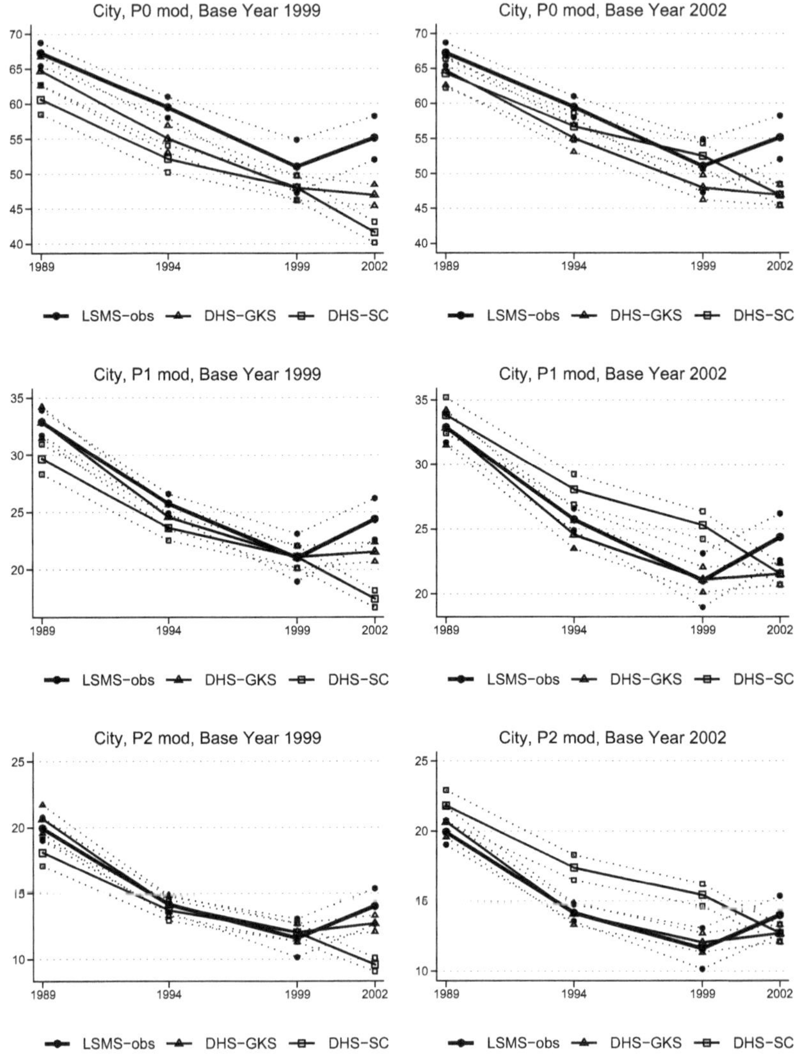

Notes: LSMS–obs: Data from LSMS using observed income; DHS–GKS: Data from DHS using GKS assumptions on dynamics; DHS–SC: Data from DHS using SC assumptions on dynamics. See notes to Figure 2.1 for details.

Source: Own calculations based on ECH, EIH, and DHS.

Figure 2.4: Inequality, Cities, 1989–2002

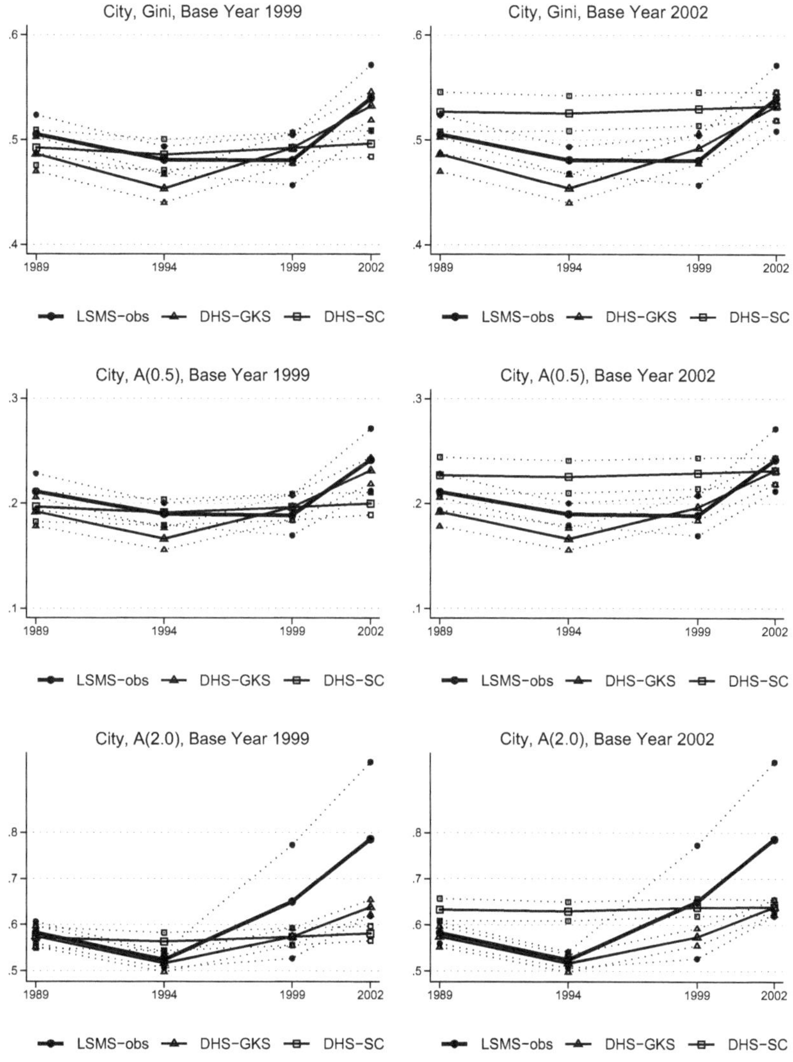

Notes: LSMS–obs: Data from LSMS using observed income; DHS–GKS: Data from DHS using GKS assumptions on dynamics; DHS–SC: Data from DHS using SC assumptions on dynamics. See notes to Figure 2.1 for details.
Source: Own calculations based on ECH, EIH, and DHS.

Figure 2.5: Moderate Poverty, Towns, 1989–2002

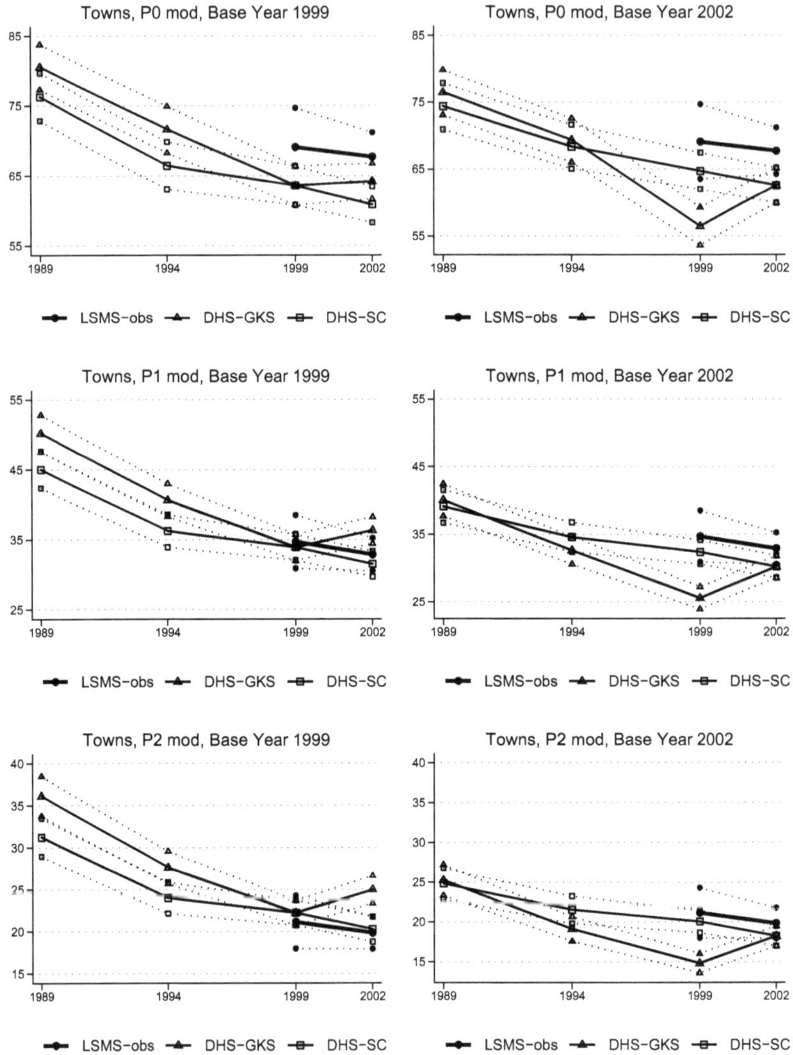

Notes: LSMS–obs: Data from LSMS using observed income; DHS–GKS: Data from DHS using GKS assumptions on dynamics; DHS–SC: Data from DHS using SC assumptions on dynamics. See notes to Figure 2.1 for details.
Source: Own calculations based on ECH, EIH, and DHS.

Figure 2.6: Inequality, Towns, 1989–2002

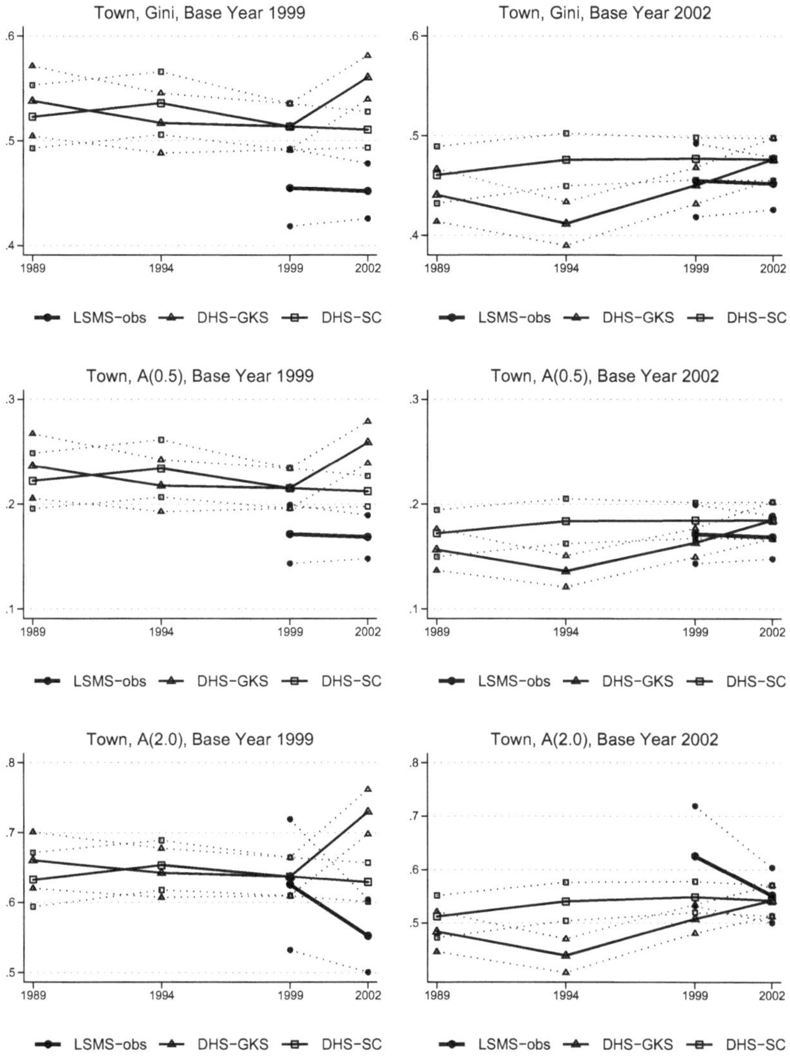

Notes: LSMS–obs: Data from LSMS using observed income; DHS–GKS: Data from DHS using GKS assumptions on dynamics; DHS–SC: Data from DHS using SC assumptions on dynamics. See notes to Figure 2.1 for details.
Source: Own calculations based on ECH, EIH, and DHS.

For P1 and P2, the downwards trend shown by observed income is replicated by SC, but not by GKS which rather suggests an important increase in poverty.[24]

Inequality measures in rural areas (Figure 2.8) present a similar picture as towns. Observed income shows almost no changes in inequality between 1999 and 2002, which highlights the fact that rural areas were less affected by the 1999 crisis. As before, SC suggests very stable figures for both years and they are relatively close to the measures based on observed income. GKS with base year 1999 shows a very different picture in 2002 as it points to an important increase in inequality, with levels well above the confidence interval for observed income. With 2002 as the base year results are closer to those with observed income, even if the levels remain higher than the observed ones.

[24]The results for extreme poverty show the same picture (Appendix Figure C.4).

Figure 2.7: Moderate Poverty, Rural Areas, 1989–2002

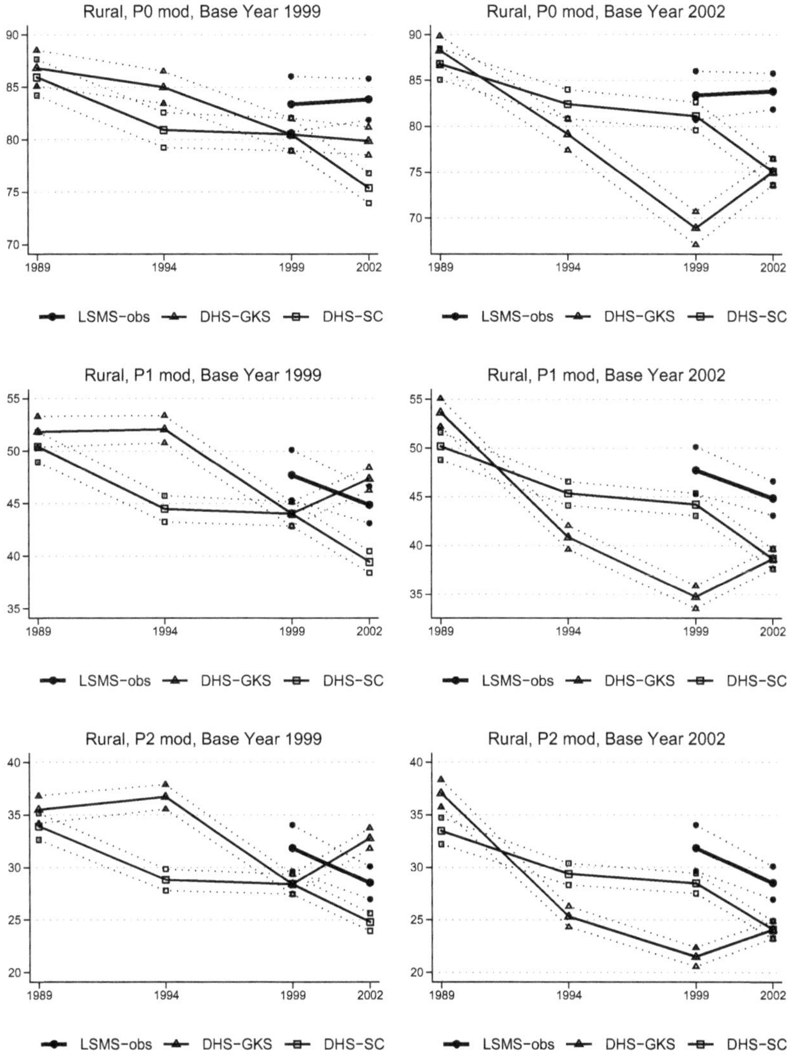

Notes: LSMS–obs: Data from LSMS using observed income; DHS–GKS: Data from DHS using GKS assumptions on dynamics; DHS–SC: Data from DHS using SC assumptions on dynamics. See notes to Figure 2.1 for details.
Source: Own calculations based on ECH, EIH, and DHS.

Figure 2.8: Inequality, Rural Areas, 1989–2002

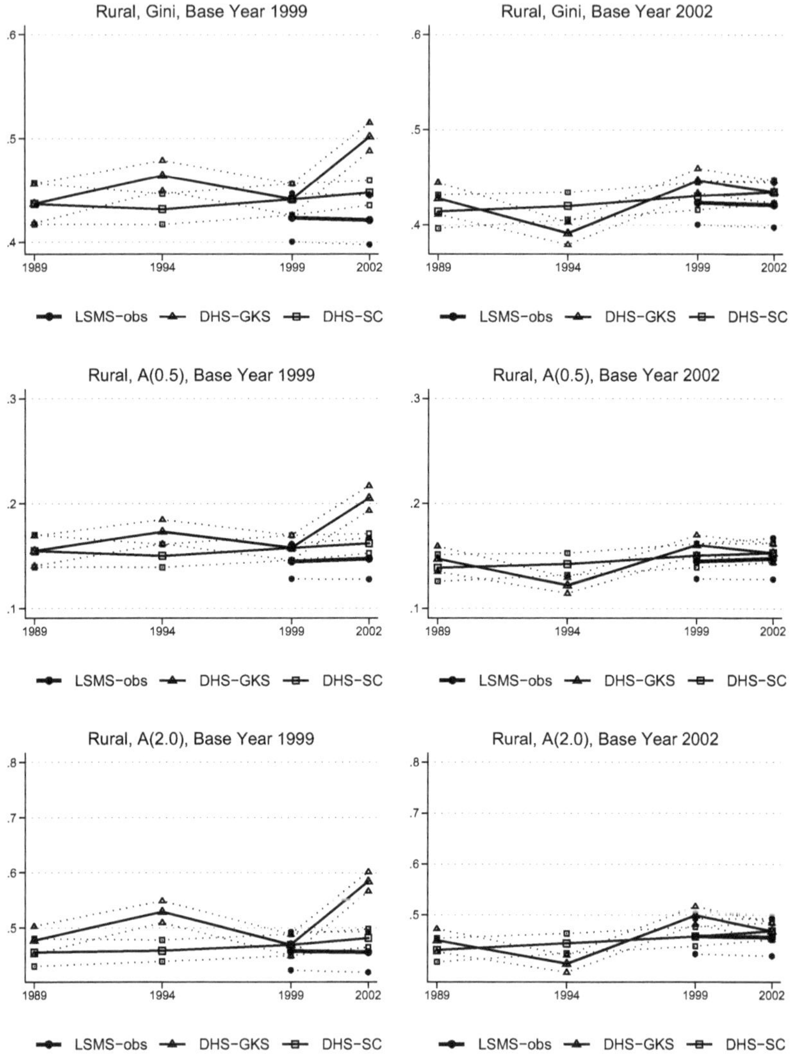

Notes: LSMS–obs: Data from LSMS using observed income; DHS–GKS: Data from DHS using GKS assumptions on dynamics; DHS–SC: Data from DHS using SC assumptions on dynamics. See notes to Figure 2.1 for details.
Source: Own alculations based on ECH, EIH, and DHS.

2.4 Discussion and Outlook

It is certainly difficult to interpret the differences of using both approaches, i.e., SC and GKS, as even using measures based on observed income do not always show a clear picture of the evolution of poverty and inequality in towns and rural areas in Bolivia between 1999 and 2002. The confidence intervals for the measures are relatively large, e.g., P0 (moderate poverty) based on observed income in rural areas is estimated to be between 81 percent and 86 percent in 1999.[25]

As the relevant regions for out-of-sample predictions are towns and rural areas by comparing the measures based on simulated income with those based on observed income, we have systematically compared the performance of GKS and SC in Table 2.4 for poverty and inequality. The idea is to check whether potential problems arise comparing the "true value", i.e., the one computed using observed income, with the values based on simulated income following either GKS or SC. The table shows (i) a simple judgment on the over-/underestimation of the true values, i.e., to see if the estimates are systematically or randomly above or below the observed values; (ii) whether the estimated numbers lie outside the 95 percent confidence interval of the true value; (iii) whether confidence intervals fail to overlap; and (iv) whether the simulated trend (between 1999 and 2002) is different than the one computed with true values. In general, (iii) and (iv) are the most problematic.

For our data, it is difficult to come to an overall judgement on wether SC performs better than GKS because the results differ for poverty and inequality measures as well as for income. In general, both methods do not yield very good results. For example, P0 is nearly always underestimated. For towns and rural areas, SC gives slightly better results. However, this does not hold for cities, where clearly GKS outperforms SC, and total Bolivia, where results are mixed. Similar results were obtained when looking at income in Chapter 2.3.3.

It can be argued that dependent on changes in regression coefficients the error terms and on changes in endowments, one or the other method performs better. First, if the regression model is very stable from period to period, the assumption of SC (of using the coefficients and error terms obtained from one period and apply them for another one) should not face many problems. However, if this is not the case, it is possible that a more flexible approach, such as assuming any kind of dynamics as GKS may yield better results, assuming that the changes between

[25]For the data used here, it is important to highlight that for both base years used (1999 and 2002), there is a one year lag between the LSMS, which are used for estimating the models, and the DHS, which are used to simulate income for towns and rural areas. This means that the previous consideration about the stability of the results from a model does not only apply for two years, but in fact for four years (1998, 1999, 2002, and 2003). Furthermore, the period itself of the late 1990s and early 2000s is characterized by significant turbulence in the economic performance.

periods are adequately modeled. If this is not the case, then GKS does not yield good results for towns and rural areas. Table 2.5 systematically compares which assumption for 1999 comes closer in terms of distance to the observed coefficients. The column "closer" indicates which estimated coefficient, β_{GKS} or β_{SC} following the Equations 2.2 and 2.3, respectively, comes closer to the "true" β_{99}. Of the total of 72 coefficients for towns and rural areas, the GKS coefficients are closer in 39 cases and the SC coefficients in 33 cases.

Second, as SC by definition always use the same coefficients and error terms, all changes in poverty and inequality measures between years are explained by changes in endowments, which yields as a general result that if endowments do not change much SC will provide measures that are rather stable over time. If true values (of income, poverty, and inequality) are not changing too much over time, SC will perform well. This is why nearly all poverty graphs show a monotonic (downward) trend and the inequality graphs nearly no trend for the SC case. As was mentioned before, Bolivia experienced an important crisis in 1999, where per capita GDP decreased almost by 2 percent after several years of positive growth. After the crisis, the economy recovered slowly, and it was only in 2004 that growth of per capita GDP was again larger than 1 percent. Therefore, one could expect that the four surveys considered in our study (1998, 1999, 2002, and 2003) depict rather different economic situations.

Coming back to the question of how to model dynamics, the constancy-of-differences assumption in Equation (2.2) can alternatively be relaxed following Grosse et al. (2009) and rearranged to:

$$(\beta_{t-1}^{T} - \beta_{t-1}^{C}) = \phi(\beta_t^{T} - \beta_t^{C}) \text{ and } (\beta_{t-1}^{R} - \beta_{t-1}^{C}) = \phi(\beta_t^{R} - \beta_t^{C}) \qquad (2.6)$$

where ϕ can be understood as a kind of "mobility parameter" that measures if the coefficients estimated separately for urban and non-urban areas become more similar towards each other or not. We present the evolution of ϕ to gain insights of the mobility of parameters over time in Chapter 2.3.1.[26]

[26]However, we do not show the results of the whole estimation procedure on poverty and inequality using this assumption.

Table 2.4: Observed and Simulated Poverty and Inequality Levels and Trends, 1999–2002

	Total				City				Town				Rural			
	1999		2002		1999		2002		1999		2002		1999		2002	
	GKS	SC	GKS	SC	GKS	SC	GKS	SC	GKS	SC	GKS	SC	GKS	SC	GKS	SC
Moderate poverty																
PO																
Over-/Underestimate (level)	u	u	u	u	u	o	u	u	u	u	u	u	u	u	u	u
Estimates are NOT in 95% CI	x		x	x			x	x	x			x	x		x	x
CI do NOT overlap	x		x	x			x	x	x			x	x		x	x
Different trend from observed		x		x	x	x	x	x	x		x			x	x	x
P1																
Over-/Underestimate (level)	u	u	o	u		o	u	u	u	u	o	u	u	u	o	u
Estimates are NOT in 95% CI	x					x	x	x	x		x		x	x	x	x
CI do NOT overlap	x					x	x	x	x				x		x	x
Different trend from observed		x				x		x	x		x		x		x	
P2																
Over-/Underestimate (level)	u	o	o	u	o	o	u	u	u	u	o	o	u	u	o	u
Estimates are NOT in 95% CI	x		x	x		x		x	x		x		x	x	x	x
CI do NOT overlap	x		x	x		x		x	x		x		x	x	x	x
Different trend from observed	x		x			x		x	x		x		x		x	
Extreme poverty																
PO																
Over-/Underestimate (level)	u		o	u	u	o	u	u	x	o	o	u	u	u	o	u
Estimates are NOT in 95% CI	x			x		x	x	x	x		x		x	x		x
CI do NOT overlap	x			x				x					x			x
Different trend from observed		x		x		x		x		x		x	x		x	
P1																
Over-/Underestimate (level)	u		o	u		o	u	u	u	o	o	o	u	u	o	u
Estimates are NOT in 95% CI	x		x	x		x		x	x		x	x	x	x	x	x
CI do NOT overlap	x		x	x		x		x	x		x		x	x	x	x
Different trend from observed	x		x			x		x	x		x		x		x	

continued on next page

Table 2.4 continued

	Total				City				Town				Rural			
	1999		2002		1999		2002		1999		2002		1999		2002	
	GKS	SC	GKS	SC	GKS	SC	GKS	SC	GKS	SC	GKS	SC	GKS	SC	GKS	SC
P2																
Over-/Underestimate (level)	u	u	o	u		o	u	u	u	u	o	o	u	u	o	u
Estimates are NOT in 95% CI	x		x	x		x		x	x		x	x	x	x	x	x
CI do NOT overlap	x		x	x		x		x			x		x	x	x	x
Different trend from observed	x		x			x		x	x		x		x		x	
Inequality																
Gini																
Over-/Underestimate (level)	u	o	o	u	o	o	u	u	u	o	o	o	o	o	o	o
Estimates are NOT in 95% CI		x	x			x		x			x	x			x	x
CI do NOT overlap						x					x	x			x	
Different trend from observed		x		x		x		x	x		x			x	x	x
A(0.5)																
Over-/Underestimate (level)	u	o	o	u	o	o	u	u	u	o	o	o	o	o	o	o
Estimates are NOT in 95% CI		x	x			x		x			x	x			x	
CI do NOT overlap						x					x	x			x	
Different trend from observed		x		x		x		x	x		x		x			
A(2.0)																
Over-/Underestimate (level)	u	u	o	u	u	u	u	u	u	u	o	o	o		o	o
Estimates are NOT in 95% CI	x							x	x		x	x	x		x	
CI do NOT overlap	x							x			x	x			x	
Different trend from observed		x		x		x		x	x		x			x	x	x

Notes: For explanation, see Chapter 2.3.4.
Source: Own calculations based on ECH and DHS.

Table 2.5: Regression Results Using Two Different Assumptions

	City		Town				Rural			
	β_{99}	β_{02}	β_{99}	β_{GKS}	β_{SC}	closer	β_{99}	β_{GKS}	β_{SC}	closer
La Paz	-0.04	-0.03	0.16	0.18	0.18	GKS	0.25	0.27	0.26	SC
Cochabamba	0.24	0.17	0.75	0.68	0.17	GKS	0.39	0.33	0.16	GKS
Oruro	-0.06	-0.23	-0.18	-0.35	-0.11	SC	0.35	0.18	0.23	SC
Potosi	-0.07	-0.08	0.18	0.17	-0.09	GKS	0.05	0.04	-0.08	GKS
Tarija	0.50	0.16	0.57	0.23	0.40	SC	0.71	0.37	0.56	SC
Santa Cruz	0.70	0.44	0.58	0.32	0.11	GKS	0.71	0.45	0.46	SC
Beni & Pando	0.62	0.31	0.29	-0.02	0.25	SC	0.74	0.44	0.59	SC
elderly dependency ratio	-0.20	-0.32	-0.18	-0.30	-0.24	SC	-0.03	-0.15	-0.08	SC
child dependency ratio	0.17	0.00	0.55	0.38	-0.01	GKS	-0.12	-0.29	0.05	GKS
hh size	-0.08	-0.05	-0.06	-0.03	-0.05	SC	-0.09	-0.05	-0.10	SC
hh head age	0.00	0.02	0.01	0.03	0.01	SC	0.02	0.03	0.03	GKS
hh head age squared	0.00	0.00	0.00	0.00	0.00	SC	0.00	0.00	0.00	SC
gender hh head	-0.05	0.03	0.22	0.30	0.06	GKS	-0.01	0.07	-0.12	GKS
access to public water	-0.08	-0.05	0.05	0.07	0.06	SC	0.00	0.03	0.13	GKS
has no toilet	-0.03	-0.04	-0.27	-0.28	0.06	GKS	-0.23	-0.25	-0.15	GKS
no partner in household	0.21	0.34	0.47	0.60	0.25	GKS	0.39	0.53	0.06	GKS
com. basic edu. (m.)	-0.16	-0.04	-0.02	0.09	0.05	SC	-0.02	0.09	0.15	GKS
incom. secondary edu. (m.)	-0.01	-0.11	-0.17	-0.27	0.07	GKS	-0.01	-0.11	0.11	GKS
com. secondary edu. (m.)	-0.05	0.06	0.29	0.39	0.07	GKS	0.05	0.16	0.19	GKS
tertiary edu. (m.)	0.39	0.43	-0.02	0.03	0.29	GKS	0.44	0.49	0.27	GKS
com. basic edu. (w.)	0.12	-0.07	-0.01	-0.20	-0.01	SC	0.26	0.06	0.22	SC
incom. secondary edu. (w.)	0.10	0.01	0.11	0.03	0.05	SC	0.27	0.18	0.26	SC
com. secondary edu. (w.)	0.24	0.02	0.12	-0.10	0.31	SC	0.44	0.22	0.33	SC
tertiary edu. (w.)	0.53	0.44	0.45	0.36	0.58	GKS	0.75	0.66	0.64	GKS

continued on next page

Table 2.5 continued

	City		Town				Rural			
	β_{99}	β_{02}	β_{99}	β_{GKS}	β_{SC}	closer	β_{99}	β_{GKS}	β_{SC}	closer
high & med. skilled white collar (m.)	0.53	0.62	1.03	1.12	0.61	GKS	0.67	0.76	0.21	GKS
skilled & unskilled manual (m.)	0.23	0.23	0.57	0.57	0.41	GKS	0.60	0.60	0.04	GKS
agriculture (m.)	-0.21	0.21	0.19	0.61	0.30	SC	0.25	0.67	-0.05	SC
sales and services (m.)	0.34	0.53	0.87	1.06	0.62	GKS	0.67	0.86	0.26	GKS
high & med. skilled white collar (w.)	0.38	0.55	0.73	0.90	0.72	SC	0.13	0.30	0.43	GKS
skilled & unskilled manual (w.)	0.14	0.19	0.51	0.57	0.17	GKS	-0.12	-0.07	0.05	GKS
agriculture (w.)	0.64	-0.14	-0.24	-1.02	-0.54	SC	-0.05	-0.83	-0.08	SC
sales and services (w.)	0.31	0.23	0.71	0.63	0.35	GKS	0.36	0.28	0.25	GKS
birth in last 12 month	0.20	-0.06	-0.29	-0.55	-0.17	SC	-0.12	-0.38	-0.03	SC
attended by doctor	-0.22	-0.02	0.68	0.88	0.10	GKS	0.20	0.40	0.02	SC
delivered in hospital	-0.10	-0.26	-0.38	-0.54	0.12	GKS	0.08	-0.08	0.15	SC
c/t/r dummy/constant	5.05	4.80	3.84	3.59	4.41	GKS	4.09	3.84	4.23	SC

Notes: See text for details.
Source: Own calculations based on ECH and EIH.

Table 2.6 gives a first insight on this question. For example, it calculates ϕ of Equation (2.6) for towns and rural areas which reveals that it is neither constant nor of the same sign or magnitude for each coefficient. What becomes evident is that a constant ϕ cannot be confirmed. In addition, it reveals that coefficients can be of different magnitude and even sign (exemplarily shown for the coefficient for cities in the last column). Of the 36 coefficients, one-third is not even stable in sign for cities. Of the remaining, many change considerably in terms of magnitude. Furthermore, several of the coefficients for cities show relatively similar values for 1989, 1994, and 2002, but not for 1999, for example from the regional variables Oruro, Santa Cruz, and Beni and Pando, but also others such as male and female secondary education, males working in agriculture, or birth in last 12 month. The question on whether this is measurement error, a structural change, or a temporal change due to the crisis in the economy remains open and cannot be answered easily with the data at hand. This could only be done using more national surveys of the other rounds of the ECH, which would be an issue to be addressed in future research (or for other countries).

Additionally worth noting is that results would have changed if we had followed the way Stifel and Christiaensen (2007) deal with the issue of underestimating poverty (by shifting the poverty line until observed and simulated poverty levels coincide). In this case the picture would look different, as the level of simulated real income would change in order to match observed levels. Such a modification would have changed the results for, for example, moderate poverty (P0) for total Bolivia (Figure 2.1) in that the GKS assumption would have nearly exactly coincided in level and trend for both base years whereas the level for 1999 (using 2002 as base year) for SC, that without shifting comes close to observed values, would overestimate P0 clearly. We suspect that the level results are driven by the regional dummy (i.e., the regional constant). Stifel and Christiaensen (2007) for example have a very large constant that is taken back and forth in time. The share of the remaining few coefficients (e.g., only 3 for the Nairobi sample) is rather negligible, besides being selected to ensure stability in themselves. In selecting variables, the authors explicitly use the ones that are expected to remain stable over time and not respond to economic conditions or policy changes. One way of dealing with such problems is suggested by Grosse et al. (2009) and consists in shifting real per capita mean income (both observed and simulated) to levels observed by national accounts.[27] This data is available for all countries (sometimes even for regional disaggregation) and can serve as a kind of neutral anchor for the level.

[27]Note that, in general, shifting per capita mean income, shifting the poverty line, or changing the intercept of the regression are all equivalent transformations. The only difference could be availability (for example, having two or more different poverty lines) or disaggregation (for example, having national account data at the departmental level).

Table 2.6: Stability of Regression Coefficients over Time

	City				Town		Rural		ϕ		sign (β) City
	β_{39}	β_{94}	β_{99}	β_{02}	β_{99}	β_{02}	β_{99}	β_{02}	Town	Rural	Constant?
La Paz	0.01	0.15	-0.04	-0.03	0.16	0.18	0.25	0.26	0.97	1.04	0
Cochabamba	0.16	0.13	0.24	0.17	0.75	0.17	0.39	0.16	-222.34	-13.85	1
Oruro	-0.17	-0.20	-0.06	-0.23	-0.18	-0.11	0.35	0.23	-0.94	0.89	1
Potosi	-0.26	-0.21	-0.07	-0.08	0.18	-0.09	0.05	-0.08	-22.22	-113.91	1
Tarija	-0.03	0.03	0.50	0.16	0.57	0.40	0.71	0.56	0.29	0.53	0
Santa Cruz	0.43	0.43	0.70	0.44	0.58	0.11	0.71	0.46	0.35	0.65	1
Beni & Pando	0.44	0.28	0.62	0.31	0.29	0.25	0.74	0.59	5.56	0.46	1
elderly dependency ratio	-0.23	-0.28	-0.20	-0.32	-0.18	-0.24	-0.03	-0.08	0.25	0.68	1
child dependency ratio	0.08	-0.08	0.17	0.00	0.55	-0.01	-0.12	0.05	-31.02	-5.39	0
hh size	-0.07	-0.05	-0.08	-0.05	-0.06	-0.05	-0.09	-0.10	12.26	0.07	1
hh head age	0.03	0.01	0.00	0.02	0.01	0.01	0.02	0.03	-1.30	0.84	1
hh head age squared	0.00	0.00	0.00	0.00	0.00	0.00	0.00	0.00	-2.30	1.32	0
gender hh head	-0.12	-0.12	-0.05	0.03	0.22	0.06	-0.01	-0.12	8.60	-0.25	0
access to public water	0.15	0.03	-0.08	-0.05	0.05	0.06	0.00	0.13	1.15	0.42	0
has no toilet	-0.20	-0.21	-0.03	-0.04	-0.27	0.06	-0.23	-0.15	-2.41	1.94	1
no partner in household	0.35	0.58	0.21	0.34	0.47	0.25	0.39	0.06	-2.77	-0.64	1
com. basic edu. (m.)	0.02	0.03	-0.16	-0.04	-0.02	0.05	-0.02	0.15	1.45	0.70	0
incom. secondary edu. (m.)	0.02	0.05	-0.01	-0.11	-0.17	0.07	-0.01	0.11	-0.94	-0.02	0
com. secondary edu. (m.)	0.10	0.10	-0.05	0.06	0.29	0.07	0.05	0.19	39.21	0.77	0
tertiary edu. (m.)	0.52	0.40	0.39	0.43	-0.02	0.29	0.44	0.27	2.83	-0.35	1
com. basic edu. (w.)	0.00	0.07	0.12	-0.07	-0.01	-0.01	0.26	0.22	-1.94	0.47	0
incom. secondary edu. (w.)	0.14	0.01	0.10	0.01	0.11	0.05	0.27	0.26	0.40	0.70	1
com. secondary edu. (w.)	0.17	0.06	0.24	0.02	0.12	0.31	0.44	0.33	-0.43	0.63	1
tertiary edu. (w.)	0.39	0.40	0.53	0.44	0.45	0.58	0.75	0.64	-0.55	1.09	1

continued on next page

Table 2.6 continued

	City				Town		Rural		ϕ		sign (β) City
	β_{89}	β_{94}	β_{99}	β_{02}	β_{99}	β_{02}	β_{99}	β_{02}	Town	Rural	Constant?
high & med. skilled white c. (m.)	0.45	0.79	0.53	0.62	1.03	0.61	0.67	0.21	-77.30	-0.33	1
skilled & unskilled manual (m.)	0.37	0.47	0.23	0.23	0.57	0.41	0.60	0.04	1.89	-1.98	1
agriculture (m.)	0.42	0.51	-0.21	0.21	0.19	0.30	0.25	-0.05	4.63	-1.74	0
sales and services (m.)	0.42	0.57	0.34	0.53	0.87	0.62	0.67	0.26	5.69	-1.20	1
high & med. skilled white c. (w.)	0.45	0.46	0.38	0.55	0.73	0.72	0.13	0.43	2.00	2.13	1
skilled & unskilled manual (w.)	0.22	0.28	0.14	0.19	0.51	0.17	-0.12	0.05	-15.70	1.81	1
agriculture (w.)	0.52	0.10	0.64	-0.14	-0.24	-0.54	-0.05	-0.08	2.18	-10.88	0
sales and services (w.)	0.34	0.30	0.31	0.23	0.71	0.35	0.36	0.25	3.37	4.07	1
birth in last 12 month	-0.13	-0.13	0.20	-0.06	-0.29	-0.17	-0.12	-0.03	4.53	-10.13	0
attended by doctor	0.07	0.04	-0.22	-0.02	0.68	0.10	0.20	0.02	7.21	9.51	0
delivered in hospital	0.03	0.00	-0.10	-0.26	-0.38	0.12	0.08	0.15	-0.72	0.44	0
c/t/r dummy/constant	4.31	4.66	5.05	4.80	3.84	4.41	4.09	4.23	3.14	1.68	1

Notes: See text for details.
Source: Own calculations based on ECH and EIH.

2.5 Conclusion

This paper aims at estimating the stability of dynamic poverty mapping approaches. Since the poverty mapping approach was established to generate data by regression-based cross-survey mapping where otherwise no other data would have been available, the results can generally not be compared to true data. With the data for Bolivia, we were able to undertake out-of-sample predictions and compare simulated data with true data. This becomes extremely relevant when using the method not only in space but also over time. Our method finds that results crucially depend on the assumptions in the regressions underlying the poverty mapping. Keeping coefficients constant over time is not the advised option. How to correctly model the coefficients in a dynamic way, however, needs to be investigated in much more detail.

Future research should continue with more exercises of testing the performance of poverty prediction methods across surveys. It should be repeated for years where the year of survey undertaken is the same and not, as in our case for Bolivia, where there is one year of time gap between the two surveys used for poverty mapping. Only in such a case, the comparison of "true" and "predicted" data is fully valid because only in this case the reliability check can be undertaken as though the data is missing, and then comparing predictions with truth. A recent paper by Christiaensen et al. (2010), using small area estimations and testing several model specifications, finds that the prediction method works well in Vietnam, badly in Russia, and partly well for China depending on the region considered.

In addition, the issue of getting correct error terms (splitting it into idiosyncratic, cluster or sampling, and model components, or even taking also measurement error into account) and, thus, confidence intervals is important in the case of countries where the full information on survey design and sampling methods is available. In any case, statistical methods on the significance should be applied, performing bootstrap methods or other methods to properly estimate standard errors of poverty and inequality measures, but they depend on having the survey information on weighting, clustering, stratification, and the steps of multistage sampling. This is, unfortunately, not the case for the Bolivian data.

Using alternative methods to predict the standard of living is another option, for example small area statistics or propensity score matching, or any other method dealing with missing data imputation. In addition, merging surveys with variables from other data sources that have an influence on income (such as weather, geographic, or policy variables) and including those variables in the estimations can improve the predictions. Furthermore, predictions could be combined with microsimulation approaches or using theories on how prices and endowments evolve over time given external or internal shocks. This holds especially for shocks that a region, sector, or the economy as a whole might affect.

Essay 3

Measuring Pro-Poor Growth in Non-Income Dimensions

A person who never made a mistake never tried anything new.
Albert Einstein (1879–1955)

Abstract: In order to track progress on MDG1 and explicitly link growth, inequality, and poverty reduction, several measures of pro-poor growth have been proposed in the literature. However, current concepts and measurements of pro-poor growth are entirely focused on the income dimension of well-being, which neglects the multidimensionality of poverty and well-being. There are no corresponding measures for tracking progress on non-income dimensions of poverty. In this paper, we propose to extend the approach of pro-poor growth measurement to non-income dimensions of poverty by applying the growth incidence curve to non-income indicators. The approach allows a much more detailed assessment of progress towards MDGs 2–6 by focusing on the distribution of progress, rather than simply focusing on mean progress. Moreover, this extension allows the assessment of the linkage between progress in income and non-income dimensions of poverty. We illustrate this empirically for Bolivia between 1989 and 1998. We find that growth was pro-poor both in the income and in the non-income dimension, but results for the non-income dimensions are less clear when the poor are ranked by income.

---

based on joint work with Kenneth Harttgen and Stephan Klasen.

3.1 Introduction

Pro-poor growth has recently become a central issue for researchers and policy makers, especially in the context of reaching the Millennium Development Goals (MDG). The various proposals to measure pro-poor growth have also allowed a much more detailed assessment of progress on reducing poverty as they explicitly examine growth along the entire income distribution.

However, one existing shortcoming of current pro-poor growth concepts and measurements is that they are completely focused on income, thus focused only on MDG1 with the aim to halve the incidence of poverty until 2015.[1] The shortcoming of the one-dimensional focus on income is that a reduction in income poverty does not guarantee a reduction in non-income dimensions of poverty, such as education or health. This means that finding pro-poor growth in income does not automatically mean that non-income poverty has also been reduced (Klasen, 2000; Grimm et al., 2002). In this context, Kakwani and Pernia (2000) note that it would be 'futile' if one operationalizes poverty reduction via pro-poor growth using just one single indicator because poverty is a multidimensional phenomenon, and thus pro-poor growth is also multidimensional. For this reasons, multidimensionality of poverty and pro-poor growth as two main research areas have to be combined. While non-income indicators have recently received more and more attention in the concept and measurement of poverty they have not in the concept of pro-poor growth and no attempts have been made to measure pro-poor growth on the basis of non-income indicators.[2] Also international organizations point to the importance of the direct outcomes of poverty reduction such as health and education (World Bank, 2000; UN et al., 2000; UN, 2000).

The aim of this paper is to introduce the multidimensionality of poverty into the pro-poor growth measurement. The basic idea of doing so goes back to Sen's capability approach (Sen, 1987, 1988). Defining human well-being in terms of functionings and capabilities,[3] Sen (1987, 1988) considers poverty as a multidimensional phenomenon and focusses on direct outcomes of human well-being. Since money-metric indicators of poverty reflect only the ability to achieve functionings, it serves only as an indirect measure of the standard of living, whereas direct measures are, for example, the status of, and access to, health and education. Based on this approach, many poverty assessments including social indica-

[1]In this paper, we exemplarily consider income as the money-metric measure of living standard and do not distinguish between income and consumption.

[2]Examples for studies examining the multidimensional casual relationship between economic growth and poverty reduction are Bourguignon and Chakravarty (2003), Mukherjee (2001), and Summer (2003).

[3]In this concept, functionings are the achievements of human well-being, and capabilities reflect the ability to achieve these functionings.

tors have been conducted using aggregate data or household-level data (UNDP, 1996; Klasen, 2000; Grimm et al., 2002). However, non-income indicators have not been considered in the pro-poor growth measurement so far.

We introduce the multidimensionality of poverty into the pro-poor growth measurement by applying the growth incidence curve (GIC) by Ravallion and Chen (2003) to non-income indicators and call our resulting graphs non-income growth incidence curves (NIGIC). We illustrate this approach using micro-data for Bolivia for 1989 and 1998. We distinguish between (i) ranking the sample by each non-income indicator, and (ii) ranking the sample by income and investigate based on this income ranking the changes of the non-income indicator with respect to the position in the income distribution. In addition to investigating growth rates, we investigate absolute changes of the non-income indicators. We find that growth was pro-poor both in the income and in the non-income dimension, but results for the non-income dimensions are less clear for the non-income development when the poor are ranked by income.

The paper is organized as follows. Section 3.2 briefly gives an overview of the concept of pro-poor growth and the need to investigate it in a multidimensional perspective. Section 3.3 explains our methodology to apply the GIC to non-income indicators and discuss some limitations. Section 3.4 presents the results of the GIC and the NIGIC for selected variables and for a composite welfare index. Section 3.5 summarizes and gives an outlook for future research.

3.2 The Concept of Pro-Poor Growth

3.2.1 Definition of Pro-Poor Growth

According to some, pro-poor growth is simply economic growth that benefits the poor (UN et al., 2000; OECD, 2001, 2006). This definition, however, provides little information how to measure or how to implement it. What remains to be specified is, first, if economic growth benefits the poor and, second, if yes to what extent. For example, Klasen (2004) provides more explicit requirements that a definition of pro-poor growth needs to satisfy. The first requirement is that the measure differentiates between growth that benefits the poor and other forms of economic growth, and it has to answer the question by how much the poor benefited. The second requirement is that the poor have benefited disproportionately more than the non-poor. The third requirement is that the assessment is sensitive to the distribution of incomes among the poor. The fourth requirement is that the measure allows an overall judgement of economic growth and not focuses only on the gains of the poor. Besides this approach there exist several other attempts conceptualizing pro-poor growth.[4]

Categorizing the different and conflicting definitions, we speak of three definitions of pro-poor growth in our paper: weak absolute pro-poor growth, relative pro-poor growth, and strong absolute pro-poor growth (Klasen, 2008a). Pro-poor growth in the weak absolute sense means that the income growth rates are, on average, above 0 for the poor. Pro-poor growth in the relative sense means that the income growth rates of the poor are higher than the average growth rates, thus that relative inequality falls (i.e., in which some indicator considering the relative gap between the rich and the poor falls). Pro-poor growth in the strong absolute sense requires that absolute income increases of the poor are stronger than the average, thus, that absolute inequality falls (i.e., some measure considering the absolute gap between the rich and the poor falls, e.g., Klasen (2004)).[5]

The different definitions of pro-poor growth are illustrated in Table 3.1, which is taken from Klasen (2008a). Table 3.1 shows a country in which the poor earn $100 per capita and the non-poor $500 per capita in the initial period. In year 1, the income of the poor grow by 3 percent and the income of the non-poor grow by 2 percent. In terms of the pro-poor growth definitions, this is pro-poor in the weak absolute sense (i.e., growth rates are above 0) and in the relative sense (i.e., the growth rate for the poor is higher than for the non-poor). In year 2, the income of the poor grow by 1 percent and the income of the non-poor also by 1 percent. This is pro-poor only in the weak absolute sense, since the the poor have only benefited proportionately from growth, which illustrates the importance of the relative and absolute definition of pro-poor growth in order to reduce inequality. In year 3, the income of the poor grow by 6 percent and the income of the non-poor by 9 percent. This illustrates the advantage of the weak absolute definition of pro-poor growth. Even if the benefit is not pro-poor in the relative sense, only the weak absolute definition captures that the poor also have made improvements (even if inequality rises). In year 4, the income of the poor grow more than the income of the non-poor showing pro-poor growth in the weak absolute and relative sense. Moreover,

[4]For a detailed review on the different definitions and measures of pro-poor growth, see, for example, Son (2003). Other approaches to define pro-poor growth are provided, for example, by White and Anderson (2000), Ravallion and Datt (2002), Klasen (2004), and Hanmer and Booth (2001). The most common measures that have evolved in pro-poor growth measurement are the 'poverty bias of growth' of McCulloch and Baulch (1999), the 'pro-poor growth index' of Kakwani and Pernia (2000), the 'poverty equivalent growth rate' of Kakwani and Son (2000), the 'poverty growth curve' of Son (2003), and the 'growth incidence curve' of Ravallion and Chen (2003).

[5]Most inequality measures, including the Gini, Theil, and Atkinson measures as well as decile or quintile ratios are relative inequality measures, but these measures can also be turned into absolute measures of inequality, e.g., absolute Gini coefficients (Ravallion, 2005). For a discussion of the merits of also considering absolute inequality measures, see Atkinson and Brandolini (2004).

the growth is also pro-poor in the strong absolute sense since the absolute increase in income for the poor ($20) is higher than for the non-poor ($15).

Table 3.1: Illustration of Pro-Poor Growth Definitions

Year	Poor	Growth	Non-Poor	Growth	Pro-Poor?
0	100	-	500	-	-
1	103	3	510	2	relative, weak absolute
2	104	1	560	10	weak absolute
3	110	6	610	9	weak absolute
4	130	18	625	2	relative, weak and strong absolute

Source: Klasen (2008a).

Table 3.1 illustrates that the definition of strong absolute pro-poor growth is obviously the strictest definition of pro-poor growth and the hardest to achieve, which is also shown empirically by White and Anderson (2000). This is why most researchers concentrate, in general, on the weak absolute and relative definitions. But this ignores that decreases in relative inequality might be—and often are—accompanied by increases in absolute inequality, which is seen as undesirable by many and can be an important source of social tension (Atkinson and Brandolini, 2004; Duclos and Wodon, 2004; Klasen, 2004). Conversely, growth that is associated with falling absolute inequality would be particularly pro-poor and, therefore, it is useful to consider this strong absolute concept as well.

This is particularly important when examining pro-poor growth in the non-income dimension of poverty where even pro-poor growth in the relative definition might not be seen as sufficiently pro-poor. Consider the case where the 'education-poor' increased their education level from 1 to 2 years, an increase of 100 percent, while the rich increased their education level from 10 to 12 years, an increase of 20 percent. This would be pro-poor growth in the relative definition as relative inequality falls, but most observers would also note the rise in absolute inequality and might, therefore, not consider this type of educational expansion 'pro-poor' since no educational degree is achieved. Furthermore, only concentrating on percentage changes in education misses that the poor should catch up to the non-poor regarding specific degrees in education. Concentrating also on absolute changes allows one to examine, for example, whether a poor individual achieved the level of primary or secondary education.[6]

[6]See also the discussion below in Section 3.3.4.

3.2.2 Multidimensionality of Pro-Poor Growth

The most glaring shortcoming of all attempts to define and measure pro-poor growth is that they rely exclusively on one single indicator, which is income. This means that they are only focussed on MDG1 but leave out the multidimensionality of poverty, which is taken into account in the other MDGs.

Income enables households and/or individuals to obtain functionings. This means, income serves to expand peoples' choice sets (capabilities) (Sen, 1987, 1988) and is, therefore, an indirect measure of poverty. In contrast, certain non-income indicators measure the functionings of households and individuals directly. Measuring poverty only with income assumes that income growth is accompanied by non-income growth. However, the problem of focussing only on MDG1 is that an improving income situation of households need not automatically imply an improving non-income situation, thus, reaching the other MDGs is not automatically guaranteed (for example, as shown in Klasen (2000) or Grimm et al. (2002)). While non-income indicators have recently received more and more attention in the concept and measurement of poverty they have not in the concept of pro-poor growth and no attempts have been made so far to measure pro-poor growth on the basis of non-income indicators.

Following Sen (1987, 1988), our conceptual approach to introduce non-income indicators in the pro-poor growth measurement starts with the selection of non-income indicators determining the most important functionings of human welfare. In line with the MDGs (UN et al., 2000) we select education, health, nutrition, and mortality as non-income indicators of poverty and, therefore, follow the spirit of the most prominent multidimensional poverty indices such as the Human Development Index, the Human Poverty Index, and the Physical Quality of Life Index by UNDP (1991, 2000). After having selected the indicators and defined related variables we investigate whether non-income growth was pro-poor between two points in time. We do this exemplarily in applying the methodology of the growth incidence curve (GIC) to non-income indicators, but non-income pro-poor growth can also be applied to other pro-poor growth measures. We also compare the results based on non-income indicators with those based on income.

3.3 Methodology

3.3.1 The Growth Incidence Curve

To answer the question if and to what extent growth was pro-poor one can investigate the growth rates of the poor, i.e., those who were below the poverty line in the initial period. A useful tool for this purpose is the GIC (Ravallion and Chen, 2003) which shows the mean growth rate g_t in income y at each percentile p of the distribution between two points in time, t–1 and t. The GIC links the growth rates of different percentiles and is given by

$$GIC : g_t(p) = \frac{y_t(p)}{y_{t-1}(p)} - 1. \tag{3.1}$$

By comparing the two points in time, the GIC plots the population percentiles (from 1–100 ranked by income) on the horizontal axis against the annual per capita growth rate in income of the respective percentile. If the GIC is above 0 for all percentiles ($g_t(p) > 0$ for all p), then it indicates weak absolute pro-poor growth. If the GIC is negatively sloped it indicates relative pro-poor growth. It is important to note that we assume anonymity throughout, i.e., we consider the growth rates of percentiles, even though they contain different households in the two points in time.[7] For a discussion of this and results when the anonymity axiom is lifted, see Grimm (2007).

Starting from the GIC, Ravallion and Chen (2003) define the pro-poor growth rate (PPGR) as the area under the GIC up to the poverty headcount ratio H. The PPGR is formally expressed by

$$PPGR = g_t^p = \frac{1}{H_t} \int_0^{H_t} g_t(p)dp, \tag{3.2}$$

which is equivalent to the mean of the growth rates of the poor up to the headcount (of the first period, thus evaluated at $t-1$). What is normally done in poverty assessments is to compare the PPGR with the growth rate in mean (GRIM). The GRIM is defined by

$$GRIM = \gamma_t = \frac{\mu_t}{\mu_{t-1}} - 1, \tag{3.3}$$

where μ is mean income. If the PPGR exceeds the GRIM, growth is declared to be pro-poor in the relative sense.

Examining pro-poor growth in the strong absolute sense, one has to concentrate on the absolute changes in income of the population percentiles between the two points in time. We define the absolute GIC by

$$GIC_{absolute} : c_t(p) = y_t(p) - y_{t-1}(p), \tag{3.4}$$

[7]One should be cautious when deducing policy implications from the GIC when assuming anonymity. In particular, the GIC allows not to show if, for example, specific policy measures were beneficial to those who where poor in the initial period, but can show if the poor over the period have benefited more from the measures than the non-poor.

which shows the absolute changes[8] for each percentile. By comparing the two periods, the absolute GIC plots the population percentiles on the horizontal axis against the annual per capita change in income of the respective percentile on the vertical axis. If the absolute GIC is negatively sloped it indicates strong absolute pro-poor growth.

Starting from the absolute GIC, we define the 'pro-poor change' (PPCH) as the area under the absolute GIC up to the headcount H. The PPCH is formally expressed by

$$PPCH = c_t^p = \frac{1}{H_t}\int_0^{H_t} c_t(p)dp, \tag{3.5}$$

which is equivalent to the mean of the changes of the poor up to the headcount. We compare the PPCH with the change in mean (CHIM), which is defined by

$$CHIM = \delta_t = \mu_t - \mu_{t-1}. \tag{3.6}$$

If the PPCH exceeds the CHIM, growth is declared to be pro-poor in the strong absolute sense.

3.3.2 The Non-Income Growth Incidence Curve

The calculation of the non-income growth incidence curves (NIGIC) broadly follows the concept of the GIC. Instead of income (y), we apply Equations (3.1) through (3.6) to selected non-income indicators to measure pro-poor growth directly via outcome-based welfare indicators. Thus, the NIGIC measures pro-poor growth not in an income sense but in a non-income sense, e.g., the improvement of the health status or the educational level between two points in time for each percentile of the distribution.

We calculate the NIGIC in two different ways. The first way we call the unconditional NIGIC in which we rank the individuals by each respective non-income variable and generate the population percentiles based on this ranking. For example, using average years of schooling of adult household members, the 'poorest' percentile is now not the income-poorest percentile but the one with the lowest average household educational attainment.

The second way, we call conditional NIGIC in which we rank the individuals by income and calculate based on this income ranking the population percentiles of the non-income variable. With the conditional NIGIC, we capture the problem that the assignment of the households to income percentiles on the one hand

[8]Note that we use the term "absolute" not in the mathematical meaning of $|-1| = 1$, but to contrast it to "relative", i.e., percentage changes.

(GIC) and to non-income percentiles on the other hand (unconditional NIGIC) might not be the same. For example, the income-poorest group might not be the education-poorest group at the same time. This is taken into account in the conditional NIGIC where the percentiles are income percentiles, thus that the 'poorest' percentile is the one with lowest income, but that the growth rates are non-income growth rates, thus, are calculated for, e.g., years of schooling of the income percentiles. With the conditional NIGIC, we measure how the development of the non-income indicators is distributed across income groups.

Both ways of calculating the NIGIC are of particular relevance for policy making. The unconditional NIGIC mirrors the development of the social indicators that are relevant for human welfare. Thus, it can monitor how the non-income MDGs (especially MDGs 2–6) have developed over time for different points of the non-income distribution. In order to reach the MDGs, improvements will be particularly important for those at the lower end of distribution of the non-income achievements and the NIGIC allows such an assessment. The conditional NIGIC give an additional tool to investigate how the progress in non-income dimensions of poverty was distributed over the income distribution. This is also of relevance when evaluating distributional impacts of aid and public spending. Standard benefit incidence studies, for example, analyze the impact of public spending by calculating shares of the total spending to each percentile and comparing the shares of the income poorest with the income richest centile (see, e.g., Van de Walle and Nead (1995), Van de Wallc (1998), Lanjouw and Ravallion (1998), Roberts (2003)). But the share of public spending for the poor serves only as a proxy for a real welfare impact in terms of non-income achievements. With the conditional NIGIC, it is possible to analyze the actual improvements in the particular social indicator over the income distribution. For example, it provides an instrument to assess if public social spending programs have reached the targeted income-poorest population groups and if the public resources are effectively allocated and used. For example, Berthélemy (2006) shows that education policies in Sub-Saharan Africa are biased against the poor. On average, policies favor the non-poor because they are concentrated on improvements in secondary and tertiary education and only little attention is paid to improvements in primary eduction, i.e., to the poor population. In this respect, the conditional NIGIC might be a useful tool in the pro-poor spending analysis to understand who benefits from public spending and to what extent.

When interpreting the NIGIC, three issue need to be discussed. First, in comparing the GIC and the NIGIC, one cannot deduce any causality between income and non-income indicators. For example, from the curves, we can neither say that an improvement in income causes an improvement in the health status nor that an improvement in the health status causes an improvement in income. They simply show how improvements in income and non-income indicators are related to each other, which might be due to causal or spurious correlations. Second, one cannot compare the absolute values of the growth rates of income and non-income variables because the variables are measured in different dimensions such as monthly income or years of schooling. One can only compare if the growth rates are positive or negative and by how much the PPGR exceeds the GRIM. Lastly, due to the different dimensions of the income and non-income indicators, and the fact that many of the non-income indicators are bounded above (i.e., there is an upper limit to survival prospects or to educational achievements),[9] it may well be plausible that different definitions of 'pro-poor growth' would be appropriate for different indicators. While one may be satisfied that income growth was pro-poor if it met the relative definition (i.e., the poor had higher income growth rates than the rich), one may only call growth in educational achievements pro-poor if the poor had higher absolute increments than the non-poor.[10]

3.3.3 Specification of the Non-Income Indicators

We calculate the unconditional and conditional NIGIC for education, health, nutrition, and for a composite welfare index (CWI) as described below. We are working with DHS data for Bolivia from the years 1989 and 1998 that do not contain information on income or consumption due to its focus on demographics, health, and fertility. However, in our DHS data set, we use simulated incomes based on a dynamic cross-survey micro-simulation methodology introduced by Klasen et al. (2007), which is also outlined in **Essay 1**.[11] The basic idea of this simulation methodology is the following. The authors use two kinds of surveys: first, the DHS (of 1989 and 1998) and, second, the Bolivian household surveys (the 2nd EIH of 1989 and the ECH of 1999). Then they estimate an income corre-

[9] See discussion in Section 3.3.4 below.

[10] A different way to deal with this problem would be to re-scale the non-income variables by, for example, transforming the education indicator into a percentage shortfall from a maximum level, say 16 years of education, and then define growth as the percentage reduction in that shortfall, which was also discussed by Sen (1981) and Kakwani (1993a). With such an indicator, one may well decide to choose the relative definition as sufficient to define pro-poor growth. As discussed below, this issue will also arise when comparing the Gini coefficients of incomes with Gini coefficients in non-income indicators. We do not apply this approach in this paper, because we do not want to give achievements at higher levels more weight than achievements at lower levels in education since we are interested into the question whether the poor can catch up to the non-poor. See Section 3.3.4 for a more detailed discussion on this particular issue.

[11] For the calculation of the PPGR in the next chapter, we use the headcount of 77 (56) percent for the moderate (extreme) poverty line as found in Klasen et al. (2007). We use the same headcount for the calculation of the PPGR of all non-income indicators.

lation in the household survey, apply the coefficients to the DHS, and predict, i.e., simulate, incomes in the DHS.[12]

For each non-income indicator, we identify alternative variables to capture particular aspects of the non-income dimension in question. For education, we specify eight different variables. We calculate average years of schooling for all adult household members and for males and females separately. Age plays an important role when analyzing changes in non-income indicators, especially for education. In particular, not much improvements in education can be expected among the adult population (the education of 30-40 year olds in 1989 should not be be very different from the education of the 40-50 year olds in 1998). To avoid misleading conclusion from potential low improvements, we, therefore, restrict the sample to women[13] aged between 20 and 30 as only this age group is likely to have experienced a change in their educational achievement (the 20-30 year olds in 1998 represent a new cohort of women who were educated later than the other cohorts). In addition, we calculate the maximal education per household instead of the average for all adults, males, females, and females aged between 20 and 30. The idea behind using these variables as an indicator is that it might be sufficient that one household member is well educated to generate income for the whole household and to invest in education of other household members (i.e., intra-household externalities) (Basu and Foster, 1998).[14] To take into account possible intra-household inequalities in education, we also calculate gender gaps

[12]See **Essay 1** for the methodology. To provide some summary here, the authors estimate an income/consumption expenditure model in the 1999 Living Standard Measurement Survey (LSMS) data, restricting the set of covariates to those which are also available in the 1998 DHS data and interacting all variables with a rural dummy. They then use the regression to predict incomes in the DHS and add a randomly distributed error term. They then repeat the procedure for the EIH of 1989, which is only available in urban areas. When imputing incomes in rural areas, they use the model for urban areas in 1989 and add the results of the rural interaction terms from 1999, assuming that the difference in the impact of income correlates between 1989 and 1999 did not change over time. There is a tendency that the simulated income growth is higher than the observed one. This overprediction should not bias the results in this paper, but it might be useful to test the results generated here with a survey that contains detailed information both on income and on non-income variables. This is done in **Essay 4**.

[13]The DHS only includes households with at least one woman in reproductive age, i.e., aged between 15 and 49 who serve as respondents in the DHS. The education for the male household members has to be taken from the memory of the respondents concerning the education of their husband or partner (with the age of the men being unknown). Households without women in reproductive age are excluded as well as unmarried men.

[14]An important issue is to be noted here: An overall problem of years of schooling as a variable for educational attainment is that years of schooling do not say anything about educational quality and, therefore, the indicator should be treated with some caution. This problem might be solved by using other data such as education test scores (like Pisa scores). However, these data are not always available and certainly not in the same data sets.

in eduction within households. In particular, we calculate the female minus male education in the households (in years of education).

For health, we specify three different variables. We calculate infant survival rates of children aged under 1 year and also for children aged under 5 years.[15] Furthermore, we take the average vaccinations of children aged between 1 and 5 per household, with a maximum of 8 possible vaccinations for each child.[16] The vaccination rate is a variable that represents access to health care and preventive medicines. A similar variable has, for example, been used in the monitoring of the health sector reform project in Bolivia in 1999 (Montes, 2003).

For nutrition, we use stunting z-scores as the variable that measures chronical undernutrition for children aged between 1 and 5 years. The stunting z-scores are defined as the difference of height at a certain age and the median of the reference population for height at that age divided by the standard deviation of the reference population. For Bolivia, it takes values between approximately -6 and 6, where values below -2 are considered as being moderately undernourished and below -3 as being severely undernourished (Klasen, 2003, 2008b). Problematic might be that the z-score contains a lot of 'genetic noise' in the sense that, for example, a low z-score interpreted as being undernourished might simply appear because the parents are genetically short and the child is also small but nevertheless well nourished and vice versa.

A further possibility to address the issue of the multidimensionality is to aggregate several indicators into a composite welfare index (CWI).[17] Here, we follow the methodology of the Human Development Index (HDI) to address the problem of difference scales of the variables (UN et al., 2000). Each variable that enters the index is normalized to be between 0 and 1 in subtracting the individual value from the minimum value observed in the data set divided by the range

$$CWI = \frac{1}{n}\sum_{i=1}^{n} \frac{individual_n - minimum}{maximum - minimum}. \tag{3.7}$$

The CWI is constructed by simply averaging the sum of the selected variable scores n. It includes four of the above explained variables: average education

[15]In our calculation, we use household child survival rates instead of child mortality rates. An improvement in child mortality comes out as a lower value but this lower value is mathematically interpreted as a deterioration. The linear transformation used is: survival rate = (mortality rate $-$ $1) * (-1)$. This means, for example that a reduction of child mortality from 40 percent to 20 percent is transformed into an increase in child survival from 60 percent to 80 percent.

[16]The possible vaccinations are 3 against polio, 3 against DPT, 1 against measles, and 1 against BCG.

[17]For a detailed overview about several composite welfare indices and how they are calculated, see, e.g., UNDP (2006).

of all adult household members, stunting z-scores, under 1 survival, and average vaccinations.[18]

As not all variables are given for all households (e.g., health and nutrition variables are only available for households who have children), we calculate the CWI for two different samples. The first sample, called small sample, is the one for which all variables are available for all households. This reduces the sample size enormously (in 1989, e.g., from 6,053 to 1,306 households) and, more importantly, in a non-random fashion.[19] The second sample, called big sample, includes all households, but the index is averaged over fewer variables for those households, which do not have data for nutrition and/or health variables. The advantage of creating the CWI based on the big sample is the higher number of observations but the disadvantage is that the results for some percentiles are driven by very few, or even only one variable. The smaller sample has fewer observations but contains for all households the same number of variables. For both, the small and the big sample, we also augment the indices by also including simulated income[20] as a fourth indicator.

3.3.4 Limitations of the Indicators

While we show below that these indicators yield important information, there arise also a number of problems when analyzing non-income indicators of welfare, which also are important to note for the use of the NIGIC, but can also be seen as general inherent limitations of non-income indicators of human well-being to be aware of. The first limitation is the informational value of the calculated growth rates of the NIGIC, where we interpret an ordinal relation in a cardinal fashion. Examining an ordinally scaled variable one can say that 6 years of schooling is better than 3 years but one cannot be sure to say that the household is twice as

[18]The latter two variables do not enter separately but form a health sub-index as the simple average of the two scores. In contrast to the HDI, we use the maximum and minimum values defined by the data sets (over both data sets, thus not separately for each data set) and do not use fixed maximum and minimum values. This might be problematic because, first, the minima and maxima might be outliers, and second, because they will (or alt least may) change if a third data set (or other countries) enter the analysis. However, for our paper it is less critical to use the minima and maxima of the two data sets because, first, our paper has a rather illustrative purpose and, second, the minima and maxima of most of the variables are the "natural ranges" of the indicators (e.g., education ranges from 0 to 18 years, vaccinations from 0 to 8 applications).

[19]This reduction in observations translates into the calculation of the percentiles resulting in higher standard errors than for the large sample.

[20]Note that we use the simulated value without adding an error term for the conditional NIGIC because this is the best income estimate for this purpose, i.e., for preserving the income ranking.

well educated.[21] This ordinal scaling leads to two different kinds of interpretation problems.

First, averaging an ordinally scaled variable leads to a ranking problem when assuming that education is one of the most important determinants to generate income and reduce poverty (Osberg, 2000). For example, comparing two households, A and B, with two adults in each household where the household members of A have 0 and 12 years of schooling and of B have 6 and 7 years of schooling, household B has a higher average education than A. Now, when B is ranked higher than A, one ignores any kind of educational degrees and the resulting differentials in returns to education. This means that the person with 12 years of schooling in A might earn disproportionately more income than both members of household B together, thus, household A should be ranked higher than B. We address this problem in also using maximal education per household.

In addition, averaging the years of schooling over the household ignores also possible intra-household inequalities in education. Taking into account the distribution of education within the household and, therefore, taking into account possible intra-household inequalities in education, we additionally focus on the individual educational attainment (instead of only on the average of the household) and on the gender gap in education of households.

Second, concerning the usual problem of absolute versus relative changes, here increases in years of schooling, just comparing growth rates might be misleading and might not reflect their true achievements. For example, Table 3.2 shows for average education an increase of 80 percent for the 2nd decile compared to 6 percent of the 9th decile, which might be overstating the improvement for the poor because the years of schooling of the poor increase from 1.31 to 2.37 years of schooling and those of the non-poor from 11.73 to 12.43. In addition, improvements in tertiary education might be harder to achieve than improvements in primary education, which should also be taken into account. This problem is related to the fact that many of the non-income indicators are bounded above, i.e., there are firm or likely upper limits on such achievements. 100 percent survival in the first year is the upper limit for health, more than 18 or 19 years of education is very rare, more than 8 vaccinations is not recommended, done, or measured, etc. One may assume 'declining marginal returns' to improvements in non-income indicators, which would suggest that a marginal year of schooling or another vaccination is less valuable when the level of schooling is already high.

This problem is also discussed by Kakwani (1993a). He derives an achievement function for non-income indicators based on the assumption that the value of the achievement increases non-linearly with the achievement level, i.e., an in-

[21]The same problem exists when interpreting income in a cardinal fashion, despite the lacking foundation for such an interpretation, but this issue is normally neglected in applied discussions.

crease in 1 year of years of schooling or life expectancy starting from a higher level reflects greater achievement than an increase starting from a lower level because the effort necessary to achieve this increase is much higher for countries that are already close to the upper limit of achievement. In particular, Kakwani (1993a) derives an improvements index, which takes into account both the asymptotic limit of non-income indicators of standard of living and the non-linearity of the values of achievements. His achievement function Q takes the lower (*min*) and upper (*max*) bounds into account in using a logarithmic transformation of the following kind, with values between 0 and 1:

$$Q = (\ln(max - x_{t1}) - \ln(max - x_{t2}))/(\ln(max - min)).$$

For example, an increase in life expectancy from 49 to 59 years gives a value of $Q = 0.10$, and an increase from 69 to 79 of $Q = 0.61$ with values of $min = 30$ and $max = 80$. However, the value of this increase is based on the effort made to achieve but does not consider the value of the outcomes of this achievement. Since we are interested in the question whether the poor can catch up to the non-poor and, therefore, rather interested in investigating improvements in direct outcomes of social indicators than in the effort of these achievements, we do not weight the improvements in relative achievements.

Besides, in addition to the relative changes, we calculate the absolute NIGIC and pro-poor changes examining directly the absolute improvements in years of education. However, even when we use absolute changes for the example of education above, which equal approximately 1, a further question remains open. An increase of 1.06 years of schooling of the 2th decile might be less beneficial because perhaps the persons are still more or less illiterate, compared to the increase of 0.70 years of schooling in the 9th decile, which might mean completing secondary schooling and getting a degree.

Another issue that arises due to the bounded-above problem of social indicators is that it may be the case (and indeed is the case in Bolivia) that some households have reached the upper limit, and further growth is not possible. However, our main focus is on the bottom of the distribution. Even if we observe improvements in, for example, education only for the lower deciles, we still can interpret these findings regarding the pro-poorness of improvements in the educational system, particularly whether the poor have benefited from these improvements.

The third type of problem in comparing relative changes relates to the stunting z-score. In our data sets, it ranges roughly from -6 to 6. Relative changes in the stunting z-score cannot be calculated because of the coexistence of negative, positive, and 0 values in the variable range. For example, how to compare the relative improvement from -2 to -1 with an improvement from 1 to 2 from the year 1989 to 1998? We reduce this problem by transforming the z-score in such a way that all values are positive, which means by adding the minimum value of both data sets to each z-score to get a range of only positive numbers.

Another limitation is the problem of weighting, which we illustrate with the example of child mortality. For example, comparing two households, A and B, where A has 1 child and B has 10 children the households should be weighted differently when in each of the two households 1 child dies. Household A has a child mortality rate of 100 percent whereas B of 'only' 10 percent. From an intrinsic point of view, it is obvious that both deaths are equally lamentable. In this case, one could think of just counting the death per household independently of the total number of children. However, it is less obvious from an economic point of view where children can be partly considered as investment goods. Here, a higher mortality rate mirrors the more heavy loss of 1 child in the 1-child household A compared to the 10-children household B. The investment-good character comes from absence or lack of social security systems in which case the children take care for the parents in the cases of unemployment, sickness, and old age (Ehrlich and Lui, 1997).[22] Following these two extreme points of view, one might think of weighting the death of children in households taking both arguments somehow into account. But any weighting would, however, be quite arbitrary and induce difficulties in justifying it with economic or welfare-theoretical judgments. Keeping this critical issue in mind we use unweighted child survival rates.

Weighting problems are also difficult with the nutrition indicator. A negative stunting z-score indicates malnourishment. But the z-score should not be interpreted as a linear variable in the sense that an increasing z-score is always equivalent to an improvement in the nutritional status. From a certain threshold onward, increasing z-scores might no longer reflect improvements of the nutritional status but indeed quite the opposite. For example, a child with a very high z-score of 3 might not be better off as one with 0 because she might be too tall for her age. This would be even stronger if one considered wasting z-scores (weight over age). Here, increasing z-scores strongly above 0 reflect obesity that negatively affects the health status (De Onis and Blössner, 2000).[23]

Another limitation when calculating the NIGIC is that some variables of the non-income indicators do not vary much between households. This holds especially for under 5 and under 1 survival in Bolivia, which is low at the household level. For both years, Table 1 shows that from the 3rd decile upwards, the max-

[22]One complicating aspect arises when taking gender preferences for the children into account. The loss of one child when considered as an investment good might depend on the cultural habits (e.g., labor market opportunities for females and males, marriage agreements, and the question who takes care of the parents in old age).

[23]In particular, several studies show that obesity in childhood negatively affects the development of the child, which is an increasing concern in developing countries (see, e.g., Dietz (1998) or Martorell et al. (1998)).

imum value of 100 percent under 1 survival is already reached in both years, so that no improvement is possible any more. This translates into growth rates of 0, so that the unconditional NIGIC becomes flat and takes the value of 0 from the 3rd decile onward. The problem of flat curves always arises when the variable values are bounded above (as for example a maximum of 19 years of schooling or 8 vaccinations). This raises the general question in which case the unconditional curves are helpful or not when analyzing non-income dimensions (see the discussion below in Section 3.4.2 and especially for Figure 3.6 on under 5 survival).

Dealing with this limitation in a more general way, the discussed variables have a more discrete or even dummy character (in the sense that a child either has survived or not) which makes it difficult to observe relative differences among individuals, households, and over time. This is why these indicators (such as mortality rates) are mostly generated and interpreted at an aggregate level. The only, but small, variation evolves from taking household averages instead of individual data. This is why these variables—and all kinds of dummy variables—show little variation for the pro-poor growth analysis using the NIGIC.

More interesting to examine in these cases is the conditional NIGIC, in which we link the non-income variables to income. Here, low variation is less problematic than for the unconditional NIGIC because the variables are ranked by income. As Table 3.3 and all figures show, there is no flat part any more. Now we generate interesting information regarding the changes on the non-income indicators when ranked according to their income situation and how improvements are distributed.

3.4 Empirical Analysis

3.4.1 Inequality

Bolivia is one of the countries with a very unequal income distribution in Latin America. Table 3.2 shows the distribution of income and the non-income indicators (unconditional) and Table 3.3 shows the distribution of the non-income indicators for the conditional case, i.e., when the non-income indicators are ranked by income.

We find high and persisting income inequality as measured with the Gini coefficient that falls from 0.56 in 1989 to 0.54 in 1998. This high inequality is also reflected in the high and only slightly falling 100:10 ratio. Turning from inequality to growth, we find that all deciles increased their incomes. Especially in the 1990s, Bolivia experienced relatively high growth rates (which also were pro-poor in urban and rural areas). However, Bolivia was and is one of the poorest countries of the region, and the positive economic trend has reversed since 1999 combined with some episodes of social and political turmoil. Bolivia used to show much worse outcomes in social indicators than other countries in the region. However, there have been notable and sustained improvements in many social indicators since the late 1980s, which continued to improve during the recent economic slowdown (Klasen et al., 2007).[24]

Looking at the unconditional case (Table 3.2), the Gini for education variables are all in the range of 0.40 to 0.50.[25] As stated above, due to the boundedness of the variable, one cannot infer directly from this that educational inequality is in some sense substantively smaller than income inequality.[26] For all educational variables, the Gini fall between 1989 and 1998, which is likely due to the fact that the rich have already reached high levels of education and the poor are catching up. Interesting to note is that the highest Gini coefficients exist for the group of all respondents both for average and maximum education indicating a gender bias in educational achievements. These findings are also reflected in the 100:10 ratio. The conditional deciles, which are shown in Table 3.3 also show that the level of schooling increases with increasing income for all educational variables, but the 100:10 ratio is much lower than in the unconditional case. We find that an improvement has been made for all educational variables in all deciles for both the unconditional and the conditional case (Tables 3.2 and 3.3). However, as already both tables show, improvements where much higher in the unconditional than in the conditional case indicating that the improvements in non-income indicators of poor, when they are ranked by income, are less clear than if the improvements are linked to the initial level in the respective non-income indicator.

The extremely low Gini for the under 1 and under 5 survival rates can be explained by the overall low incidence of child mortality in Bolivia at the household level. For both age groups, child mortality is below 10 percent. The conditional deciles indicate that mortality seems to be more or less randomly distributed over the income distribution (Table 3.3).[27] For vaccination, the Gini falls strongly from 1989 to 1998, and we find clear improvements, especially for the lower deciles (except the lowest decile), which is also due to the fact that the best vaccinated

[24]See also the **Introduction and Overview** section of this book.

[25]All non-income indicators show in generally lower Gini coefficients compared to income. As Klasen (2008b) notes, this is only the case for countries (like Bolivia), where the richest groups are already close to the upper bound. This is, for example, not the case for many African countries as shown by Thomas et al. (2000) who calculate Gini coefficients for education.

[26]One should also be aware of the fact that the calculation of the Gini of the social indicators are based on discrete variables. Although income also is strictly discrete, it has a much more continuous character then social indicators like years of education. Thus, it is much more difficult to calculate a Lorenz curve for years of schooling given the lower boundary (0) and upper boundary (18), and the Gini should be interpreted with caution. An attempt to face this problem as addressed by Thomas et al. (2000).

[27]As explained below, reasons for this might be the overall low mortality risk in Bolivia and the tendency for underreporting among poorer population groups.

deciles had only limited room for improvements. The inequality of the stunting z-score is relatively low and falls slightly. Malnutrition decreases with an increasing position in the income distribution, but the differences for the income deciles are quite low.

Table 3.4 shows the distribution of the composite welfare index. The CWI reflects the findings from above where the Gini coefficients decrease for the selected variables. For the CWI (both excluding and including income), the Gini coefficient is higher for the big sample than for the small sample indicating between-group inequality.[28] Table 3.4 also illustrates the difference in the values of the indices if income is included and excluded. If income is included into the index, the level of values decreases, both in the unconditional and the conditional case, which is driven by the high and persisting income inequality in Bolivia.

[28]This between-group inequality is driven by the higher degree of homogeneity in the small sample.

Table 3.2: Deciles of Income and Non-Income Indicators (Unconditional), 1989 and 1998

	1	2	3	4	5	6	7	8	9	10	Mean	100:10	Gini
	Mean of the Deciles (unconditional), 1989												
Income	21.88	40.27	57.50	77.33	100.61	132.39	177.08	246.12	368.36	863.39	213.39	39.46	0.56
Education													
Ave. educ.	0.22	1.31	2.26	3.20	4.28	5.61	7.32	9.38	11.73	15.20	6.03	69.09	0.43
Ave. educ. all respondents	0.00	0.00	1.29	2.27	3.34	4.72	6.24	8.58	11.56	15.13	5.31	n.d.	0.51
Ave. educ. respondents (20-30)	0.13	1.72	2.95	4.10	5.18	7.01	8.92	11.25	12.00	14.48	6.69	111.38	0.39
Ave. educ. partners	0.00	1.35	2.83	4.13	5.30	6.52	8.57	11.35	12.70	16.77	6.95	n.d.	0.42
Max. educ. household	0.48	2.52	3.52	4.82	5.88	7.50	9.78	11.99	13.87	16.98	7.64	35.36	0.38
Max. educ. household (respondents)	0.00	0.00	1.29	2.27	3.34	4.72	6.24	8.58	11.56	15.13	5.40	n.d.	0.51
Max. educ. household (20-30)	0.11	1.67	2.90	3.86	5.00	6.64	8.65	11.11	12.00	14.70	6.58	133.63	0.40
Max. educ. of partners	0.00	1.37	2.85	4.25	5.40	6.75	8.88	11.64	12.84	16.89	7.09	n.d.	0.42
Health													
Under 5 child survival rate (%)	38.43	64.06	75.81	94.64	100.00	100.00	100.00	100.00	100.00	100.00	87.04	2.60	0.11
Under 1 child survival rate (%)	41.51	88.31	100.00	100.00	100.00	100.00	100.00	100.00	100.00	100.00	92.55	2.41	0.07
Ave. vacc. per child (age>=1)	0.08	1.88	3.49	4.67	5.67	6.46	7.10	7.98	8.00	8.00	5.30	100.00	0.28
Nutrition													
Stunting z-score	-4.17	-3.01	-2.50	-2.11	-1.70	-1.33	-0.90	-0.25	-0.00	0.88	-1.54	n.d.	0.19

continued on next page

Table 3.2 continued

	1	2	3	4	5	6	7	8	9	10	Mean	100:10	Gini
	Mean of the Deciles (unconditional), 1998												
Income	36.37	63.60	89.26	119.22	155.89	203.15	269.64	369.20	555.27	1242.66	312.10	34.17	0.54
Education													
Ave. educ.	0.87	2.37	3.51	4.78	6.06	7.34	8.70	9.81	12.43	16.04	7.21	18.44	0.35
Ave. educ. respondents	0.00	1.36	2.72	3.95	5.16	6.68	8.34	9.42	10.75	16.39	6.48	n.d.	0.41
Ave. educ. respondents (20-30)	0.99	3.45	5.00	6.45	7.98	8.99	9.99	9.99	13.71	16.59	8.05	16.76	0.31
Ave. educ. partners	0.54	2.23	3.85	5.13	7.51	8.58	9.50	10.00	14.23	17.04	7.86	11.59	0.36
Max. educ. household	1.47	3.48	4.87	6.44	8.23	9.01	10.00	10.71	15.76	17.04	8.74	11.60	0.31
Max. educ. household (respondents)	0.00	1.36	2.72	3.95	5.16	6.68	8.34	9.42	10.75	16.39	6.58	n.d.	0.41
Max. educ. household (20-30)	0.89	3.00	4.45	5.35	7.08	8.40	9.28	10.00	12.70	16.46	7.82	18.49	0.32
Max. educ. partners	0.54	2.25	3.89	5.19	7.64	8.73	9.66	10.00	14.69	17.04	7.96	31.56	0.36
Health													
Under 5 child survival rate (%)	46.03	70.36	90.70	100.00	100.00	100.00	100.00	100.00	100.00	100.00	90.62	2.16	0.08
Under 1 child survival rate (%)	43.67	93.29	100.00	100.00	100.00	100.00	100.00	100.00	100.00	100.00	93.63	2.29	0.06
Ave. vacc. per child (age>=1)	0.09	2.13	3.74	4.92	5.88	6.74	7.14	8.00	8.00	8.00	5.48	88.89	0.26
Nutrition													
Stunting z-score	-3.61	-2.43	-1.92	-1.55	-1.19	-0.79	-0.30	-0.00	0.05	1.11	-1.06	n.d.	0.16

Notes: The explanation for the variables is the following. Income: Real household income per capita in Bolivianos per month (CPI of 1995=100). Education: All variables for education are measured in average single years per household. Respondents and partners are only couples, for which the respondent knows the education of her partner. Health: Under 5 (1) survival rates are estimated with life table estimations taking the sample of children born 10 (5) years prior to the sample. Survival rates are averaged over the household. Vaccinations: Average vaccinations of the children in the household older than 1, where the possible vaccinations are 3 against polio, 3 against DPT, 1 against measles, and 1 against BCG. Nutrition: Stunting z-score of the last born child of each respondent (averaged over the household). A a child is defined as stunted if her z-score is below -2.
Source: Own calculations based on DHS.

Table 3.3: Deciles of Income and Non-Income Indicators (Conditional), 1989 and 1998

	1	2	3	4	5	6	7	8	9	10	Mean	100:10
	Mean of the Deciles (conditional), 1989											
Income	21.88	40.27	57.50	77.33	100.61	132.39	177.08	246.12	368.36	863.39	213.39	39.46
Education												
Ave. educ.	3.04	3.48	4.11	4.47	5.54	6.07	6.99	7.94	9.37	11.47	6.03	3.77
Ave. educ. respondents	2.20	2.93	3.25	3.75	4.69	5.41	6.34	7.19	8.70	10.68	5.51	4.85
Ave. educ. respondents (20-30)	3.30	4.62	5.20	5.91	6.78	8.06	8.32	8.84	9.24	10.47	6.69	3.17
Ave. educ. partners	3.88	4.03	4.96	5.20	6.40	6.73	7.65	8.68	10.04	12.26	6.98	3.16
Max. educ. household	4.41	4.77	5.52	5.91	7.08	7.75	8.70	9.73	11.23	13.29	7.64	3.00
Max. educ. household (respondents)	2.20	2.93	3.25	3.75	4.69	5.41	6.34	7.19	8.70	10.68	5.63	4.85
Max. educ. household (20-30)	3.19	4.50	4.83	5.72	6.55	7.52	8.48	8.16	9.53	10.82	6.58	3.39
Max. educ. partners	4.00	4.10	5.02	5.31	6.52	6.91	7.84	8.85	10.18	12.40	7.11	3.10
Health												
Under 5 child survival rate (%)	84.54	86.94	86.83	85.02	85.82	87.44	88.16	88.41	91.06	91.00	87.04	1.08
Under 1 child survival rate (%)	91.46	91.03	91.96	92.74	92.34	93.85	93.45	94.35	93.39	92.43	92.55	1.02
Ave. vacc. per child (age>=1)	5.19	4.79	5.07	5.35	5.09	5.47	5.77	6.82	6.16	6.39	5.30	1.23
Nutrition												
Stunting z-score	-1.75	-1.73	-1.89	-1.71	-1.52	-1.57	-1.27	-1.26	-1.18	-0.82	-1.54	n.d.

continued on next page

Table 3.3 continued

	1	2	3	4	5	6	7	8	9	10	Mean	100:10
	Mean of the Deciles (conditional), 1998											
Income	36.37	63.60	89.26	119.22	155.89	203.15	269.64	369.20	555.27	1242.66	312.10	34.17
Education												
Ave. educ.	3.92	4.47	5.20	6.45	6.45	7.10	8.09	8.82	9.85	12.35	7.21	3.15
Ave. educ. respondents	3.10	3.72	4.48	4.84	5.83	6.51	7.62	8.20	9.29	11.74	6.53	3.79
Ave. educ. respondents (20-30)	4.59	5.35	6.22	7.35	7.91	8.71	9.28	9.88	10.43	11.84	8.05	2.58
Ave. educ. partners	4.74	5.22	5.92	6.26	7.06	7.69	8.56	9.44	10.40	12.96	7.82	2.73
Max. educ. household	5.34	5.86	6.63	6.97	7.99	8.78	9.72	10.46	11.44	13.79	8.74	2.58
Max. educ. household (respondents)	3.10	3.72	4.48	4.84	5.83	6.51	7.62	8.20	9.29	11.74	6.63	3.79
Max. educ. household (20-30)	4.34	5.05	5.77	7.07	7.53	8.47	8.54	9.71	10.37	12.12	7.82	3.03
Max. educ. partners	4.79	5.29	5.99	6.32	7.18	7.78	8.68	9.56	10.55	13.06	7.92	2.73
Health												
Under 5 child survival rate (%)	86.98	90.13	89.29	88.94	90.82	89.76	90.44	93.06	92.21	95.24	90.62	1.10
Under 1 child survival rate (%)	92.42	94.43	94.15	93.21	92.01	94.19	92.61	95.22	94.69	96.09	93.63	1.03
Aver. vacc. per child (age>=1)	5.19	5.26	5.02	5.17	5.34	5.40	5.74	5.99	5.93	6.43	5.48	1.24
Nutrition												
Stunting z-score	-1.56	-1.48	-1.30	-1.37	-1.17	-1.15	-1.01	-0.90	-0.79	-0.44	-1.06	n.d.

Notes: For the explanation for the variables, see Table 3.2.
Source: Own calculations based on DHS.

Table 3.4: Deciles of the Composite Welfare Index, 1989 and 1998

	1	2	3	4	5	6	7	8	9	10	Mean	100:10	Gini
	Mean of the Deciles (unconditional), 1989												
Composite welfare index													
Small sample	0.29	0.35	0.39	0.43	0.47	0.50	0.54	0.59	0.64	0.74	0.49	2.55	0.15
Big sample	0.11	0.29	0.38	0.45	0.51	0.56	0.61	0.66	0.74	0.86	0.52	7.82	0.23
Composite welfare index (including income)													
Small sample	0.22	0.27	0.30	0.32	0.35	0.38	0.41	0.45	0.49	0.57	0.37	2.66	0.16
Big sample	0.10	0.23	0.29	0.33	0.36	0.39	0.43	0.47	0.53	0.63	0.37	6.52	0.22
	Mean of the Deciles (unconditional), 1998												
Composite welfare index													
Small sample	0.32	0.40	0.44	0.48	0.52	0.55	0.59	0.63	0.67	0.74	0.53	2.31	0.13
Big sample	0.18	0.36	0.43	0.49	0.53	0.58	0.63	0.68	0.74	0.86	0.38	4.78	0.19
Composite welfare index (including income)													
Small sample	0.25	0.31	0.34	0.37	0.40	0.42	0.46	0.49	0.53	0.61	0.42	2.48	0.14
Big sample	0.14	0.27	0.32	0.37	0.40	0.43	0.47	0.51	0.55	0.65	0.41	4.81	0.20
	Mean of the Deciles (conditional), 1989												
Composite welfare index													
Small sample	0.44	0.43	0.45	0.46	0.47	0.50	0.53	0.53	0.58	0.63	0.50	1.43	-
Big sample	0.45	0.45	0.46	0.48	0.51	0.53	0.56	0.59	0.61	0.68	0.53	1.51	-
Composite welfare index (including income)													
Small sample	0.32	0.31	0.32	0.33	0.36	0.38	0.40	0.41	0.46	0.53	0.37	1.66	-
Big sample	0.31	0.29	0.31	0.34	0.35	0.37	0.39	0.42	0.47	0.56	0.37	1.77	-
	Mean of the Deciles (conditional), 1998												
Composite welfare index													
Small sample	0.45	0.48	0.49	0.49	0.52	0.53	0.56	0.58	0.60	0.65	0.53	1.44	-
Big sample	0.46	0.48	0.48	0.50	0.52	0.54	0.58	0.59	0.63	0.69	0.55	1.44	-
Composite welfare index (including income)													
Small sample	0.33	0.34	0.36	0.38	0.39	0.41	0.44	0.46	0.51	0.58	0.42	1.77	-
Big sample	0.32	0.32	0.35	0.37	0.38	0.40	0.42	0.45	0.49	0.59	0.41	1.83	-

Notes: The composite welfare index includes average education per household, under five survival rate, average vaccination per child (age>=1), and stunting. See text for details.
Source: Own calculations based on DHS.

3.4.2 Pro-Poor Growth

Figure 3.1 shows the relative and absolute GIC for income. The relative GIC plots the annual growth rates in monthly household per capita income for each household of the distribution. The absolute GIC plots absolute increases in real Bolivianos for the whole period 1989–1998 for each percentile. Included are (also in all other figures) the bootstrapped 95 percent confidence intervals[29] and the moderate and extreme poverty headcounts for 1989 of 77 and 56 percent, respectively.

Figure 3.1: GIC (absolute and relative), 1989–1998

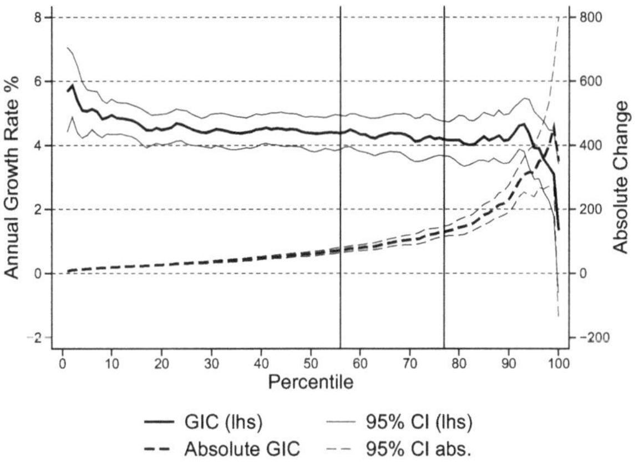

As can be seen from the position and slope of the GIC, income growth was pro-poor in the weak absolute and relative sense since the curve is above 0 for all and negatively sloped for nearly all percentiles. As expected, we do not find strong

[29] In particular, based on the households in both surveys, the bootstrap draws 200 weighted random samples with replacement for each period and calculates the respective percentiles and growth rates (and absolute changes) so that we obtain 200 values per percentile, so to say: 200 GIC and NIGIC. Based on these 200 values, we draw the mean and the standard deviation per percentile and calculate the respective 95 percent confidence intervals. Alternatively, the confidence intervals could be estimated not using mean and standard deviation (which are based on normality assumptions) but to use directly the bootstrapped values (given by the p5 and p95 values). Including the further sampling information was not possible (strata, cluster) since this information is not available in the 1989 survey. Thus, confidence intervals are expected to be too narrow. For the GIC and NIGIC, it it not possible to say how much they are too narrow. (Deaton, 1997, Chapter 1.4) gives an example for data on Pakistan in how the inclusion of strata and cluster influences the standard error.

absolute pro-poor growth since the absolute GIC is positively sloped meaning that absolute increases in income were much higher for the non-poor than for the poor. Turning to the absolute GIC, the absolute GIC in Figure 3.1 clearly shows that income growth in Bolivia was strongly anti-poor using the strong absolute definition. The absolute increments of the rich far exceed those of the poor.

Figure 3.2a shows the relative and absolute unconditional NIGIC for average education per household. Figure 3.2b shows the relative and absolute conditional (smoothed[30]) NIGIC for this variable. Note that the confidence intervals of the unconditional NIGIC lie very tight around the NIGIC. The reason for this lies in the discrete character of the social indicator. Each percentile contains households with nearly the same level of years of education, which results in low variations within percentiles and which leads to the very tight confidence intervals around the unconditional growth rates (and absolute changes).

Whereas for the unconditional NIGIC the growth rates and absolute changes are shown for percentiles (1-100), for the conditional NIGIC the growth rates and absolute changes are shown for vintiles (1-20). The reason for using vintiles instead of percentiles is to get a higher number of observations for each group when households are ranked by income. For example, if a percentile contains only 50 households (ranked by income) and if we assign to these households the respective mean years of education, then it is possible to obtain huge variations within each percentile, which results in very wide confidence intervals between the growth over the period, and we will miss to show the income gradient.

For the unconditional NIGIC, Figure 3.2b, we find pronounced weak absolute as well as relative pro-poor growth.[31] The relative pro-poorness of average education is reflected comparing the PPGR with the GRIM where the PPGR for moderate poverty is 3.89 percent and the PPGR for extreme poverty 4.88, both much higher than the GRIM of 1.80 percent (Table 3.5).

The conditional NIGIC is more volatile than the unconditional NIGIC and also shows weak absolute and relative pro-poor growth but to a lower extent. Thus, the conditional NIGIC shows that the income-poor have experienced slightly higher educational growth than the average. This is also reflected in the higher PPGR (2.00 percent for moderate and 2.24 percent for extreme poverty) compared to the GRIM (1.80 percent).

[30]As the conditional are very volatile, we only include the smoothed conditional NIGIC in the figures to show the major trend of the curves.

[31]A noteworthy point appears when looking at the upper part of the unconditional NIGIC and their absolute changes. In the range of the 7th and 8th decile, all curves for the education variables fall below 0 and become positively sloped afterward. This reduction might not be a deterioration but might be due to a reform of the schooling system, i.e., in the number of years necessary to complete schooling grades.

Figure 3.2: NIGIC for Average Education, 1989–1998

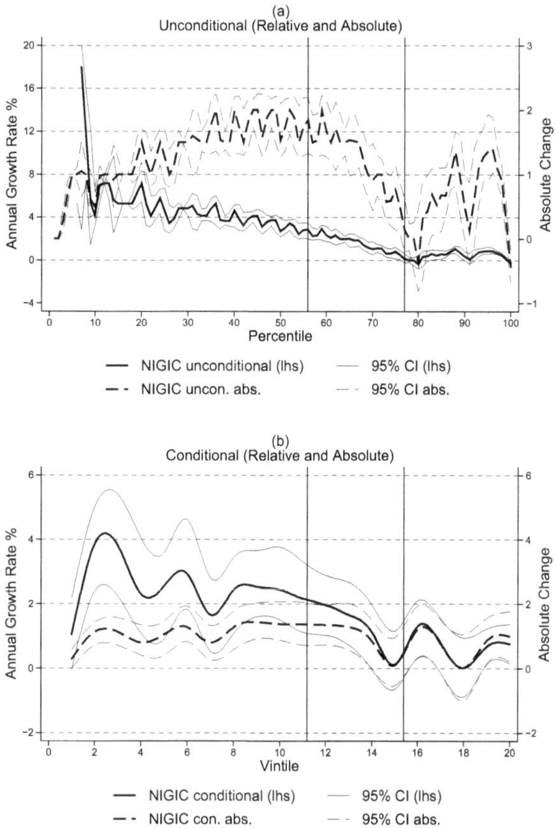

Table 3.5: Pro-Poor Growth Rates, Bolivia, 1989–1998

		NIGIC 1989-1998 (unconditional)		NIGIC 1989-1998 (conditional)			NIGIC 1989-1998 (unconditional)		NIGIC 1989-1998 (conditional)	
	GRIM	PPGR moderate	PPGR extreme	PPGR moderate	PPGR extreme	CHIM	PPCH moderate	PPCH extreme	PPCH moderate	PPCH extreme
Income	3.88	4.54	4.63	4.54	4.63	98.71	53.82	37.02	53.82	37.02
Education										
Ave. educ.	1.80	3.89	4.88	2.00	2.24	1.18	1.30	1.34	1.01	1.01
Ave. educ. respondents	2.30	4.84	6.08	2.48	2.80	1.33	1.59	1.38	1.07	1.06
Ave. educ. respondents (20-30)	1.87	3.47	4.75	1.75	2.02	1.36	1.38	1.74	1.03	1.09
Ave. educ. partners	1.41	2.65	3.61	1.66	1.86	1.03	1.11	1.33	0.95	0.95
Maximal education per household	1.36	2.60	3.74	1.55	1.73	1.10	1.08	1.58	1.01	1.03
Max. educ. household (respondents)	2.24	4.69	5.88	2.37	2.69	1.31	1.52	1.37	1.05	1.04
Max. educ. household (20-30)	1.73	3.42	4.66	1.64	1.89	1.23	1.27	1.58	0.92	0.95
Max. educ. partners	1.35	2.55	3.57	1.57	1.76	1.00	1.05	1.34	0.91	0.92
Health										
Under 5 child survival rate (%)	0.40	0.70	0.96	0.37	0.40	3.57	4.54	6.25	3.19	3.45
Under 1 child survival rate (%)	0.12	0.14	0.19	0.11	0.15	1.07	1.29	1.78	1.00	1.35
Ave. vacc. per child (1-3)	0.34	0.66	0.91	0.15	0.20	0.18	0.21	0.27	0.07	0.09
Nutrition										
Stunting z-score	1.05	1.63	1.87	0.82	0.78	47.71	54.60	55.38	35.12	32.32
Composite welfare index (CWI)										
Small sample	0.82	1.08	1.16	0.72	0.72	0.04	0.05	0.05	0.33	0.34
Big sample	0.58	1.83	2.41	0.35	0.34	0.03	0.04	0.05	0.02	0.02
CWI (including income)										
Small sample	1.08	1.25	1.31	0.88	0.85	0.04	0.04	0.04	0.03	0.03
Big sample	0.97	1.69	1.98	0.82	0.84	0.04	0.04	0.04	0.03	0.03

Notes: Notes: For the explanation of the variables, see Table 3.2. We are using two poverty lines. The moderate poverty line leads to an income headcount of 77 percent and the extreme poverty line to an income headcount of 56 percent, which we also use for the non-income indicators. GRIM: Growth rate in mean; PPGR: Pro-poor growth rate; CHIM: Change in mean; PPCH: Pro-poor change. Changes are for the entire period and not annualized.

Source: Own calculations based on DHS.

To take into account also possible intra-household inequalities, in addition, Figures 3.3a and 3.3b show the unconditional and conditional NIGIC for individual education in single years. Both figures reflect the picture that was found for average education per household showing relative pro-poor growth both for the unconditional and for the conditional case. This indicates that intra-household inequalities have not a substantial impact on the pro-poorness in the improvements in education attainment in Bolivia over the period.

Figure 3.3: NIGIC for Individual Education, 1989–1998

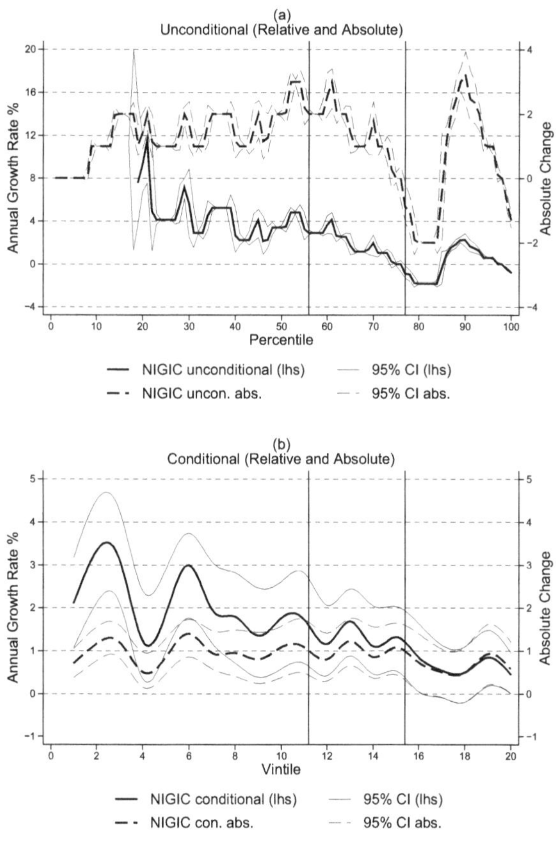

Turning to the absolute NIGIC, we do not find strong absolute pro-poor growth for the absolute unconditional NIGIC for education as the slope of the absolute curves in Figures 3.2 and 3.3 is not negative, but even positive for the poorest deciles. This is quite interesting because it puts the findings of the relative unconditional NIGIC in Figure 3.2a in perspective where we have found high relative pro-poor growth for the first 3 deciles. This seemingly contradictory finding is largely due to the high growth rates for the lower deciles which results from the very low base in 1989. The absolute conditional NIGIC is virtually flat, meaning that the income-poor have not been able to improve their educational attainment by more than the average. These findings are also reflected in comparing the PPCH with the CHIM. As Table 3.5 shows, the unconditional PPCH is still larger than the CHIM, however, only slightly: the average years of schooling only increased by 1.18 years in mean, and by 1.30 years for the moderately poor and 1.34 for the extremely poor. For the absolute conditional changes and for both poverty lines, the CHIM is higher than the PPCH of 1.01.

Another way to look at intra-household inequalities is to look at the gender gaps in education of individual couples within households. To remind, we calculate the female minus male education in the households in years of education, thus the maximum distance would be 16 years (translating in an indicator ranking theoretically from -16 (for the case of a man with full and a woman with no education) to +16). In 1989, the first 60 percentiles exhibit a negative gap (thus, a better educated husband), the next 20 percentiles show the same level of education, and the last 20 percentiles exhibit a positive gap (thus, a better educated wife). In 1998, this unequal distribution of education is slightly reduced, with the same level of education reached at the 55th percentile and the positive gap at the 77th percentile.

Ranking the households by this gap, we plot in Figure 3.4 the unconditional and conditional absolute change in the gender gap. We find that the intra-household gender gaps were reduced for nearly all households except for those between the 10th and the 20th percentile. Again, especially households in the middle of the distribution showed the strongest reductions (Figure 3.4a). The large flat part between percentile 60 and 80 show the part of the distribution where the gap is the same for around 20 percentiles. When looking at the conditional NIGIC, we find no clear trend meaning that the reduction in gender gaps is equally distributed across all income groups (Figure 3.4b).

Figures 3.5a and 3.5b show the results for average vaccination. The unconditional NIGIC shows pro-poor growth in the weak absolute sense and is also slightly negatively sloped. Table 3.5 confirms the pro-poorness in the relative

Figure 3.4: NIGIC for Gender Gap in Education, 1989–1998

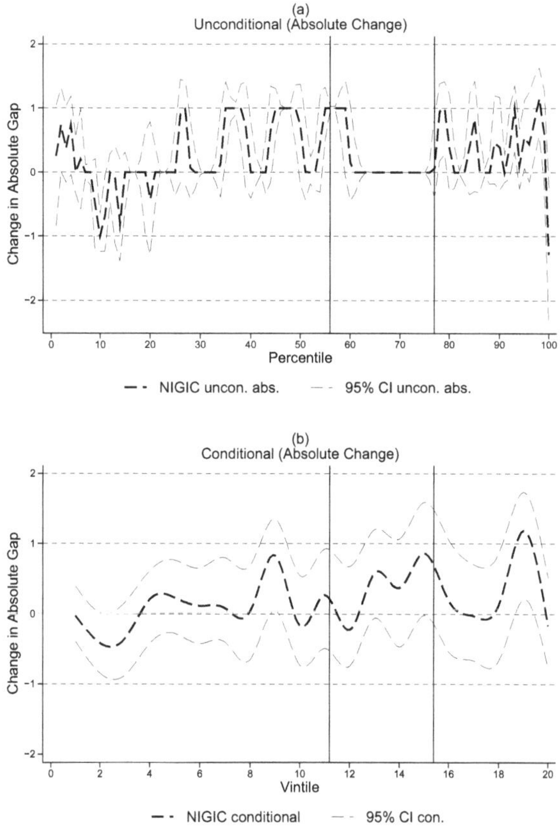

sense. Here, both PPGR exceed the GRIM. However, improvements are relatively low, which was also shown in Table 3.2.[32]

The conditional NIGIC shows no clear pro-poor growth trend, also visible in the wide confidence intervals. In addition, the PPGR are lower than the GRIM and

[32] Interesting to note is the bump around the 70th percentile. Whereas the flat parts of the curves before and after the bump show the percentiles that had 7 and 8 vaccinations in both periods respectively, the bump shows the improvements of those who had vaccinations between 7 and 8 in the initial period.

Figure 3.5: NIGIC for Vaccinations, 1989–1998

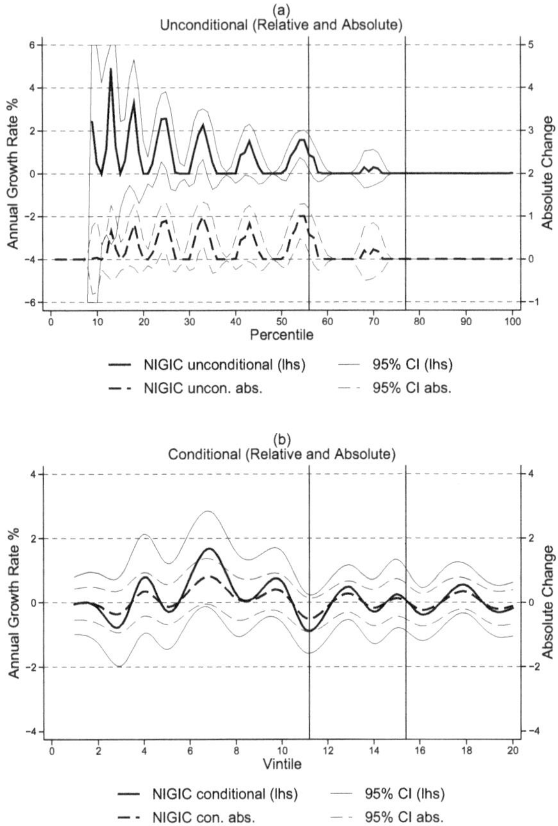

for some deciles we even find a deterioration. The same findings also hold for the absolute curves. This reveals that relative pro-poor growth might not be enough for the poor and that absolute increases (the amount of additional vaccinations) are of particular weight. Finally, it is essential for the health status of children to have all possible vaccinations. The conditional absolute NIGIC shows that the improvements are relatively equally distributed among the income groups.

When examining the high relative growth in the unconditional NIGIC for education and vaccinations, Figures 3.2a and 3.5a do not report growth rates for the very poor deciles. This is due to two reasons. First, the very poor began and ended with no education and no vaccinations (see discussion below). Second, the slightly better off started with no education or no vaccination and ended up having positive levels of education and vaccinations in the second year. But in this case the growth rate is not defined and, thus, not reported. Remember that the very high growth rates that appear on the graphs at the left are, therefore, based on percentiles who had some small amount of education and vaccinations, and even a moderate absolute expansion translates into a very high growth rate.

Examining the absolute unconditional NIGIC for education and vaccinations also reveals an important finding regarding the very low tail of the distribution. As Figures 3.2a, 3.3a, and 3.5a show, the very education-poor (vaccination-poor) had no education (vaccinations) in the first year and this continued to be the case in the second year. This is true for the first few deciles in the education indicator and nearly the entire first decile in the vaccination indicator. Thus, whatever expansion has taken place in non-income improvements, it bypassed a core group of very poor.[33]

For all the other educational variables, we confirm the findings above. Comparing the results for females with males, we find some signs for gender inequality, which are most obvious in the lower percentiles. But we find that the gender inequality seems to have been reduced because the average and maximal education for females increased by more years than for the other groups, especially for males (Tables 3.2 and 3.5). However, the women in the all respondents sample started from a lower level and are on average still worse educated.

For both survival variables, the unconditional NIGIC and the absolute NIGIC are only interpretable for the first few deciles where they show clear improvements in the sense of weak absolute and relative pro-poor growth, but they become flat from the 4th decile onward in the case of under 5 survival since 100 percent survival is already reached as shown in Figures 3.6a and 3.6b. Also the conditional NIGIC, which oscillate closely to 0 but always above, reflects the moderate and more or less equally distributed mortality risk for the income groups. Also, the deciles of Table 3.3 show only a small income gradient of mortality risk. The example of survival rates shows that unconditional curves are less helpful in some of the non-income dimensions compared to conditional curves. This holds for variables that have a low variation in the data, and the extreme example where the unconditional curves are hardly useful are dummy variables. This is why Grosse

[33]The findings with the education indicator have to be treated with some caution as they may simply say that adult women that had no education in the first survey continue to have no education in the second survey, which is to be expected in the absence of adult education programmes. This is not the case, however, with the vaccination indicator as it refers to children between ages 1 and 5 and, thus, it is indeed worrying that a new cohort of children has grown up without any vaccinations.

et al. (2008b) only use conditional curves when monitoring the MDGs, since most of the indicators monitored are dummy variables. However, the more complex the indicators are measured (for example on a scale from 0 to 10), the more interesting it becomes to use both conditional and unconditional curves.

Figure 3.6: NIGIC for Under Five Survival, 1989–1998

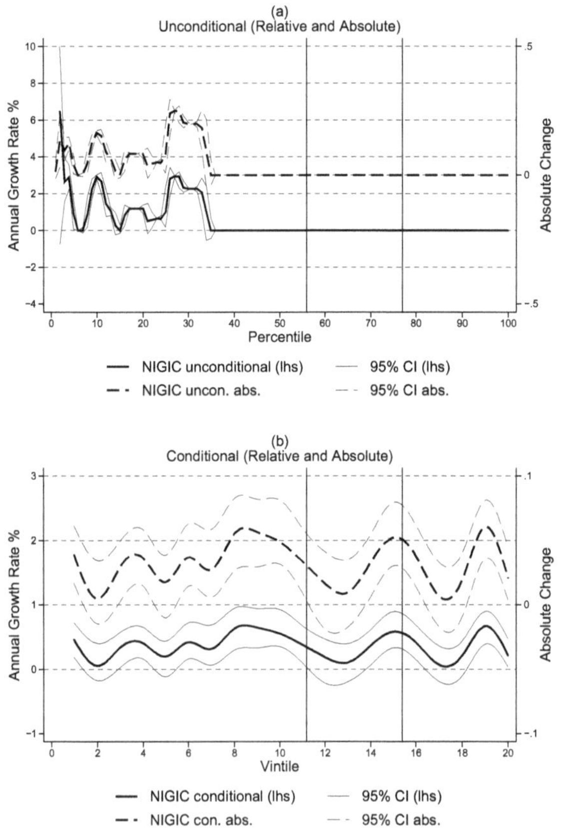

Figures 3.7a and 3.7b show the NIGIC for stunting. The unconditional NIGIC indicates weak absolute and relative pro-poor growth. For the conditional NIGIC, we only find weak absolute but no relative pro-poor growth. These results are

also found when looking at the PPGR and the GRIM for the improvements in the stunting z-score. Both absolute NIGIC show that the absolute changes are distributed nearly equally over the sample.

Figure 3.7: NIGIC for Stunting, 1989–1998

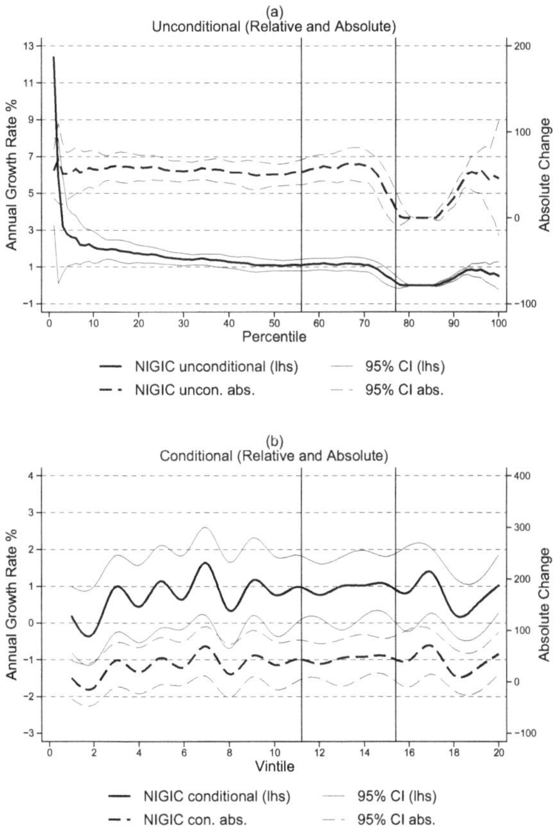

Aggregating the several variables in the CWI, Figures 3.8a and 3.8b summarize the development of the social indicators in one single NIGIC. As expected, we find pro-poor growth in the weak absolute and relative sense for the unconditional NIGIC. Looking at Table 3.5, we find very high relative pro-poor growth as both PPGR clearly exceed the GRIM. As being somewhat more volatile the conditional NIGIC shows also pro-poor growth in the weak absolute but not in the relative sense. Asking for pro-poor growth in the strong absolute sense, we find an anti-poor trend for the lower end of the distribution for the unconditional absolute NIGIC and a more or less equally distributed trend for the conditional absolute NIGIC.

Figure 3.8: NIGIC for the Composite Welfare Index, 1989–1998

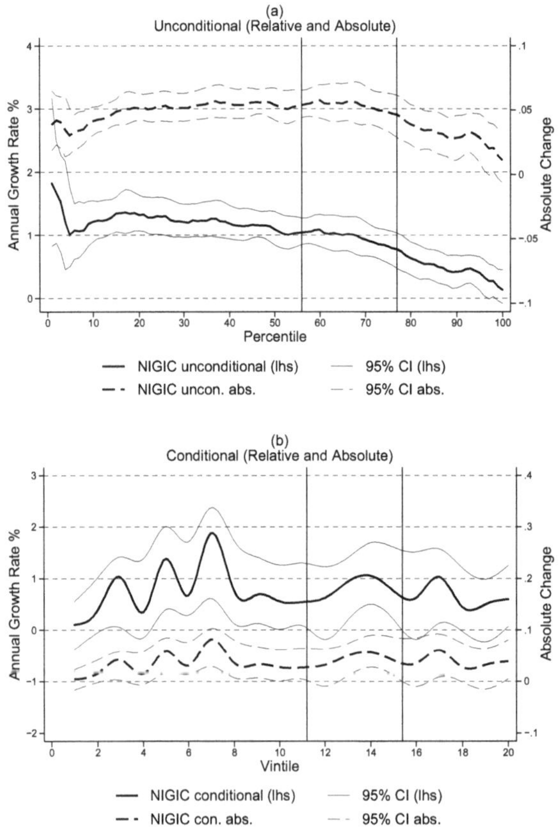

Altogether, for nearly all variables, we find the strongest increases in the unconditional absolute NIGIC for some medium groups but not for the poorest groups. For most of the percentiles, we find weak absolute pro-poor growth, but we do not find relative pro-poor growth, especially not for the poorest. These outcomes mirror the findings of previous analysis about poverty in Bolivia (Republic of Bolivia, 2001; INE, 2004; World Bank, 2004), which also find improvements in income and non-income poverty but not for the very poor.[34] Nevertheless, Bolivia remains one of the poorest countries in Latin America in the income as well as in the non-income dimension.

However, one should bear in mind that the findings regarding the NIGIC come from a period when there were great improvements made in social indicators, particularly among middle and lower income groups. When translating these measures to other countries (particularly in Africa) it could well be that the NIGIC would show that growth rates were not pro-poor as was found by Günther et al. (2006) for Mali from 1995-2001. To illustrate this, we additionally present the NIGIC for individual education of the household head and partner for Burkina Faso between 1994 and 2003 in Figures 3.9a and 3.9b.[35]

Figure 3.9a nicely illustrates that the improvements in education between the two periods have been made only for the upper 30 percentiles, whereas all other groups are bypassed from improvements. This means that no pro-poor growth is found for Burkina Faso between 1994 and 2003 and that only the initially educated population group has experienced relative and absolute improvements, which was not found for Bolivia. When looking at Figure 3.9b, we see that the relative and absolute improvements in years of education show no significant income gradient.

[34]Most of the improvement furthermore benefited mainly the urban population with little improvement in the rural areas.

[35]For the calculation of the NIGIC, we use the Enquête Prioritaire sur les Conditions de Vie des Ménages (EPM) household survey data sets from 1994 and 2003.

Figure 3.9: NIGIC for Education (Burkina Faso), 1994–2003

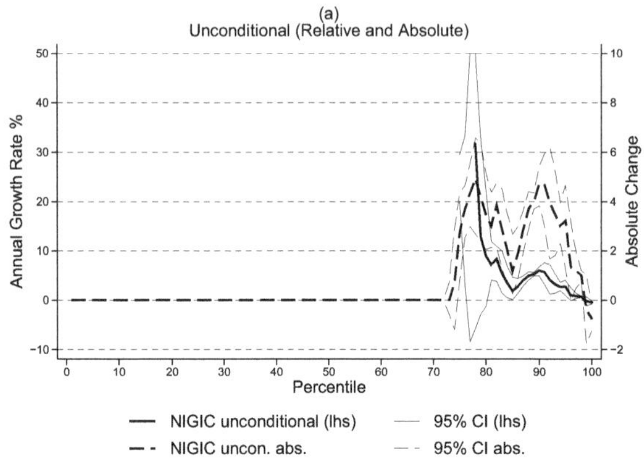

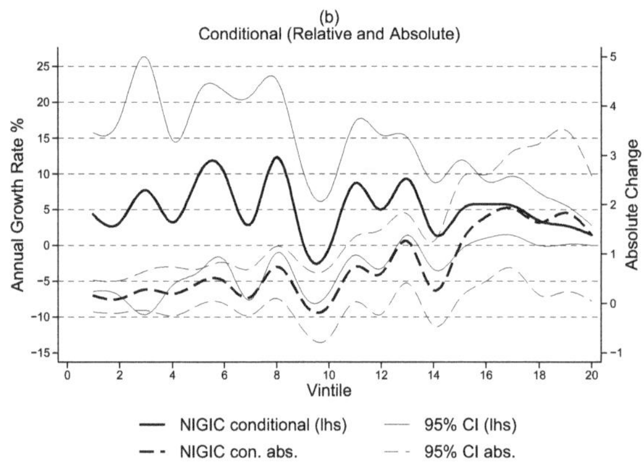

3.5 Conclusion

We introduced the multidimensionality of poverty into the pro-poor growth measurement. The purpose is to overcome the major shortcoming of the existing pro-poor growth measurements, which are exclusively focussed on income but give no information on how social indicators changed over time for poor population groups. The aim is to better monitor the MDGs and not only to focus on the income dimension of poverty.

In our approach, we apply the methodology of the GIC to non-income indicators and investigate pro-poor growth of non-income indicators using the NIGIC. We analyze how income and non-income indicators changed in favor of the poor. Also, we analyze how social indicators have developed when they are linked to their position in the income distribution. This is of special interest when evaluating distributional welfare impact of aid and public spending. Furthermore, we take absolute inequality explicitly into account and analyze if absolute improvements are large enough for the poor to catch up. Reducing absolute inequality in social indicators is crucial for sustainable development and for equal choices.

We exemplarily illustrate this approach using data for Bolivia from 1989 to 1998. Using the GIC and the unconditional NIGIC, we find improvements both in the income and non-income dimensions of poverty which is a common finding for Bolivia. Growth was pro-poor in the weak absolute and the relative sense both for income and non-income indicators, whereas we find no pro-poor growth in the strong absolute sense for income and only limited strong absolute pro-poor growth for the middle percentiles for non-income indicators. However, in general this is not the case when using the conditional NIGIC, where the social indicators were sorted by the initial income.[36] Thus, there is not at all a perfect overlap of income-poor and of non-income-poor households. These findings suggest that the improvements in non-income dimensions were more focussed on the initially poor in those indicators, whereas they were not focussed on the initially income-poor. The absolute changes show that the poor have not benefited disproportionately more from the improvements. This means that relative pro-poor growth does not automatically mean that the poor catch up with the non-poor in absolute terms because we find that relative income and non-income inequality have fallen, but not absolute inequality.

When calling for pro-poor growth as the most significant policy measure to achieve the MDGs, policy makers should not only focus on income pro-poor growth rather on multidimensional dimensions of pro-poor growth and, therefore, take non-income indicators explicitly into account. We have shown that the income-poor are not automatically the ones that benefit most from growth in social indicators, which is an important and new finding. In addition, policy makers should also give attention to pro-poor growth in the strong absolute sense in order to accelerate progress in meeting the MDGs.

[36]One has to note again that the data used is not panel data. Additionally, for the two-dimensional view of the conditional NIGIC it is even more crucial to keep in mind that we do not consider the same households, and that the trends of social indicators of the income-poor have nothing of a panel character (Grimm, 2007).

Essay 4

Pro-Poor Growth in Multidimensional Poverty Indicators: An Application to Colombia

Happiness is when what you think, what you say, and what you do are in harmony.
Mohandas Gandhi (1869–1948)

Abstract: Empirical multidimensional poverty assessment poses three important challenges: The first is the selection of indicators that best reflect basic capabilities. The second is the aggregation of variables in composite multidimensional poverty indicators, especially the weighting procedure applied. The third is to follow the multidimensional poverty indicators over time to judge whether or not the poor have achieved improvements in multidimensional welfare. We illustrate these three challenges empirically for Colombia and investigate how the distribution of particular dimensions of welfare has changed between 1997 and 2003. We also investigate if there is a relation between changes in income and non-income dimensions, and whether this depends on the weights applied. We use two opposed methodologies to calculate weights: one based on statistical procedures and the other based on normative criteria. We apply an extension of the pro-poor growth measurement for multidimensional poverty indicators to investigate the distributional pattern of progress in these indicators.

---

based on joint work with Adriana Cardozo.

4.1 Introduction

One of the major issues concerning poverty analysis during the last decades was the recognition that poverty should not be defined only as lack of income, but that there are multiple dimensions by which deprivation can be observed. In the case of Colombia, multidimensional poverty has been approached using the Human Development Index (HDI), the Unmet Basic Needs Index (NBI), and the Life Conditions Index (ICV).[1] However, all three have methodological and conceptual shortcomings. Moreover, research combining income growth with multidimensional poverty and inequality trends is scarce.

The objective of this paper is to analyze how the distribution of particular dimensions of welfare in Colombia changed between 1997 and 2003, and if there was a relation between changes in income and non-income dimensions. We create indicators reflecting some of the most important non-income dimensions such as human and physical capital (education and assets), health status, and subjective welfare and track relative changes in these indicators along quantiles of the population, for example deciles and vintiles. By applying the recently developed methodologies on multidimensional pro-poor growth (Klasen, 2008a) to the Colombian Living Standard Measurement Survey (LSMS) we discuss whether changes in assets, education, health, and subjective welfare were more beneficial to the poor than to the non-poor. For constructing indices, we select a subset of variables and apply principal component analysis (PCA) in a recently modified version known as polychoric PCA, suggested by Kolenikov and Angeles (2009) to define weights. This methodology allows to correctly calculate the correlation matrix before applying traditional PCA, diverging from the standard procedure used up to now in the literature. Results are compared to the same indicators using normatively selected weights to enrich the discussion about the right weighting procedure.

Although the time span is short and covers a turbulent economic period with a large recession, it is quite relevant because it gives an insight into how the overall economic situation affected non-income dimensions like education, health, assets ownership, and access to public services. Non-income dimensions of poverty are expected to react more slowly and to be less sensitive to short-term shocks compared to income or consumption. The method applied in this paper allows us to assess in detail the progress in the reduction of multidimensional poverty and to combine it with trends in the entire income distribution.

The paper is structured as follows. Section 4.2 explains the foundations of multidimensional poverty analysis and of non-income pro-poor growth measurement. Section 4.3 describes the Colombian background and the data used. This

[1] NBI and ICV are the abbreviations in Spanish, which we will keep using.

section also explains in detail the multidimensional indicators and highlights some limitations. Section 4.4 presents the results, and Section 4.5 concludes.

4.2 Multidimensional Poverty Analysis: Concept and Measurement Issues

4.2.1 Foundations of Multidimensional Poverty Analysis

Multidimensional poverty analysis is primarily concerned with poverty assessment in attributes different than income. Many authors argue that the different dimensions of poverty are generally weakly correlated with income (or expenditures) and that links between income and indicators such as malnutrition, mortality, and school enrollment are difficult to identify empirically (for example Klasen (2000); Günther and Klasen (2009)). Other authors argue that multidimensional welfare indicators and income give similar overall pictures of poverty (von Maltzahn and Durrheim, 2007). Overall, a consensus about the existence of multiple dimensions of poverty has emerged and has gained attention among academics and policy makers in the last two to three decades.

Conceptually, multidimensional welfare analyses are inspired by seminal work of Sen (1979, 1980, 1985), who has developed what is known in the literature as the capabilities approach. According to this approach, poverty is understood as deprivation of capabilities, or substantive freedoms, suggesting that poverty measures based solely on income and material status do not represent all aspects of human being nor give information about people's capacities to achieve basic functionings. The capabilities approach also focuses on the individual's ability to participate in society, move across different spheres of life, and access markets, something that can hardly be captured by traditional income-based poverty measures (Clark, 2005). Based on Sen's work, several attempts have been made to empirically measure multidimensional poverty and inequality (Atkinson and Bourguignon, 1982; Bourguignon and Chakravarty, 2003; Duclos et al., 2006; Alkire and Foster, 2009). Among the questions to be addressed, the most important ones are: the dimensions to be included, the procedure for judging whether an individual is poor or not, and the aggregation (or not) of multidimensional poverty outcomes.

Dimensions frequently included are health, nutrition, education, and dwelling characteristics or asset endowment, taken as tangible outcomes that reflect functionings. However, there are many dimensions that can hardly be measured but affect the ability of an individual to escape out of poverty. Typical examples are freedom, human rights, or absence of violence. For each dimension, a threshold needs to be specified below which an individual is considered to be poor. For example, children could be defined as being poorly nourished if their stunting z-score falls below a critical value,[2] or adults could be considered as being poorly educated if their schooling level falls below the minimum years for a primary or secondary education degree. Similar to income poverty measurements, the multi-dimensional poverty measure can be rather crude (such as the poverty headcount), be more sensitive to inequality (such as poverty gap or poverty severity), or could take the form of a more axiomatic index such as the Sen index (Bourguignon and Chakravarty, 2003).

Some authors argue that combining dimensions by some aggregation function into an index shrinks multidimensional poverty analysis back to a one-dimensional analysis. A better way to keep the multidimensional view is to refrain from aggregation but to find other ways of presenting multidimensional poverty results. For example, Atkinson and Bourguignon (1982) use a stochastic dominance approach of Lorenz curves to measure multidimensional inequality (in this case, two-dimensional using country averages of income and life expectancy) reflecting not only the individual threshold levels but also how much the dimensions of poverty happen to be correlated with each other (an increase in correlation is interpreted as being worse since it becomes more likely to be poor in both dimensions at the same time). Bourguignon and Chakravarty (2003) use micro data on income and education for rural Brazil and apply different weights reflecting substitutability or trade-offs between the two dimensions. Duclos et al. (2006) follow a dominance approach that is robust to the aggregation procedure and the poverty line. They present for example graphical results by dominance surfaces using two dimensions (expenditures and nutrition compared for urban and rural Vietnam) and three dimensions (survival, undernutrition, and asset endowment in Ghana). The latter example already becomes difficult to be graphically presented and interpreted, not to speak of even higher orders. Duclos et al. (2006) also highlight that the interaction and correlation plays an important role in judging poverty, so that for example the increase of a poor person should be valued higher if that person is also deprived in other dimensions, or, to put it differently, the higher the correlation between poverty in the various dimensions is, the poorer the person is. Alkire and Foster (2009) follow the same argument and present an intuitive counting approach. In each dimension, a person is considered to be deprived if she falls below a certain threshold. The number of deprived dimensions determine if a person is finally considered to be poor: (i) under a union approach, it is sufficient to be deprived in one dimension to be considered as poor, (ii) under an intersection approach, it is necessary to be deprived in all dimensions to be considered as poor. Of course, the choice of one extreme (or an intermediate approach) depends also on the number of dimensions. With an increasing number of dimensions, more

[2]See **Essay 3** for more details on stunting, as well as for other health indicators.

and more people are considered poor in a union approach leading to a too high number of poor people (because one single deprivation is enough to be poor), whereas less and less people are considered to be poor in an intersection approach leading to a too low number of poor people (because it misses the poor that are deprived in many but not in all dimensions).

Despite the fundamental critique, an important range of studies on multidimensional poverty aggregate variables that reflect physical, human, and social capital to create a composite index. The internationally best known indicator trying to capture multidimensional poverty is UNDP's Human Development Index (HDI), which combines indicators of longevity, education, and living standards. This indicator has been criticized for having weak conceptual foundations and using an equal weight for each component. However, it has gained a key role in policy debate given its comparability across countries and the easy way of understanding and communicating it (Kanbur, 2002). Grimm et al. (2008) have addressed some of the critiques raised against the HDI by extending the analysis from the macro level of between country comparisons, i.e., of national averages, to the micro level in breaking down the HDI for comparisons within countries.

Beyond using arbitrary weights, like setting all weights equal to one, it is possible to define weights through statistical procedures to generate an overall index. A frequently used technique in recent research is principal component analysis (PCA) suggested by Filmer and Pritchett (2001), which extracts the linear combinations between variables that best explain their variance and covariance structure.[3] Intuitively, one or few variables underlie the covariance structure in the data, and it thus allows aggregating several variables into a single dimension, giving each one a weight resulting from the eigenvalues and eigenvectors of the covariance matrix.[4]

As discussed for example by Kolenikov and Angeles (2009), PCA has some shortcomings and was originally developed for variables that are multivariate normal and applied to continuous data, which does not hold when data are discrete (most of them binary or categorical, only very few continuous), as also relevant in our case. Breaking down categories into dummy variables results in perfectly negatively correlated variables, introducing spurious correlations. Additionally if the

[3]Other authors using this procedure are for example Ram (1982), Sahn and Stifel (2000, 2003), and Klasen (2000) using the closely related factor analysis. Kolenikov and Angeles (2009) provide an overview over the literature and over the variables typically included. See also **Essay 1** and especially Chapter 1.6 for some further critique on PCA weights.

[4]An alternative to weight selected variables is to use the price of assets and value them in terms of the monetary welfare they provide. This is only possible if prices, quantities, and the current monetary value of each item are available, which is not the case for our data. However, even if prices were given, they would surely not exist for all dimensions of multidimensional poverty such as non-market goods or might be misleading such as goods with external effects.

majority of the data points are concentrated in a single category, the method assigns larger weights to the most skewed variables and creates a biased correlation matrix.

Several ways have been proposed to overcome the shortcomings of PCA. Kolenikov and Angeles (2009) suggest using polychoric correlations in order to estimate the correlation matrix before applying PCA. Polychoric PCA (PPCA) assumes that the observed ordinal variable has an underlying continuous variable (assuming normality) and uses maximum likelihood to calculate how that continuous variable would have to be split up in order to produce the observed data. The resulting polychoric correlation matrix is used to calculate the eigenvectors. This procedure is particularly useful for ordinal data.[5] Moreover it allows computing weights not only on owning but also not owning an asset (Moser and Felton, 2009) (since weights are not symmetric), and it generates a larger percentage of explained variance by the first component as shown by Kolenikov and Angeles (2009). An alternative to overcome the problem inherent in PCA for discrete data is multiple correspondence analysis (MCA). As outlined by Booysen et al. (2008) MCA poses less constraints on the data and makes overall fewer assumptions about the distribution of the variables that are selected for the analysis than PCA.

Both PPCA and MCA overcome some of the shortcomings of traditional PCA analysis. However, both are data-driven approaches, thus the weights are determined by statistical procedures. A more fundamental critique is that weights should be derived from either economic theory or be based on welfare theoretical arguments. Thus, the researchers themselves should determine the most important aspects to be included in multidimensional poverty indices, and also their weights. What is criticized by, e.g., Grimm et al. (2008) for the HDI, is the weighting scheme by which each component gets the same arbitrary weight.

In this paper, we address this critique and define the weights based on our own evaluation, thus on normative procedures, outlined in Section 4.3.3, and compare them with data-driven weights using PPCA. The definition of normative weights is delicate, and thus might expose us to some discussions. However, equal weighting, despite being a popular weighting scheme, should be exposed to even more discussion and critique because it also sets weights normatively, in this case equal to each other. In general, we refrain from aggregating several dimensions of poverty into a single index but instead combine only several variables of the same dimension into a "dimension-index", see below.

[5]However, it would not be suitable for truly categorical variables such as gender, race, or geographic region.

4.2.2 Multidimensional Poverty Dynamics: Pro-Poor Growth

Evident from above is the point that poverty is a multidimensional phenomenon that should be measured by one or several multidimensional indices. Furthermore, the within- and between-country distribution of multidimensional welfare is an important point having gained more attention in the last years. The HDI by income quintile of Grimm et al. (2008) is a one-time, static snapshot on this point. The next step is to look beyond statics and turn to dynamics, thus at multidimensional poverty and inequality over time.

Since the early 2000s, the concept of pro-poor growth has gained attention in research and policy. The term pro-poor growth refers broadly to economic growth that benefits the poor, and has been measured empirically mainly through household income or consumption expenditures changes, i.e., in the traditional income-based dimension of poverty. Several ways have been proposed to define and measure pro-poor growth.[6] We focus on two definitions: For the weak (also called general) definition, any growth path leading to poverty reduction is considered pro-poor, so any positive income growth is defined as being pro-poor. For the strong (also called strict) definition, growth is pro-poor only when both poverty and inequality decrease, thus when income gains of the poor are higher relative to those of the non-poor (thus, also called relative approach when looking at growth rates).[7]

As shown by Grosse et al. (2008a)[8] and Klasen (2008a) for Bolivia, it is possible to extend existing pro-poor growth measurement tools such as the growth incidence curve (GIC) of Ravallion and Chen (2003) to non-income variables such as education or health by specifying non-income growth incidence curves (NIGIC). The income-based GIC graphs the rate of growth of real income (shown at the y

[6]For a detailed review on the different definitions and measures of pro-poor growth, see, for example, Son (2003). Other approaches to define pro-poor growth are provided, for example, by White and Anderson (2000), Ravallion and Datt (2002), Klasen (2004), and Hanmer and Booth (2001). The most common measures that have evolved in pro-poor growth measurement are the 'poverty bias of growth' of McCulloch and Baulch (1999), the 'pro-poor growth index' of Kakwani and Pernia (2000), the 'poverty equivalent growth rate' of Kakwani and Son (2000), the 'poverty growth curve' of Son (2003), and the 'growth incidence curve' of Ravallion and Chen (2003).

[7]The strong approach to pro-poor growth can be further subdivided into relative or strong absolute. The relative approach focuses on proportional changes in income between poor and non-poor and considers growth to be pro-poor when relative inequality decreases. This is only possible if incomes of the poor rise by a higher proportion than incomes of the non-poor. For the strong absolute approach, growth is pro-poor if absolute income gains of the poor are higher than those of the non-poor, meaning that absolute inequality (defined as the absolute difference in income between the poor and non-poor) decreases. Numerical examples for difference between changes in relative and absolute inequality are given by Ravallion and Chen (2003) and Klasen (2008a).

[8]Note that Grosse et al. (2008a) is equivalent to **Essay 3**.

axis) for each quantile of the distribution (shown the x axis with increasing order by income) between two points in time. The formal derivation can be found in **Essay 3**, Section 3.3.1. A curve below 0 at all points of the distribution indicates that all households suffered income losses. The contrary indicates income gains for all percentiles and consequently a poverty decrease compared with the initial period, satisfying the weak definition of pro-poor growth. An upward-sloping curve indicates that rich households benefited more than others, while a downward-sloping curve indicates that the poor benefited relatively more, giving evidence of pro-poor growth in a relative sense.

The graphical analysis of the GIC would not demand using a poverty line to determine whether growth was beneficial to the poor. However, this is only possible when the slope of the curve has a clear trend. In practice, the GIC often has different slopes at different points and switches sign along percentiles, making it impossible to draw clear conclusions. To overcome this problem Ravallion and Chen (2003) suggest calculating the pro-poor growth rate (PPGR) as the area below the GIC up to the poverty headcount of the initial period. This area equals total income growth of the poor, or, to put it differently, the PPGR reflects the average of the growth rates of the poor. It can be compared to the growth rate in mean (GRIM), and if the PPGR is higher than the GRIM growth is pro-poor in the relative sense, while the opposite result indicates that distributional changes negatively affected the poor.

When applying the GIC to non-income indicators is particularly interesting to depict changes in variables expressing non-income welfare (or functionings of households) by income percentiles (e.g., educational progress conditional of the position in the income distribution, thus, ordered from the income-poor to the income-rich), and thus investigating how the educational progress was distributed over the income distribution (Grosse et al., 2008a).[9] It is also useful to present results unconditional to income, which means percentiles are created based on the non-income variable itself (e.g., progress of education ordered from the education-poor to the education-rich) to follow the outcome-based multidimensional poverty measure directly.

[9]Grosse et al. (2008a) show that it is interesting to analyze absolute changes in non-monetary indicators, which is additionally informative to using only growth rates. With absolute changes, it is possible to track if growth is pro-poor in the strong absolute sense. Thus, it is possible to measure pro-poor growth using the three definitions of weak absolute, weak relative, and strong absolute. Here, we only focus the first two definitions, and just exemplarily present absolute results for income. See Cardozo and Grosse (2009) for absolute NIGIC for Colombia.

4.3 Application to Colombia

4.3.1 Macroeconomic Trends and Public Policies

At the beginning of the 1990s, Colombia undertook several political and economic reforms by which the economic model moved from an import substituting to an open and liberalized one. Several changes in the labor, financial, and exchange rate markets were undertaken, together with drastic reductions in average tariffs and the removal of barriers to foreign direct investment and capital exports (Cardozo, 2008). The role of the state in providing education and health was also modified. The constitution of 1991 accelerated the fiscal decentralization process. The new model increased the responsibility of departments and municipalities in the administration of resources and placed them as primary providers of basic services to the population, particularly in education and health (Sánchez, 2006; Bès et al., 1998). Reforms were expected to increase public spending efficiency through participation of local governments and had positive effects on access to basic services, although not in the expected magnitude. Changes in the education system contributed to progressive increases of gross enrollment rates, particularly concerning secondary education, but the quality of public education continued to be very low and even weakened, showing dramatic differences compared to private schools.[10] In the health sector coverage increased, especially after further reforms undertaken in 1993, moving from 20 percent of the total population in 1993 to 32 in 1995 and 75 in 2004 (Sánchez, 2006). However, the goal of achieving universal health coverage by 2000 as well as equal access for all individuals was not reached, and quality of services remained largely dependent on the purchasing power of the households.[11]

At the end of the 1990s, the economic and political environment became particularly difficult due to the combination of the second largest recession experienced during the 20th century and the dramatic escalation of the internal armed conflict. Large unemployment rates due to the crisis as well internally forced displacement due to violence increased poverty to levels last observed in 1985. The economic deceleration started in 1996 and lasted until 2001, achieving a peak in 1999 with a contraction of -5.52 percent in per capita GDP. All poverty indica-

[10]Access to pre-school education increased from 51 percent in 1995 to 88 percent in 2006. Widespread primary education explains high literacy rates (of 98 percent) among the youth. Gross enrollment rates in middle and secondary education also rose, although there is still an important lag in achievements of secondary schooling, especially in rural areas, where even though gross enrollment rates almost doubled since 1995 they were only 55 percent in 2006 (Sánchez, 2006).

[11]Recent studies show that only 48.1 percent of population in the 1st quintile of the income distribution are covered by the health system, compared to 83.7 percent of the 5th quintile (Jazmín et al., 2004) and that public spending in health benefits the richest (4th and 5th) quintiles (González, 2001).

tors increased up to 1999 (headcount of 57 percent), slowed down from 2000 to 2001, rose again in 2002, and improved since then. By 2005, national poverty and inequality indicators as well as real income had returned to the levels of the early to mid-1990s, but unemployment remained higher than in 1996, at around 12 percent.

The temporary effects of the recession on households were channeled through unemployment and reduction of income. It is not clear in how far that affected non-income dimensions, particularly those in which the government was increasing public spending. The final outcome on other dimensions of poverty might have depended on the counteracting effect of reforms at that time. One could expect households in the upper quintiles of the income distribution to have overcome the crisis easily, restructuring expenditures towards maintaining education and health status but reducing luxurious expenditures. The effect on middle income groups is much harder to be predicted: the most vulnerable might have become at least temporarily poor, others might have turned to using more public services, particularly in education, as suggested by Barrera and Domínguez (2006). Finally, income-related deprivation of the poorest quintiles might have had accelerated the drop out of students, reduced asset ownership, and slowed down the pace of improvement in access to public services (Sarmiento et al., 2005).

Periodic analysis of multidimensional poverty in Colombia is done using the Human Development Index (HDI), the Unmet Basic Needs Index (NBI),[12] and the Life Conditions Index (ICV)[13] as proxies. The NBI has several well known shortcomings. The selection of the included basic needs is subjective as well as the fact that they have the same weight. Thus, two households are equally poor if the first lacks good dwelling characteristics and if schooling-age members of the second do not attend school. Moreover, it does not allow to make assessments on the depth of poverty nor judgements on the amount of poor persons as it is calculated by household, making the classification dependent on the demographic characteristics of it. Finally, components of the NBI are strongly oriented towards infrastructure conditions, some of which are not relevant to measure poverty in urban areas due to nearly full coverage of service infrastructure there (DNP, 2006;

[12]The NBI for Colombia includes five basic needs: inadequate dwelling, dwellings without basic services, households being overcrowded, no attendance to school, and high economic dependence. It classifies a household as poor if it lacks one of these basic needs, and extremely poor if it lacks two or more. Using Census data, the NBI can be calculated at the municipal level (the smallest administrative unit) and is used to determine distribution of transfers from the central government (for example to infant primary health care and education (DNP, 2008)), to target social programs, and also to create poverty maps, thus to assess the geographical distribution of poverty.

[13]The ICV ranks from 0 to 100, with the latter representing the highest possible welfare. It captures in a single measure variables corresponding to quality of housing, access to public services, education, and the size and composition of the household.

Feres and Mancero, 2001). For the ICV, the corresponding weights are calculated using PCA. This index has become an important tool for targeting of social programs, but is criticized for leaving completely aside the income dimension and being built based purely on statistical procedures.

Recent research on multidimensional poverty has been done by Vélez and Robles (2008), who apply axiomatically derived poverty indices to three socioeconomic dimensions (consumption, education, and security) in order to explain improvements of welfare perceptions by Colombians between 1997 and 2003. The authors apply seven types of three-dimensional poverty indicators to the mentioned dimensions and test four types of normative weights using the Colombian LSMS from 1997 and 2003. The authors conclude that the negative effects on welfare induced by the lower per capita consumption due to the economic recession of the late 1990s were more than compensated by the increasing progressiveness of subsidies due to social programs and the improvement in the educational endowments of household heads. However, conclusions are very sensitive to the chosen normative weights among dimensions, and the relation with improvement in self-reported welfare cannot be directly derived from the resulting reduction in the multidimensional poverty indices.

4.3.2 Data

For this paper, we use the Living Standard Measurement Survey (LSMS) (Encuesta de Calidad de Vida, ECV) of 1997 and 2003, which has a very rich questionnaire in non-income aspects. Moreover, the ECV includes income and expenditures, which are calculated in per capita monthly terms and reported in Colombian pesos constant of 1997, corresponding to an average of 2000 pesos per USD. We used as deflator the consumer price index for low income groups, available separately for each of the 13 metropolitan areas, rest of urban areas, and rural areas. This same deflator is used to update the poverty lines, which exist for the same subdivisions (Official poverty lines version 2005).[14]

The total amount of observations included in 1997 is 37,735 individuals and in 2003 is 83,757. The sample of 2003 is larger because it is also representative for suburban areas of Bogota and subregions of the department of Valle. The ECV is representative at the national, urban, rural, and regional level (five regions) in both years. Monthly household per capita expenditures include all expenditures on food, clothes, leisure, household durables, health, education, services, and finance costs.[15] We could not correct it for agricultural home production because this

[14]For methodological details on the poverty lines, see DNP (2006). For details on effects of price deflators on pro-poor growth measurement, see Günther and Grimm (2007).

[15]A check for outliers in income and expenditures was done constructing box plots by subgroups, as well as scatter plots of income versus expenditures to track implausible values. Extreme

information is only partially available in the 2003 round. We also did not include imputed rents because the variable needed for that (property of a house and it's value) has a large variation in value and therefore in interpretation, as well as because that information is available only for urban areas in the two survey rounds.

4.3.3 Multidimensional Poverty Indicators

Our approach consists of creating multidimensional indices reflecting four key areas of welfare: (i) basic assets and infrastructure endowment of the household (including private goods' ownership and access to public services), (ii) health, (iii) living conditions and welfare self-perception, and (iv) education (split up into education of children in schooling age, education of adults, and education of the subgroup aged 20–30, called twens).[16] The indices on assets, health, and subjective welfare were created using two weighting alternatives: PPCA weights and normative own weights (Table 4.1). PPCA weights were calculated using the STATA routine proposed by Kolenikov and Angeles (2009). The baseline PPCA results shown here are generated using a pooled sample.[17]

(i) Basic assets. The first index comprises durables ownership, dwelling characteristics, and access to services, combined together into what we call an asset index. This dimension is intended to reflect accumulated long-term welfare that goes beyond short-term fluctuations in income. Calculated at the household level, this index reflects items and services shared by all members and allows complementing the income dimension by overcoming problems of seasonality and high variability in income. It is also useful to overcome income measurement error (Moser and Felton, 2009). To construct the asset index, we selected a subset of eight basic household items, five dwelling characteristics, number of rooms per person, and access to public services (Table 4.1). Each household item and dwelling characteristic corresponds to a binary or ordinal variable, in which hav-

cases where the difference between income and expenditures is large, checked using scatter plots, were double checked for consistency and possible mistakes in the original information. Outliers were finally identified as values greater or less than three standard deviations from the median of log income or log expenditures and were not used for the analysis. These outliers coincide with those showing large difference between income and expenditures, so no additional cases had to be excluded. Zeros and missing values were not taken into account to calculate the medians. This procedure skipped out of a total of 854 households in 1997 and 1476 in 2003, corresponding to 2 percent and 1.7 percent of each sample.

[16]Note that we do not generate an "overall" index, combining the four areas of welfare, but only "dimension-indices".

[17]For sensitivity, and due to different sample designs, sample sizes, and weighting of the 1997 and 2003 surveys we also calculated them separately for each year. Resulting weights in both years are very similar to the ones shown in Table 4.1.

ing it is associated with higher welfare. We calculated the number of rooms per person and created five groups on it to capture overcrowding.

Access to public services includes electricity, piped gas (which is a relatively newly available service in Colombia), water, sewage, litter collection, and telephone (fixed line network). We included these services into the overall asset index. In addition to presenting results on the overall asset index, we separate it into a "private goods" and "public services" part for the pro-poor growth analysis. In doing so, we are able to show if any progress in the overall asset ownership is mainly driven by an increase in privately owned goods and dwelling characteristics or by an increase in state provision of public services.

Normative weights for the asset index were assigned according to two criteria: the importance of each item inside the corresponding subindex composing a specific index, what we call scores, and the value inside the index, what we call weights. The final normative weight is achieved by multiplying the score with the weight. The welfare of a household is calculated as the sum of final weights.[18] The same logic applies for the health and subjective welfare indices. When using normative weights, of course both scores and weights are of subjective choice. Innumerable alternative weighting schemes are possible, including some that are not necessarily additive as the one proposed.

Using PPCA weights, the assets having the highest scoring factor for the average Colombian household are: having high quality floor, having a car, and using electricity as cooking material. Among public services, piped gas has the highest weight followed by phone connection. The variables strongly diminishing the household's score are: lack of access to electricity and water, lack of toilet, low quality wall material, and lack of shower facility.

(ii) Health. With the second non-income dimension we capture health using six variables: reported health status of the person, having a chronic health disease, having a sickness in the last month, being affiliated to a medical service, going to a routine health checkup once per year without being acutely ill, and having been to hospital last year due to a serious disease or injury. Although the first variable

[18] For example, within the asset index, owning a fridge enters with a score of 5 into the subindex of household durables, and the subindex enters with the weight of 2 into the overall asset index. Thus, the overall importance of owing a fridge is 10 compared to, e.g., having a flush toilet which is 12. Due to lack of information on the amount of each of the eight selected durables a household might have, as well as the value, we gave this subset of variables the lowest weight (2) for constructing the asset index. These minimal basic items facilitate household functioning, thus the importance relies on having them, while lack of them is indicating deprivation. However, some of them are rather luxury items and not reflecting missing basic requirements. We assign the highest weights to dwelling characteristics, such as floor material (7), wall material (6), and type of toilet (6) for constructing the asset index, followed by material used for cooking (5), rooms per person (5). Access to public services receive an overall medium weight (4) since the household itself has no direct influence on them but most of them rely on public provision.

Table 4.1: Composition of Variables of Non-Income Indices

	1997 mean	2003 mean	Normative weights Score	Weight	Final	PPCA pooled
ASSETS						
Household durables						
Fridge	65.4	63.9	5	2	10	0.13
No	34.6	36.1	0	2	0	-0.23
Mixer	75.4	67.8	1	2	2	0.10
No	24.6	32.2	0	2	0	-0.25
Color TV	69.5	73.0	3	2	6	0.11
No	30.5	27.0	0	2	0	-0.28
Radio	43.4	40.9	2	2	4	0.19
No	56.6	59.1	0	2	0	-0.14
Car	12.7	10.1	8	2	16	0.32
No	87.3	89.9	0	2	0	-0.04
Oven	21.5	17.5	7	2	14	0.28
No	78.5	82.5	0	2	0	-0.07
Washing machine	19.3	23.1	6	2	12	0.29
No	80.7	76.9	0	2	0	-0.10
Video	17.2	13.8	4	2	8	0.32
No	82.8	86.2	0	2	0	-0.07
Dwelling quality						
Cooking material						
Electricity	19.5	10.5	3	5	15	0.33
Gas tube	18.8	35.0	2	5	10	0.12
Gas cylinder	37.1	33.9	1	5	5	-0.06
Kerosene, coal, other, wood	24.6	20.6	0	5	0	-0.27
Wall material						
Brick, block, stone, prefabricated, polished wood	76.5	81.2	3	6	18	0.08
Adobe, compressed earth material	6.8	4.8	2	6	12	-0.21
Bahareque (cane + mud)	10.6	6.5	1	6	6	-0.27
Crude wood, guadua (bamboo), organic material, zinc, cardboard, residuals, plastic	6.1	7.6	0	6	0	-0.43
Floor material						
Marble, parquet, polished wood	3.4	2.6	3	7	21	0.48
Carpet	2.0	1.7	2	7	14	0.35
Vinyl, sheet or ceramic tiles, brick	40.2	42.2	1	7	7	0.13
Crude wood, wood planks, concrete, fine gravel, earth, sand	54.5	53.5	0	7	0	-0.18
Toilet facility						
Toilet to sewer	66.9	68.7	3	6	18	0.13
Flush toilet	12.9	14.4	2	6	12	-0.17

continued on next page

Table 4.1 continued

	1997 mean	2003 mean	Normative weights Score	Weight	Final	PPCA pooled
Toilet without connection, latrine	9.1	8.1	1	6	6	-0.27
No facility	11.1	8.9	0	6	0	-0.44
Shower facility						
Watering can in shower room	74.1	74.2	2	4	8	0.10
Room without watering can	12.4	14.1	1	4	4	-0.23
No Shower room	13.5	11.7	0	4	0	-0.40
Number of rooms per person						
Up to one-third	16.9	12.9	0	5	0	-0.23
One-third to one-half	9.1	8.4	1	5	5	-0.13
One-half to three-quarters	26.9	27.3	2	5	10	-0.05
Three-quarters to one	29.5	31.5	3	5	15	0.06
More than one	17.6	19.9	4	5	20	0.20
Access to services						
Electricity	93.5	95.4	2	4	8	0.03
No	6.5	4.6	0	4	0	-0.55
Piped gas	20.3	36.4	1	4	4	0.22
No	79.7	63.6	0	4	0	-0.11
Water	84.1	85.7	2	4	8	0.07
No	16.0	14.3	0	4	0	-0.35
Sewage	67.9	69.5	1	4	4	0.12
No	32.1	30.5	0	4	0	-0.28
Litter	70.2	72.1	1	4	4	0.12
No	29.8	28.0	0	4	0	-0.31
Phone	46.3	55.9	1	4	4	0.17
No	53.7	44.1	0	4	0	-0.23
HEALTH						
Health status of the person						
Very good	12.6	9.1	3	7	21	0.87
Good	57.3	63.0	2	7	14	0.13
Regular	26.5	25.0	1	7	7	-0.53
Bad	3.7	2.9	0	7	0	-1.12
Chronic health disease	88.4	86.0	1	5	5	0.14
No	11.6	14.0	0	5	0	-0.92
Sick in the last month	83.8	88.5	1	1	1	0.11
No	16.2	11.5	0	1	0	-0.73
Affiliated to medical service	57.4	61.8	1	3	3	-0.10
No	42.6	38.2	0	3	0	0.17
Health check up once per year	43.5	46.1	1	4	4	-0.12
No	56.5	53.9	0	4	0	0.15
Hospitalized last year	92.8	93.5	1	2	2	0.06
No	7.2	6.6	0	2	0	-0.80

continued on next page

Table 4.1 continued

	1997 mean	2003 mean	Normative weights Score	Weight	Final	PPCA pooled
LIVING CONDITIONS AND SUBJECTIVE WELFARE						
Life compared to 5 years ago is						
Better	36.6	33.4	2	4	8	0.65
Equal	32.5	36.5	1	4	4	-0.02
Worse	30.9	30.1	0	4	0	-0.68
Household income is						
More than enough	6.7	6.0	2	4	8	1.19
Just enough	50.3	52.5	1	4	4	0.30
Not enough	43.0	41.5	0	4	0	-0.59
Household / Household members						
Had no severe health problem (last year)	86.4	92.4	1	4	4	0.08
Had	13.6	7.6	0	4	0	-0.72
Had not experienced a death (last year)	94.7	96.1	1	2	2	0.02
Had	5.3	4.0	0	2	0	-0.53
Feels safe in neighborhood	77.7	73.2	1	5	5	0.09
Does not	22.3	26.8	0	5	0	-0.23

Notes: The first two columns show the sample means (of 1997 and 2003). For normative weights, we show the two steps of generating them: Final normative weights are calculated multiplying scores (reflecting the "valuation" for each item within each sub-index) and weights (reflecting the weight of the sub-index within the overall three dimension-indices, i.e., assets, health, and living conditions and subjective welfare). PPCA pooled: Scoring factors based on polychoric principal component analysis.
Source: Own calculations based on ECV.

is subjective in nature, it is the only one available giving an overall judgement of each person's health and thus is a good proxy for health status, and we assign the highest normative weight to the health status.[19]

The variables adding the highest weight using PPCA are the following: the best subjective health status of the person has the largest weight inside the index. A strong negative weight is given to having a chronic disease, having been in hospital, and having had a disease recently. It is interesting to note that the two variables are treated differently by the weighting schemes: whereas we consider it as desirable to be affiliated to a medical service and to frequently go a health

[19]The variables for the health index are not strongly correlated to each other (the opposite could have been expected, i.e., all variables measuring the same thing), so all of them were taken into account for the final analysis. For example, the correlations with the reported health status range from 0.06 to 0.34 in 1997, and the correlations hardly change over time.

checkups without being ill, this is not reflected in the PPCA weights: the signs are opposite than expected. This is also most likely the reason for the differing results in the pro-poor growth analysis below (see also Section 4.3.4 for more details).

(iii) Living conditions and subjective welfare. The index measuring life satisfaction and subjective welfare combines the variables on current living conditions compared to 5 years before,[20] perception of whether income is enough for household needs, having problems with death or serious illness of a family member in the last year, and safety perception in the neighborhood. This combination captures four important aspects: changes in the general welfare perception and in the subjective judgement of income (which we consider most important and assign the highest weight to), the effects of violence and criminality, and major events (death, illness) affecting the whole household. The variables adding the highest PPCA weights in the subjective welfare index are: having more than enough money for household needs is the one contributing with the largest weight, while having had a severe health problem and the general perception of life being worse than 5 years ago subtracts the most.

(iv) Education. We created three separate indices: First, an index for children (including young adults up to age 20), second, an index for all adults older than 20 years old, and third, an index for adults aged between 20 and 30 years old (shortly called: twens). The main objective of the first is to track progress of the population in schooling age taking two aspects into account: years of schooling and being in the right class for the corresponding age. This indicator is similar to calculating net enrollment rates in cross-country studies since it gives a penalty to being in a lower class than to the one that a child should be at a given age.[21] By subtracting the age of each individual younger than 20 years from the reported years of schooling (*YOS*) we should ideally get a difference of 6, indicating the student started schooling at 6 and never repeated any class nor stopped studying.

[20]Note that in this way, we look at changes of changes in the pro-poor growth analysis. This might be problematic since it is a relative judgement. However, there are only minor changes in this variable. Furthermore, the variable should give a broad idea of how people judge their current living conditions, see also Section 4.3.5.

[21]According to Law 115 of 1994, all Colombians should receive a minimum of 1 year of preschool education and 9 years basic education divided into 5 of primary schooling and 4 of basic secondary schooling. Schooling grades 10 to 11 are considered as middle education classes ending up into complete secondary schooling. Upper and lower age bounds for each class can be defined by each school, but most of them expect children to finish mandatory preschool at age 5, primary at 10, basic secondary at 14, and middle education at 17. We, thus, assume that children are expected to start primary education at the age of 6, which would drive them to have completed at least 1 year of primary education by the age of 7. If the education process is continuous, at the age of 17 students must be finishing secondary education (11th class).

We allow individuals up to age 20 to fall into these indicators, to capture young adults still enrolled in school.[22]

Students enrolled in classes lower than the right one for their age are considered overaged, and would get a value higher than 6. The maximum and minimum possible values for this indicator are 4 and 20, the first one accounting for a child having started school early or having skipped one year and the last one accounting for an illiterate young adult.[23] Note that the same result, for instance a value of 15, can have different meanings for different individuals. It can be a 20 years old person with 5 years of education, or a 15 years old without education. Both are, however, overaged in the sense that they do not have the education level expected for their age.

For adults older than 20 years, we calculate the average years of education of all adult household members.[24] The same formula is applied to twens, averaging YOS only over the household members who are aged between 20 and 30. With the distinction between all adults and twens we can better track cohort effects with the latter group since the overall adult group reacts too slowly to changes in the education system or in public provision of education because the education level hardly ever changes among the adult population, but with twens a new cohort has entered the surveys.

The detailed overview of all variables used[25] and their weights according to each procedure is shown in Table 4.1.[26] To transform all indices into the same scale and ease comparability we normalize them from 0, the worst observed achievement, to 10, the best following the methodology of the Human Development Index (HDI) and Grosse et al. (2008b) (also using a pooled data set to determine the minima and maxima).[27] Once normalized, results are averaged by

[22]The indicator is defined as: $E_{children} = Age - YOS$.

[23]One might question if 4 is really better than 6 or if 4 is rather as good as 6. We suggest that 4 is better than 6 since it reflects that the child has higher abilities than others to be able to complete the educational system more quickly and to enter the labor market earlier.

[24]It is defined as $E_{adults} = \sum YOS_{adults} / \sum adults$.

[25]Education is not shown in the table because the three education indicators are based on one variable (years of schooling). Aggregating them into an "overall education" index is problematic because not all households have children or twens which would cause either missing values or reducing sample size, so we opted against this. The mean of the education variables can be found in Table 4.3.

[26]The normatively assigned weights correspond to weights for each index independently of the others, since we do not calculate an overall index which would not be interpretable given that some indices are presented at the household level and others at the individual. Furthermore, it might hide more information that providing additional one.

[27]$Index = 10 * \frac{1}{n} \sum_{i=1}^{n} \frac{individual_n - min}{max - min}$. Another possible standardization is dividing by the standard deviation. However, the proposed range between 0 and 10 is simple to understand, and it allows the reader to intuitively and quickly see the distributional difference between each indicator. This standardization has some limitations as well, see also **Essay 3** for more discussion.

vintile to draw the corresponding NIGIC. We draw for each indicator two types of curves: sorted conditional to income (e.g., education outcomes from the income-poorest to the income-richest) and unconditional (e.g., education outcomes from the education-poorest to the education-richest). Both conditional and unconditional will be presented only in relative terms, showing annualized growth rates between 1997 and 2003 for each indicator.

4.3.4 Correlation with Income and Consumption

The multidimensional poverty indicators are, as mentioned above, likely to be correlated with income and consumption, but not perfectly. Exemplarily, we show the correlation coefficient for 1997 for the entire set of indicators investigated (Table 4.2). As expected, the correlation between income and consumption is highest, but also not perfect, with a correlation coefficient of 0.73. For the multidimensional poverty indicators, the correlation with income is highest for asset ownership especially for the subgroup of private goods (0.55 and 0.53 for normative weights and PPCA weights, respectively) and for adults' education (0.52). This reflects the ability to purchase these goods as well as the ability to earn more income the higher the education of adults in the household is (or the ability to pay for education the higher the income is). Less correlated to income and consumption is subjective welfare and living conditions (for both weighting schemes around 0.3), and even less the education of children and twens (0.15). Especially the results on education show that households are able to send their children to school relatively independently from the income level. The coefficients goes further down in 2003 (results not shown in the table), giving some evidence on the success of increasing public spending in the education sector, thus of more households being able to benefit from increased public schooling opportunities.

Interesting to note is that the two different weighting schemes result in roughly the same magnitudes concerning the value of the correlation coefficient. The only notable difference is health. The two different weighting procedures render a correlation coefficient of 0.24 for normative weights and of 0.03 for PPCA weights where the latter intuitively seems to be too low. In general, the health indicator using PPCA weights is hardly correlated with any other indicator (ranging from -0.01 for twens' education to 0.10 for subjective welfare) in contrast to the one using normative weights (ranging from 0.10 for twens' education to 0.31 for private goods's ownership). Also the correlation between normative weights and PPCA weights for health is rather low (0.67) compared to the other indicators with correlation coefficients raging from 0.96 to 0.99.

Table 4.2: Correlation Structure of Income and Multidimensional Poverty Indices, 1997

			Normative weights					PPCA weights					Education		
	Inc.	Cons.	Ass.	Priv.	Publ.	Hea.	S.W.	Ass.	Priv.	Publ.	Hea.	S.W.	Chi.	Ad.	Tw.
Income	1.00														
Consumption	0.73	1.00													
Normative weights															
Assets	0.53	0.58	1.00												
Private goods	0.55	0.61	0.99	1.00											
Public services	0.32	0.35	0.83	0.75	1.00										
Health	0.24	0.25	0.30	0.31	0.22	1.00									
Subjective welfare	0.28	0.26	0.24	0.26	0.12	0.21	1.00								
Polychoric PCA weights															
Assets	0.48	0.53	0.98	0.96	0.90	0.29	0.22	1.00							
Private goods	0.53	0.58	0.99	0.99	0.78	0.31	0.26	0.97	1.00						
Public services	0.33	0.37	0.84	0.77	0.99	0.23	0.12	0.91	0.79	1.00					
Health	0.03	0.01	0.02	0.02	0.00	0.67	0.10	0.02	0.02	0.00	1.00				
Subjective welfare	0.32	0.31	0.31	0.32	0.18	0.24	0.96	0.29	0.32	0.18	0.10	1.00			
Education															
Children	0.15	0.20	0.39	0.38	0.35	0.19	0.12	0.40	0.40	0.36	0.03	0.15	1.00		
Adults	0.52	0.57	0.71	0.71	0.56	0.34	0.28	0.70	0.71	0.58	0.06	0.34	0.34	1.00	
Twens	0.15	0.20	0.29	0.29	0.22	0.10	0.05	0.27	0.28	0.22	-0.01	0.06	0.17	0.26	1.00

Source: Own calculations based on ECV.

Going into detail, we investigated the correlation of the variables included in the health index with income and consumption (results not shown in the table). We find that health status, affiliation to medical service, and going to checkups is positively correlated to income and consumption (of a magnitude of around 0.2) whereas chronic and recent disease and hospitalization due to serious injury or illness are not correlated at all with money-metric indicators, most of them slightly below 0. Affiliation to medical service might depend on formal employment and the ability to pay for such a service. There seems to be no obvious reason why medical affiliation should have any negative impact on welfare, thus, the negative weight resulting from PPCA (Table 4.1) seems to be implausible. Going to checkups might depend on the availability or quality of hospitals or health posts as well as on the ability to pay. Furthermore, it might depend on the health status of the person. However, the data does not support this hypotheses since neither health status, nor chronic disease, nor recent disease, nor hospitalization are correlated to the checkup question. The only correlation of checkups exists with medical affiliation which furthermore increases over time (from 0.14 to 0.28). Thus there is also no obvious reason why checkups should have a negative weight on welfare (as assigned by PPCA weights) and we tend to believe more in the normative weights.

4.3.5 Limitations of the Indicators

Before turning to pro-poor growth, we underline some limitations of the indicators.[28] The first one is that many variables are bounded due to questionnaire design and concepts. Even if the household has, for example, a large and varied set of assets, only 18 possible are listed in the survey. Thus, middle income and rich households who already have all items do not show improvements in the data set, although they might have had in real life. Concerning access to public services, the variables included are all bounded: It is not possible to have more than "one" access to a service. Once having access, differences depend on the consumption and tariff paid for it. Thus, once having reach the maximum value (such as the maximum years of education), improvements are not possible any more, thus leading to a flat part (0 growth rates) in the curves. This can be seen below for twens' education in the unconditional case, but there is not a real solution this problem as long as there is no other information, for example, on quality or price given in the data. However, conditional curves are more interesting in this case as there is no flat part any more since income and education are not perfectly correlated to each other, thus income-poor households are not automatically the same as education-poor households.

[28] See also **Essay 3**, Section 3.3.4 for more discussion on limitations.

Another argument to be taken into account for assets would be to think about transforming them in per capita terms, similar to the rooms per person. It makes a difference to share a TV with one other family member or with ten. In this case, larger households would be worse off. However, the questionnaire does not ask about the amount of each asset but only about ownership, but maybe (and likely) some households have more than one. However, transforming some variables into per-capita terms would give a kind of lower bound. Looking at the list of variables included in the asset index, we would identify some, but only a few, to exhibit rivalry in consumption: TV, radio, car, video, toilet, shower, phone. For the others, rivalry is not convincingly given. Rerunning the calculation leads to no big changes, neither in weights nor in pro-poor growth findings.

Except for education, all other non-income indices are constructed as composite multidimensional poverty indicators consisting of several variables. Tracking each variable separately would have also been interesting, but given the large number of variables this would take too much space. An example by Grosse et al. (2008b) shows how to track several individual MDG-related variables for income vintiles of Bolivia over time. In this paper, we exemplarily show the access to public services separately for 1997 and 2003, see below.

Another important issue to keep in mind is that while facing income variations and temporary draw backs during economic crisis, dwelling characteristics and access to services might not change as rapidly as income, given that the initial response of the household is to reduce expenditures, take credits (also in form of delaying debt payments), and use savings. A simple tabulation of the question on how households responded to the loss of employment or income sources during the five years previous to the 2003 survey showed that 23 percent of them opted for reducing expenditures in clothing, 21 percent in food, 21 percent took credits, and 10 percent confirmed having used savings, but only 4 percent moved to a cheaper dwelling and 3 percent enrolled their children in a less expensive school.

The subjective welfare index has also some limitations. Ideally the question on current living conditions should be in the index, but this question in 2003 is not comparable to the one in 1997.[29] We used only variables that had the same response alternatives in both years, in this case we selected the variable how the person values the current household's situation compared to that 5 years before. The three available response categories (better, equal, worse) have each a share of around one-third in both years, raising doubts on whether responses are driven by each person's understanding on the question and what each one consider as "better", rather than by a conscious and comparable answer across households.

[29]The number of possible answer options changed from 3 to 4.

4.4 Results

4.4.1 Trends and Inequality in Multidimensional Indicators

Table 4.1 shows a first snapshot of mean trends of multidimensional welfare indicators from 1997 to 2003. Of the durables included in the assets index, TV and washing machine ownership go up, the other six go down. Stronger changes can be observed for some elements of the dwelling quality, with a strong increase of piped gas as cooking material at the expense of electricity. Minor improvements are found in wall material, toilet facility, and crowding. Hardly any change show wall material and shower facility. Public services and access to infrastructure increase for all six services. For the variables forming the health index (which is the only one that can be evaluated at the individual level), we find an overall but minor general improvement.

Concerning health status, there is an increase in those reporting having good health, and less reporting very good, regular, or bad health status. People reporting having a chronic disease slightly increase while temporary diseases go down. The affiliation to a medical service system improves. Concerning subjective welfare, the amount of households reporting that life was better than 5 years before decreased slightly. But in general, changes in the answers to this variable are minor. The share of households that consider their household income as being enough or more than enough for fulfilling their needs goes down. Severe health problems or even death of a family member, which affect the household as a whole, go down. The strongest deterioration occurred for the safety perception which goes down more strongly. Education (Table 4.3) has remained rather stable for adults' and children's education with the former going slightly down and the latter going slightly up, whereas twens' education clearly increases.

We calculate for each indicator the sample deciles means (Table 4.3), first sorted by income (conditional) and second sorted by the indicator itself (unconditional). For each indicator, the table shows also inequality measures: the ratio of the richest to poorest decile (10:1 ratio), the Gini coefficient (in the conditional part of the tables), and the Theil Index (in the unconditional part). Three main issues emerge in these tables: (i) indicator means calculated using normative and PPCA weights are similar, (ii) there are minor improvements in almost all deciles with means staying nearly equal between 1997 and 2003, and (iii) inequality in multidimensional poverty indicators is lower compared to income and expenditures (Table 4.4), the latter all being above 0.5 for the Gini coefficient.[30]

[30]Lower inequality in non-income indicators compared to income or expenditures must be interpreted cautiously, given that those indicators have a natural upper bound while income does not. As already mentioned, inequality measures of income and expenditures are pretty high. The Gini coefficient is above 0.5 in both cases, although it decreases over time (Table 4.4). The 10:1 ratio

Among multidimensional poverty indicators, inequality measured by the Gini is highest for adult education (0.35 in 1997 compared to 0.34 in 2003) and assets (decreasing from 0.25 to 0.23). Inequality is lowest for children's education but increases over time (for all three inequality indices, i.e., 10:1 ratio, Gini coefficient, and Theil index). For all other variables, the indicators show the same trends: slightly decreasing inequality with the notable difference of twens' education going strongly down from 0.22 to 0.13 for the Gini coefficient and from 0.11 to 0.06 for the Theil index. Overall, particularly regarding changes in the 10:1 relation for both weighting schemes, all show decreases in inequality both in the conditional and unconditional case, with the only notable exception of unconditional children's education.

Concerning mean trends, results are similar between PPCA and normative weights. For assets and health, the mean increases but in different magnitudes. For subjective welfare, however, PPCA weights show an increase while normative weights show a slight decrease. As expected, we find an income gradient. This means that non-income outcomes increase the higher the income decile. However, there is an imperfect correlation between income-poor and non-income poor, thus indicating that there are reasons beyond income facilitating or impeding access to certain assets and services.[31] This might be of course related to geographic location, public policies, and the existence of markets for non-income indicators. The gradient is strongest for adults' education and asset ownership, and lowest for health and children's education. The different outcome between indicators sorted or not by income is evident in adults' education: approximately 3 versus 20 in both years for the 10:1 ratio (Table 4.3). While low inequality in children's education outcomes reflects the nearly full coverage of primary schooling, irrespective of the income decile, high inequality in adult's education can be explained by the limited access to public tertiary education, thus depending on households' ability to pay for it in the private sector. It can also reflect persisting low education levels (or even illiteracy) of older cohorts, which do not catch up once they enter the labor force. This is confirmed by the inequality of twens' education which is lower and also shows the highest reduction in inequality. The second most unequally distributed indicator, assets, also seems to have an important relation to income, partly explained by the households' ability to pay for public services. Breaking down this indicator to track access to services, one finds low coverage rates for the first income deciles but almost full coverage for the last (see also below).

also decreased over time. As explained by Klasen (2008a), inequality in non-income indicators turns out lower, given that most likely rich households already achieved the upper limit while poor households are getting closer to it.

[31]Similar results are also found in Grosse et al. (2008a) and Klasen (2008a) for Bolivia.

Table 4.3: Non-Income Deciles, 1997 and 2003

	1	2	3	4	5	6	7	8	9	10	10:1	Gini/Theil[a]	Mean
	Normative weights												
	Mean of the Deciles (conditional), 1997												
Assets	2.75	3.06	3.44	3.79	4.18	4.84	5.20	5.78	6.49	7.39	2.69	0.25	5.02
Health	5.74	5.87	5.96	6.04	6.16	6.35	6.41	6.68	6.99	7.32	1.28	0.16	6.40
Subjective welfare	5.25	5.33	5.40	5.61	5.82	6.03	6.08	6.35	6.70	7.31	1.39	0.19	5.93
	Mean of the Deciles (unconditional), 1997												
Assets	1.03	2.40	3.53	4.33	4.92	5.48	6.00	6.60	7.38	8.49	8.23	0.11	5.02
Health	2.91	4.38	5.26	6.08	6.19	6.90	7.04	7.68	8.06	9.30	3.20	0.04	6.40
Subjective welfare	2.26	3.88	4.22	5.40	5.56	6.33	7.04	7.07	8.49	8.93	3.96	0.07	5.93
	Mean of the Deciles (conditional), 2003												
Assets	3.21	3.51	4.06	4.54	4.98	5.45	5.85	6.28	6.84	7.76	2.42	0.23	5.12
Health	5.97	6.09	6.22	6.41	6.51	6.62	6.77	6.95	7.12	7.54	1.26	0.15	6.54
Subjective welfare	5.16	5.27	5.37	5.60	5.62	5.75	5.96	6.09	6.31	6.85	1.33	0.18	5.92
	Mean of the Deciles (unconditional), 2003												
Assets	1.17	2.76	3.84	4.54	5.09	5.55	6.02	6.54	7.24	8.50	7.25	0.09	5.12
Health	3.11	4.54	5.49	6.11	6.31	6.94	7.23	7.94	8.06	9.29	2.98	0.04	6.54
Subjective welfare	2.30	3.82	4.28	5.21	5.56	5.98	7.04	7.04	8.17	8.83	3.84	0.06	5.92

continued on next page

Table 4.3 continued

	1	2	3	4	5	6	7	8	9	10	10:1	Gini/Theil[a]	Mean
	Polychoric PCA weights												
	Mean of the Deciles (conditional), 1997												
Assets	2.88	3.25	3.72	4.11	4.55	5.30	5.69	6.32	6.99	7.76	2.69	0.25	5.47
Health	7.19	7.15	7.17	7.16	7.14	7.14	7.16	7.09	7.16	7.29	1.01	0.13	7.17
Subjective welfare	4.84	4.95	5.02	5.25	5.53	5.79	5.86	6.19	6.57	7.29	1.51	0.20	5.70
	Mean of the Deciles (unconditional), 1997												
Assets	0.89	2.45	3.78	4.83	5.59	6.23	6.78	7.35	7.99	8.79	9.83	0.12	5.47
Health	3.25	5.33	6.34	7.00	7.49	7.81	8.08	8.33	8.60	9.47	2.92	0.04	7.17
Subjective welfare	2.21	3.45	4.11	4.88	5.40	6.19	6.66	7.02	8.13	8.78	3.96	0.07	5.70
	Mean of the Deciles (conditional), 2003												
Assets	3.49	3.86	4.52	5.10	5.59	6.15	6.54	6.97	7.46	8.19	2.34	0.23	5.61
Health	7.20	7.21	7.19	7.19	7.19	7.13	7.12	7.14	7.11	7.21	1.00	0.12	7.18
Subjective welfare	4.90	5.07	5.20	5.44	5.50	5.66	5.90	6.08	6.32	6.95	1.42	0.19	5.77
	Mean of the Deciles (unconditional), 2003												
Assets	1.07	2.78	4.11	5.06	5.73	6.30	6.86	7.37	7.96	8.89	8.31	0.10	5.61
Health	3.65	5.51	6.35	7.09	7.57	7.58	8.08	8.13	8.60	9.11	2.50	0.03	7.18
Subjective welfare	2.52	3.50	4.44	4.96	5.49	6.09	6.42	6.92	8.07	8.75	3.47	0.06	5.77

continued on next page

Table 4.3 continued

	1	2	3	4	5	6	7	8	9	10	10:1	Gini/Theil[a]	Mean
Education													
Mean of the Deciles (conditional), 1997													
Adults	1.99	2.25	2.51	2.89	3.03	3.68	4.12	4.83	5.93	6.95	3.49	0.35	4.07
Children	7.30	7.49	7.56	7.50	7.43	7.79	7.89	7.95	8.30	8.48	1.16	0.10	7.85
Twens	6.79	6.53	6.53	6.51	7.00	7.05	7.43	7.91	8.23	8.53	1.26	0.22	7.37
Mean of the Deciles (unconditional), 1997													
Adults	0.44	1.39	2.07	2.78	3.37	4.08	4.91	5.81	6.90	8.79	20.02	0.20	4.07
Children	4.33	6.36	7.17	7.66	8.05	8.47	8.67	8.89	9.30	9.51	2.20	0.02	7.85
Twens	1.41	3.22	4.78	6.49	7.67	9.95	10.00	10.00	10.00	10.00	7.10	0.11	7.37
Mean of the Deciles (conditional), 2003													
Adults	2.49	2.63	2.96	3.42	3.84	4.17	4.67	5.19	5.65	6.33	2.54	0.34	4.00
Children	7.49	7.61	7.73	7.76	7.76	7.90	8.02	8.08	8.13	8.18	1.09	0.12	7.88
Twens	7.53	7.69	7.90	8.15	8.51	8.73	9.01	9.27	9.46	9.68	1.28	0.13	8.57
Mean of the Deciles (unconditional), 2003													
Adults	0.42	1.42	2.10	2.75	3.30	4.07	4.83	5.65	6.70	8.56	20.32	0.20	4.00
Children	3.55	6.15	7.12	7.71	8.15	8.65	8.87	9.20	9.33	9.69	2.73	0.03	7.88
Twens	2.37	5.39	7.96	9.98	10.00	10.00	10.00	10.00	10.00	10.00	4.22	0.06	8.57

Notes: [a]Two inequality measures are shown. For simplicity, the Gini Index can be found in the conditional parts of the table, the Theil Index can be found in the unconditional parts. This does not mean, however, that the indices are calculated conditionally or unconditionally.
Source: Own calculations based on ECV.

Table 4.4: Income and Expenditures Deciles, 1997 and 2003

	1	2	3	4	5	6	7	8	9	10	10:1	Gini	Mean
	Mean of the Deciles (conditional). 1997												
Inc.	20	39	55	72	92	117	152	208	319	798	38.95	0.55	191
Cons.	47	48	60	70	81	101	116	170	239	446	9.52	0.53	145
	Mean of the Deciles (unconditional). 1997												
Cons.	17	32	45	59	76	96	124	164	245	570	33.65	0.53	145
	Mean of the Deciles (conditional). 2003												
Inc.	20	36	49	64	80	101	129	172	256	642	32.41	0.52	153
Cons.	41	45	54	67	82	95	118	152	213	431	10.40	0.51	125
	Mean of the Deciles (unconditional). 2003												
Cons.	16	30	42	54	68	85	109	146	213	502	31.84	0.51	125

Notes: Income (Inc.) and consumption expenditures (Cons.) are in 1000 Pesos, constant of 1997.
Source: Own calculations based on ECV.

Comparison of decile means among indicators shows that twens' education is the closest to the upper bound (for almost all deciles, for some even reaching the upper bound) followed by children's education, health, and subjective welfare, while the asset index and adults' education are the most distant from the upper bound. Disparities between indicators in the lower income deciles indicate that poor people have access to education, at least for children and twens (the first income deciles already have a value of over 7 and 6, respectively), but cannot afford basic assets (decile value of around 3) such as good dwelling characteristics or access to public services.

4.4.2 Pro-Poor Growth Analysis

Income and Expenditures

We present in this section GIC and NIGIC by vintiles including the 95 percent confidence intervals using bootstrap techniques.[32] Analysis based on PPGR and GIC show that mean income and expenditures by vintiles decreased from 1997 to 2003. However, the contraction was higher for the richest in relative as well as in

[32]In particular, based on the households in both surveys, the bootstrap draws 200 weighted random samples with replacement for each period and calculates the respective percentiles and growth rates so that we obtain 200 values per percentile, so to say: 200 GIC and NIGIC. Based on these 200 values, we draw the mean and the standard deviation per percentile and calculate the respective 95 percent confidence intervals. See Chapter 3.4.2 in **Essay 3** for more discussion on confidence intervals.

absolute terms (growth rates and absolute changes).[33] Table 4.5 shows PPGR for the moderate and the extreme poverty line, both divided into unconditional and conditional to income.

Table 4.5: Growth Rates in Mean and Pro-Poor Growth Rates, 1997–2003

	Relative NIGIC 1997-2003				
		(unconditional)		(conditional)	
	GRIM	PPGR mod.	PPGR extr.	PPGR mod.	PPGR extr.
	Income and consumption				
Income (EH)	-0.95	1.72	3.69	1.72	3.69
Income (ECV)	-3.65	-1.73	-0.82	-1.73	-0.82
Consumption (ECV)	-2.45	-1.56	-1.26	-1.18	-1.91
	Non-income indices using normative weights				
Assets	0.35	1.51	2.63	2.73	2.35
Health	0.35	0.69	1.20	0.78	0.56
Subjective welfare	-0.02	0.38	1.05	-0.24	-0.16
	Non-income indices using PPCA weights				
Assets	0.42	1.74	3.66	3.29	2.88
Health	0.02	0.59	1.53	0.08	0.04
Subjective welfare	0.20	0.76	1.17	0.34	0.35
	Education				
Education of children	0.07	-0.82	-2.86	0.47	0.37
Education of adults	-0.28	-0.65	-2.29	3.21	3.29
Education of twens	2.54	7.94	9.46	2.96	2.15

Notes: GRIM: Growth rate in mean; PPGR: Pro-poor growth rate (moderate and extreme poverty line).
Source: Own calculations based on EH and ECV.

The table shows that growth rates in mean (GRIM) for income and expenditures were negative, but contraction was stronger in income (-3.65 versus -2.45). Both poverty lines result in PPGR that were higher than the GRIM but still negative, confirming the contraction of income and expenditures for households below the poverty line. Results indicate that, on average, households below the extreme poverty line were affected to a lesser extent from contraction in income and expenditures than those up to the moderate poverty line. As a result, when analyzing income and expenditures, growth was neither pro-poor according to the weak

[33]Note that we only show absolute changes for income and expenditures. For the non-income variables, we focus on relative changes, thus we present only growth rates. To get an idea on absolute changes, one should refer to Table 4.3.

(general) nor to the absolute approach. However, losses were lower for the poor relative to the non-poor. The richest vintiles of the distribution experienced the hardest contraction, while households below the extreme poverty line seemed to be less affected by the 1999 economic recession in absolute and relative terms.

Figure 4.1 shows the graphical result for the GIC based on income and on expenditures. Growth rates are below 0 for almost all income vintiles, and the GIC is downward sloping indicating higher rates of income losses for the richer households. Although relative losses of the poor were less than those of the non-poor, negative growth rates for almost all vintiles point to an increase in poverty. The poverty headcount using income increased from 54 to 60 percent for moderate poverty and from 18 to 21 percent for extreme poverty between 1997 and 2003 (Table 4.6), and using consumption from 55 to 63 percent for moderate poverty and 19 to 24 percent for extreme poverty. Income poverty has been slightly lower in urban areas as compared to expenditure poverty. The opposite holds for rural areas where expenditure poverty is higher than income poverty. At the national level, these differences nearly cancel out. This is also confirmed when looking at deciles (Table 4.4).[34] Consumption expenditures go down less strongly over time compared to income, giving evidence for consumption smoothing (Table 4.5). The absolute GIC is also decreasing by vintile and below the 0 axis, showing large absolute losses for the richest. Relative and absolute GIC for expenditures are also downward sloping and below 0 for all vintiles. It is not surprising to observe larger absolute decreases in expenditures the higher the vintiles, given that poor households have less scope for reducing expenditures.

Assets, Health, and Subjective Welfare

Figure 4.2 shows relative NIGIC for assets and for the subdivision into private goods and public services. The left graphs corresponds to indicators using normative weights, while the right graphs to those using PPCA weights. Concerning growth rates and sorted by income the evolution of asset ownership is pro-poor according to the weak approach (NIGIC above 0). According to the relative approach, growth can also be declared to be pro-poor since growth rates are higher for income-poorer households. For the first half of the distribution, there is no clear trend and the conditional NIGIC oscillates around 3, but growth is clearly

[34]The poverty indices for income and consumption are very similar both in levels and trends. The absolute difference is a few percentage points. This is similar to findings by Chen and Ravallion (2004) who have compared income and consumption for Latin American countries. They find consumption to have a lower mean but also a lower inequality. For the 1$ a day line, consumption poverty is slightly lower, for the 2$ a day line, income poverty is slightly lower. However, the differences are not statistically different. Unfortunately, Chen and Ravallion (2004) do not provide the disaggregation to rural/urban areas and also not for the individual countries.

Figure 4.1: GIC National, 1997–2003

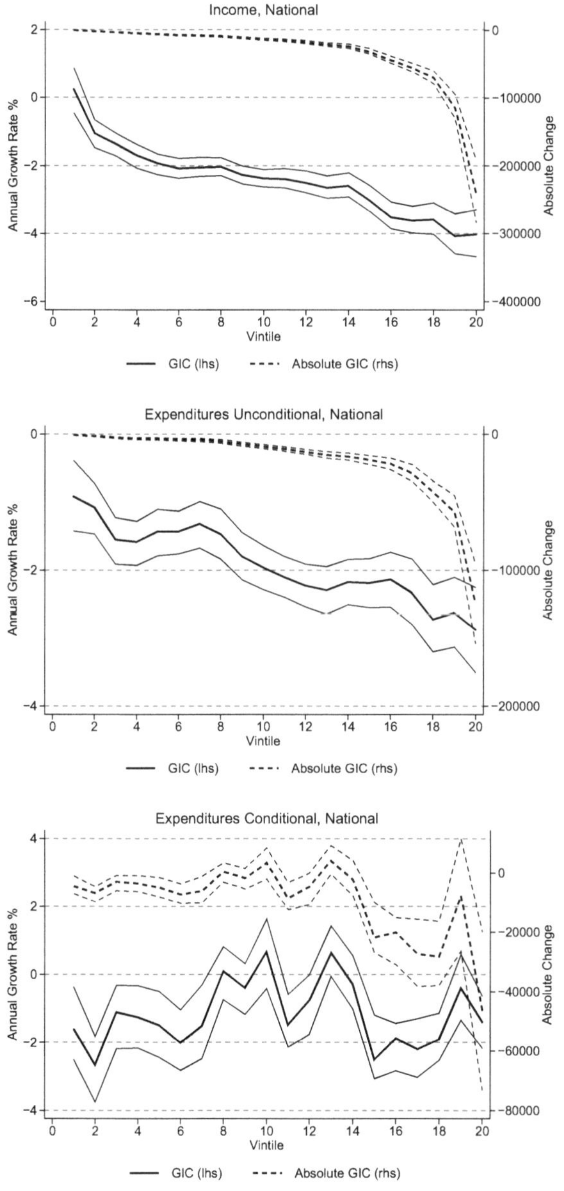

Source: Own Calculations based on ECV.

Table 4.6: Poverty and Inequality Measures by Area, 1997–2003

	Moderate poverty line			Extreme poverty line			Inequality measures		
	FGT0	FGT1	FGT2	FGT0	FGT1	FGT2	Gini	Theil	PS
	Income based using ECV data								
National									
1997	54.06	24.85	14.64	18.02	6.40	3.29	0.55	0.59	100
2003	60.34	27.85	16.28	20.53	6.83	3.32	0.52	0.52	100
Urban									
1997	46.46	20.23	11.59	13.11	4.65	2.41	0.53	0.53	72.14
2003	55.37	24.75	14.25	16.66	5.45	2.67	0.51	0.47	73.61
Rural									
1997	73.71	36.78	22.53	30.72	10.96	5.56	0.45	0.39	27.86
2003	74.19	36.81	22.53	31.32	10.65	5.13	0.44	0.38	26.39
	Expenditure based using ECV data								
National									
1997	55.18	25.55	15.09	19.05	6.63	3.28	0.53	0.52	100
2003	63.13	30.62	18.50	23.83	8.56	4.27	0.52	0.49	100
Urban									
1997	45.41	18.25	9.76	10.44	3.09	1.39	0.49	0.44	72.14
2003	57.10	25.74	14.75	43.16	17.08	9.05	0.48	0.42	73.61
Rural									
1997	80.47	44.44	28.87	41.33	15.81	8.19	0.45	0.38	27.86
2003	79.95	44.24	28.97	16.89	5.55	2.56	0.47	0.41	26.39

Notes: FGT: Foster-Greer-Thorbecke measures of poverty (headcount, gap, severity). PS: Population Share.
Source: Own calculations based on ECV.

higher than for the second half where we find a clear downward sloping trend. Breaking the overall results down, private goods' ownership and public services show different levels but same trends: The conditional NIGIC oscillates around 2 for private goods for the first half and around 4 for public services, and both NIGIC clearly show a decreasing trend for the second half of the distribution going down to nearly 0 for private goods and to 2 for public services. No curve turns negative, thus both subdivisions are pro-poor according to the weak approach.

Sorted by the non-income indicator, the unconditional NIGIC are downward sloping for the overall asset index regardless of the weighting system, although with some differences for the first few vintiles. However, according to both sys-

Figure 4.2: Assets, Private Goods, Public Services: NIGIC, 1997–2003

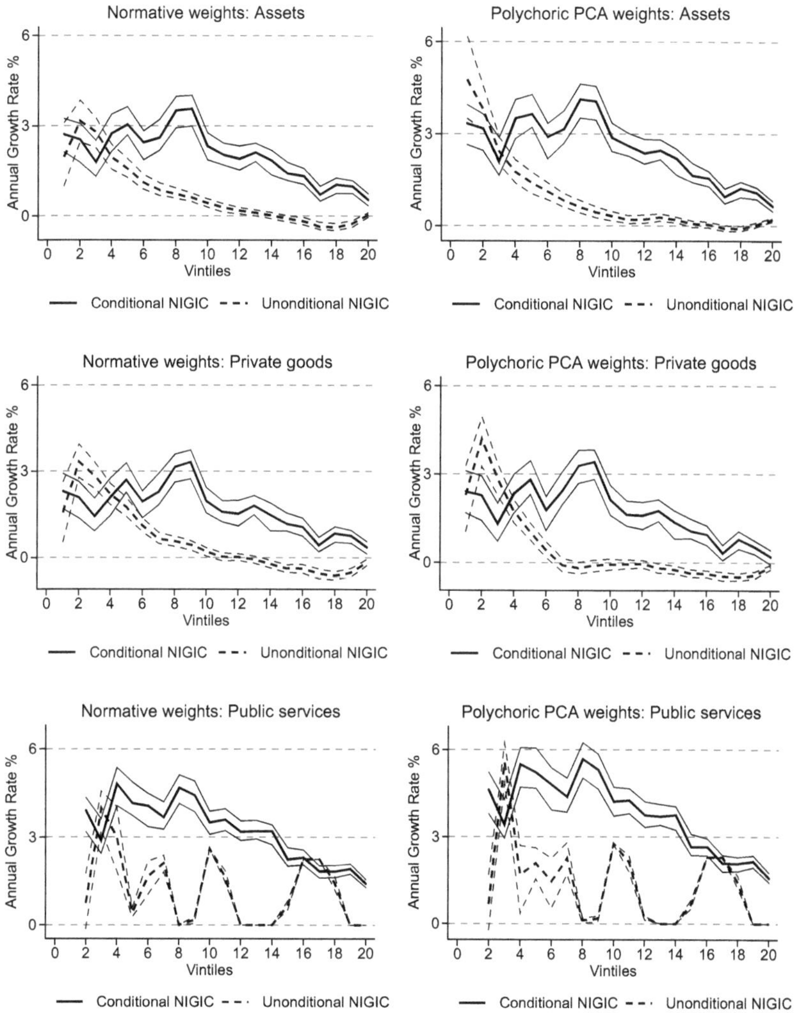

Source: Own Calculations based on ECV.

tems growth is pro-poor according to the weak and relative approaches. For private goods, the NIGIC is positive and downward sloping for the first half of the distribution, but turns negative for the second. This change in sign occurs earlier for the PPCA weights compared to normative weights. Public services are positive throughout the whole distribution. Due to the relatively low variation in the data (since only 6 public services can be evaluated), we find "flat" parts in the unconditional NIGIC where for both years the value is the same, thus the growth rate is 0 for several vintiles.

Research on particular services (Figure 4.3) shows the improvements between 1997 and 2003.[35] Natural piped gas became available to households in the major cities at the beginning of the 1990s and its access increased considerably since then (Libhaber and Foster, 2003). Table 4.1 confirms these results, for example the percentage of households having access to piped gas increased from 20 percent in 1997 to 36 percent in 2003. This explains why it adds up one of the largest weights inside the asset index but it is not a major deprivation if a household does not have it. Electricity had already high coverage rates in 1997, thus large improvements on it between 1997 and 2003 were not feasible. In light of privatization and decentralization reforms undertaken in the early 1990s, designed to improve coverage and efficiency in the provision of basic services, one would have had expected higher improvements in the asset index. But the combined effect of implementation problems and the economic crisis slowed the progress, particularly due to the reduction of public funds. However, increases in access to public services are important, and poor households had a pro-poor share in this increase.

For health, although the shape of the curves is similar regardless of the weighting system, the conditional NIGIC is clearly above 0 when using normative weights and around 0 when using PPCA weights (Figure 4.4). The unconditional NIGIC of health show slightly different results depending on the weighting system. One is above 0 (normative weights) for the first three-quarters of the distribution, while the other close to 0 (for the second quartile of the distribution) and below it for the second half of the distribution (PPCA weights). The summary statistics (Table 4.1) confirmed an increase in affiliations to a medical service, but this category does not have a large weight in the index using PPCA weights. The outcome variable, subjective health status, is the one having the largest weight. In that variable we see that the average health status had no major changes, and that most Colombians report having good health in both years. The small changes do not affect

[35]See Sánchez (2006) for more details on public services for the slightly longer time period 1993–2003.

Figure 4.3: Access to Public Services, by Income Percentile, 1997–2003

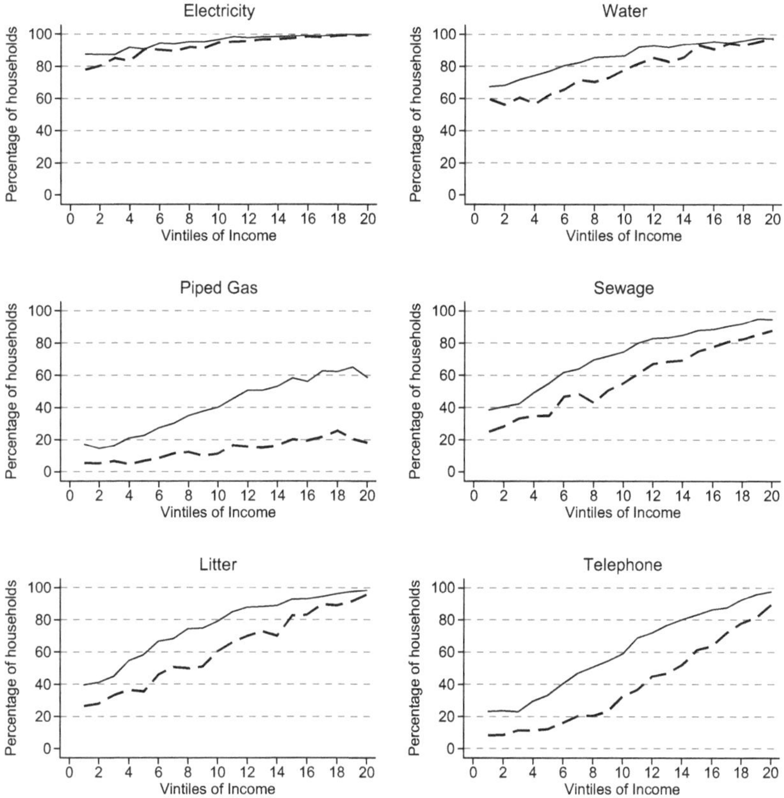

Legend: - - **1997** – 2003
Source: Own Calculations based on ECV.

poor households more or less than rich ones, and inequality in health according to this index is low.[36]

[36]However, interpretation should consider that the included questions reflect perceptions, and are not complemented by objective health measures like infant mortality rates, prenatal care, or nutritional status which use to be inversely correlated with income. Furthermore, the way people value their own health status and that of their family members can differ considerably from a physician's valuation.

The conditional NIGIC for living conditions and subjective welfare (shortly: life) in Figure 4.4 is nearly always below 0 and downward sloping when using normative weights, but above 0 for approximately the first half of the distribution and then changes sign to negative for richer households in the case of PPCA weights, also having a downward sloping trend. Using the unconditional NIGIC, there are positive but volatile growth rates for the first 7 (normative weights) or 10 (PPCA weights) vintiles, thus the distribution shifts favoring the poor. Also the downward trend of all curves suggest relative improvements.

Figure 4.4: Health, Subjective Welfare: NIGIC, 1997–2003

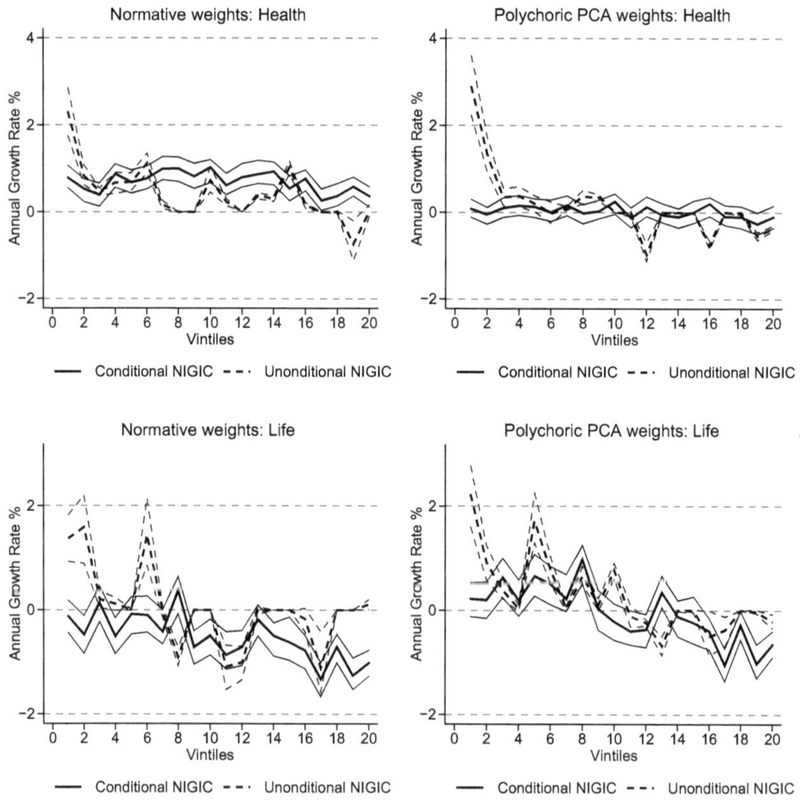

Source: Own Calculations based on ECV.

A more rigorous analysis is possible using PPGR, presented in Table 4.5. For comparison purposes we use the percentiles derived from the moderate and extreme headcount index based on income poverty lines to calculate PPGR: 54 percent (corresponding to vintile 11) for moderate poverty and 18 percent (corresponding to vintile 4) for extreme poverty. The GRIM are overall rather low, in the range of -0.02 (subjective welfare using normative weights) and 0.42 (assets using PPCA weights). For assets, PPGR for the moderate and extreme poverty lines are higher than the GRIM for both weighting systems and also for conditional and unconditional, indicating that the poor exhibited larger increases in assets. For health, we obtain different results depending on the weighting scheme: using normative weights we clearly find pro-poor growth both conditionally and unconditionally, but using PPCA weights we find pro-poor growth for the unconditional and only slightly pro-poor but rather no growth at all for the conditional case. The GRIM for the subjective welfare indicator is slightly below 0 using normative weights and at 0.20 using PPCA weights. For both weighting schemes in the unconditional case, the poorest have positive and higher growth rates, thus PPGR above GRIM. For the conditional case, the income-poorest vintiles have negative growth rates using normative weights, thus anti-poor growth, but for PPCA weights, the conditional case shows pro-poor growth in the weak absolute and the relative sense.

Education

As a lagged result of the economic crisis in the late 1990s, gross enrollment rates declined by 2001 (Table 4.7). The largest fall was in pre-school enrollment rates, followed by secondary education. There is also evidence of decreases in net enrollment of the poorest quintiles in secondary education, as well as higher demand from middle income households for public instead of private education (Barrera and Domínguez, 2006).

Figure 4.5 shows the NIGIC for the three education indicators. Observing results lined up by income, children being overaged is clearly more relevant the poorer the household is (see also Table 4.3). However, between 1997 and 2003 one observes minor but positive growth rates for the income-poorest vintiles, in contrast to the negative growth rates observed in the unconditional case. As a consequence, inequality between the first and last income deciles of the education distribution decreased. The PPGR confirms these results (Table 4.5). The GRIM is positive but very close to 0 with the conditional PPGR both being above. The unconditional NIGIC shows large decreases for the education-poorest children (up to the extreme income-poverty headcount). This is reflected in a PPGR of -2.86 when using the extreme poverty line and of -0.82 for the moderate poverty line and confirms higher overage rates for children sorted in the lowest vintiles

Figure 4.5: Education: NIGIC, 1997–2003

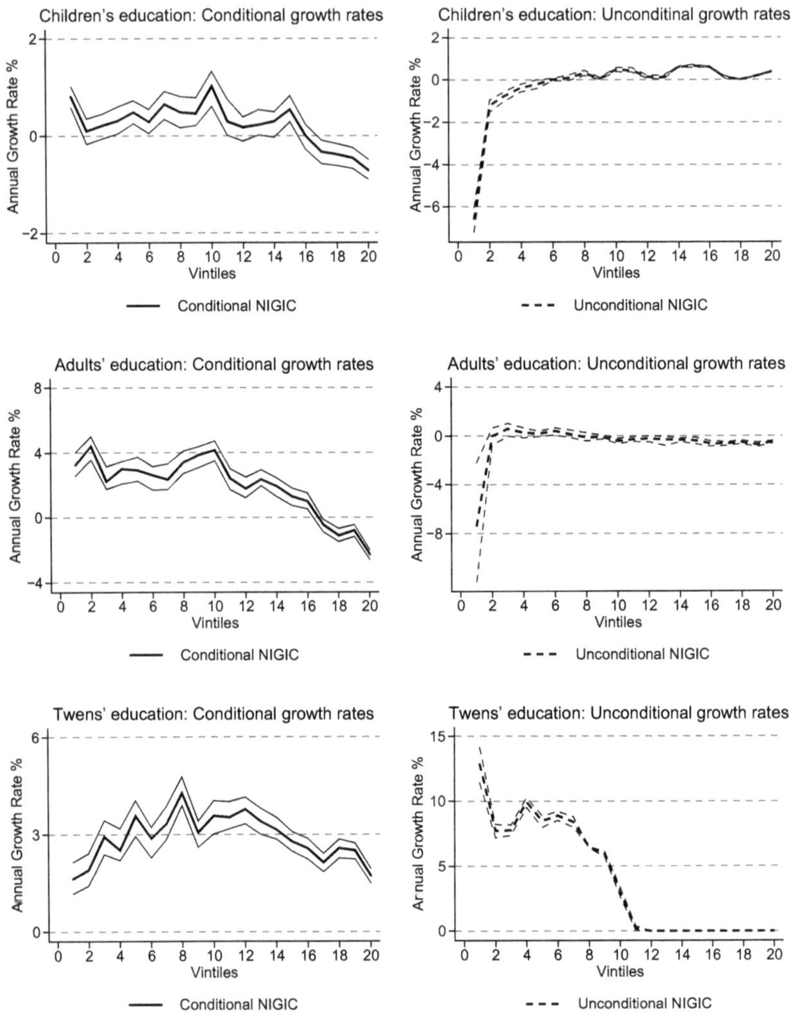

Source: Own Calculations based on ECV.

Table 4.7: Gross and Net Enrollment Rates, 1995–2006

	Gross enrollment					Net enrollment	
Year	Pre-scholar	Primary	Media	Secondary	Total	Primary	Secondary
1995	51	114	72	46	77	n.a.	n.a.
1996	55	108	72	47	75	n.a.	n.a.
1997	58	108	72	51	76	n.a.	n.a.
1998	64	115	78	57	81	91	55
1999	66	115	78	58	82	93	56
2000	69	114	78	57	82	94	58
2001	54	112	73	51	79	92	55
2002	71	112	79	56	82	93	57
2003	84	112	83	60	84	n.a.	n.a.
2004	82	111	83	61	85	89	58
2005	89	111	86	65	88	93	63
2006	88	112	88	69	90	92	68

Notes: Gross school enrolment ratio corresponds to the number of children enrolled in a level regardless of age, divided by the population of the age group that officially corresponds to the same level.
Source: Gross enrollment rates: Ministry of Education. Net enrollment rates: World Development Indicators.

in 2003. All other vintiles show no major variation, and growth rates are slightly above 0.

Figure 4.5 also shows NIGIC of adults' and twens' average years of education. The adults' NIGIC conditional to income is above 0 and downward sloping up to the 16th vintile, thus covering people below both poverty lines. The PPGR is way higher than the GRIM indicating that the poorest percentiles in 2003 had higher average adult education. Sorted by average years of education, the resulting PPGR are negative (-0.65 and -2.29) and lower than the GRIM (-0.28), due to the sharp fall in the first few vintiles. This result points to a fall in the average years of adult education for the poorest few vintiles of the distribution in 2003 compared to 1997 (Table 4.5). A very different picture is shown by twens' education, which shows an inverted-u-shaped NIGIC in the conditional case giving highest growth rates to the medium income groups. This explains why only when using the moderate poverty line, the conditional PPGR is higher (2.96) than the GRIM (2.54), but not when using the extreme poverty line (2.15). Unconditional twens' education shows a very interesting pattern since it is clearly pro-poor. Education growth rates are very high for the education-poorest, leading to very high PPGR of 7.94 and 9.46, compared to the GRIM of 2.54.[37]

[37] In this case, it is interesting to look at absolute changes. While growth rates are very much higher for the first few vintiles, absolute changes are highest for the 3rd and 4th decile (of around

The puzzling result of the educational poorest regardless of income raises the question about their socioeconomic characteristics. The generational effect of improvement in access to education in recent years can be seen in higher average years of schooling for younger generations, where the younger adults show higher average years of education and growth rates compared to the elderly. However, educational outcomes are still much better for those ranking higher in the income distribution with the poorest 10 percent of households having on average much fewer years of education compared to the richest. Although this average increased slightly from 1997 to 2003, differences between poor and rich remained the same.[38]

Summarizing, average years of adult education went slightly down in the period of analysis, although these changes were proportionally larger for the income poor. However, it is not clear in how far this result is driven by better-educated adults who became poor in 2003.[39] Unambiguously, twens' education went up, on average by more than 1 year, and for some groups by much more. Interesting to note is also the flat part in the unconditional case where growth rates go down to 0 from the 11th vintile onwards. This is driven by the fact that the upper bound of the indicator is reached, so that no increases are possible any more, which can also be seen in Table 4.3 showing the maximum value of 10 from decile 7 and 5 onwards for 1997 and 2003, respectively.

With respect to the education indices, the low growth rates found in children's education sorted by income can be linked to stagnation in enrollment rates in primary and secondary schooling during the crisis, as well as quality deterioration leading to high repetition rates. This combined effect is stronger the higher the educational level. Thus, although gross enrollment rates increased, net enrollment (which takes into account children's age for the class they are attending) did not (Table 4.7). Studies focusing on education show that public schools absorbed part of the enrollment decline of high income groups in private schools, while the lower-income students dropped out. As a consequence the educational gap

3) rather than for the 1st decile (of less than 1) using Table 4.3. For similar results, see also Grosse et al. (2008a) and Klasen (2008a) for Bolivia.

[38]Coverage of tertiary education shows a much lower participation of the poorest quintiles, with only 6 percent of the 18-25 years old students enrolled in 2003 belonging to the 1st quintile of income. New entrance to tertiary education was also affected by the crisis, when the number of new entrants from 1997 to 1999 declined by 19 percent (World Bank, 2003).

[39]Further tests to explain why education seems to be anti-poor, especially for children's education in the case in the unconditional case, reveal that there might be some sampling problem. For the departments of Bogota and Valle, the sample size was strongly increased in 2003 compared to 1997 to gain significant insights at lower geographical levels. Even with the sample weights, results are strongly influenced by these departments. However, even excluding them still results in some negative growth rates for the first few vintiles, but to a lesser extend. Adults' education growth rates also increase when excluding Bogota and Valle.

between poor and rich increased, particularly due to immense quality differences between private and public schools (Velez et al., 2003).

4.5 Conclusion

Empirical multidimensional poverty assessment poses tree important challenges: The first challenge is the selection of indicators that best reflect basic capabilities. When looking for implementation of indices in the literature one finds a large variety and combination of variables, usually focused on education, health, and asset ownership. Few studies or indices include proxies for political and social participation, burden of violence, and environmental issues, due to lack of appropriate data among others. In this paper, we selected four important aspects of multidimensional wellbeing: asset ownership (including access to public services), health, subjective welfare, and education.

The second challenge is the aggregation of variables in composite multidimensional poverty indicators, especially the weighting procedure applied. We offered in this paper two opposed methodologies to calculate weights: one based on statistical procedures (PPCA) and the other based on our researchers' criteria. Given that household needs as well as valuation of those needs change in time, the weights obtained by any selected procedure need to be revised regularly, particularly when using such indices for selecting social program beneficiaries. An example of this is the provision of piped gas which was almost non-existing in the 1980s and has now a large weight in the asset index. Another classical example is the valuation of a black-and-white television 20 years ago with its value today.

The third challenge is to follow the multidimensional poverty indicators over time to judge whether or not the poor have achieved improvements in multidimensional welfare. We have used an extension of the pro-poor growth measurement for multidimensional poverty indicators to investigate the distributional pattern of progress in these indicators. Of special interest was to look at the trends of multidimensional indicators when they are conditioned on the position in the income distribution, since we have found weak to medium correlations between income and non-income dimensions of wellbeing. Dynamic results using the NIGIC approach show improvements in the asset index that had positive growth rates, especially the provision of public services, and larger so for the poorer. Results on health and subjective welfare depended on the weighting schemes, where health was more positive using normatively selected weights, whereas subjective welfare was more positive using PPCA weights. For education, children's education (calculated similar to net enrollment rates) showed some major deteriorations in the unconditional case (indicating some drop outs or repetitions), but minor improvements in the conditional case (indicating that not automatically the income-poor were hurt most). Adults's education also showed different pictures: improvements in the conditional case but a deterioration or hardly any change in the unconditional one. Twens' education showed a pro-middle-class improvement in the conditional case, and very strong and pro-poor increases in the unconditional case indicating the success of schooling policies in the new cohorts entering the labor force.

Although non-income indicators are easier to measure and less prone to error as discussed by Günther and Klasen (2009), low variation, the existence of upper bounds, and the fact that some of them depend on public policies are challenging for interpreting them. A limitation for Colombia is that the time period of analysis is too short for some indicators that might need even decades to exhibit significant changes. However, our results are consistent with previous analysis on multidimensional pro-poor growth using longer time spans (Grosse et al., 2008a): inequality in multidimensional poverty indicators is lower than in income indicators and they change less as time passes.

Bibliography

Alkire, S. and J. E. Foster (2009). Counting and multidimensional poverty measurement (revised and updated). OPHI Working Papers 32, Queen Elizabeth House, University of Oxford.

Atkinson, A. B. (1970). On the measurement of inequality. *Journal of Economic Theory 2*(3), 244–263.

Atkinson, A. B. and F. Bourguignon (1982). The comparison of multi-dimensioned distributions of economic status. *Review of Economic Studies 49*(2), 183–201.

Atkinson, A. B. and A. Brandolini (2004). Global world inequality: Absolute, relative or intermediate. Presented at the 28th General Conference of the International Association for Research in Income and Wealth, August 22-28, Cork, Ireland.

Barrera, F. and C. Domínguez (2006). Educación básica en Colombia: Opciones futuras de política. Report. Departamento Nacional de Planeación, DNP-MERDP.

Basu, K. and J. E. Foster (1998). On measuring literacy. *Economic Journal 108*(451), 1733–1749.

Berthélemy, J. (2006). To what extent are African education policies pro-poor? *Journal of African Economies 15*(3), 434–469.

Bès, M., R. Hernández, and C. Oliva (1998). Descentralización en Colombia: Nuevos desafíos. Estudios Económicos y Sectoriales 52159, Banco Interamericano de Desarrollo. Departamento Regional de Operaciones 3, División de Países 5.

Biewen, M. (2002). Bootstrap inference for inequality, mobility and poverty measurement. *Journal of Econometrics 108*(2), 317–342.

Biewen, M. and S. P. Jenkins (2006). Variance estimation for generalized entropy and Atkinson inequality indices: The complex survey data case. *Oxford Bulletin of Economics and Statistics 68*(3), 371–383.

Binder, D. and Z. Patak (1994). Use of estimating functions for estimation from complex surveys. *Journal of the American Statistical Association 89*(427), 1035–1043.

Booysen, F., S. van der Berg, R. Burger, M. von Maltitz, and G. du Rand (2008). Using an asset index to assess trends in poverty in seven Sub-Saharan African Countries. *World Development 36*(6), 1113–1130.

Bourguignon, F. and S. Chakravarty (2003). The measurement of multidimensional poverty. *Journal of Economic Inequality 1*(1), 25–49.

Bourguignon, F., F. H. G. Ferreira, and N. Lustig (2005). *The microeconomics of income distribution dynamics in East Asia and Latin America*. New York: World Bank and Oxford University Press.

Branisa, B. (2006). Wealth, poverty, and inequality in Bolivia using different methods and data sets. Master's thesis, University of Göttingen.

Cardozo, A. and M. Grosse (2009). Pro-poor growth using non-income indicators: An empirical illustration for Colombia. Ibero-America Institute for Economic Research Discussion Paper (Courant Research Centre 'Poverty, Equity and Growth' Discussion Paper) 192 (9), University of Göttingen.

Cardozo, A. R. (2008). Pro-poor growth in Colombia from 1996 to 2005. In S. Klasen and F. Nowak-Lehmann D. (Eds.), *Poverty, Inequality and Migration in Latin America* (Göttingen Studies in Development Economics ed.), Volume 20, pp. 87–107. Frankfurt: Peter Lang.

Chen, S. and M. Ravallion (2004). How have the world's poorest fared since the early 1980s? *World Bank Research Observer 19*(2), 141–169.

Chen, S. and M. Ravallion (2008). The developing world is poorer than we thought, but not less successful in the fight against poverty. World Bank Policy Research Working Paper 4703. August 2009 revised version.

Christiaensen, L., P. Lanjouw, J. Luoto, and D. Stifel (2010). The reliability of small area estimation prediction methods to track poverty. WIDER Working Paper 2010/99, UNU-WIDER.

Clark, D. (2005). Sen's capability approach and the many spaces of human well-being. *Journal of Development Studies 41*(8), 1339–1368.

Datt, G. and M. Ravallion (1992). Growth and redistribution components of changes in poverty measures: A decomposition with applications to Brazil and India in the 1980s. *Journal of Development Economics 38*(2), 275–295.

Davidson, R. and E. Flachaire (2007). Asymptotic and bootstrap inference for inequality and poverty measurement. *Journal of Econometrics 141*(1), 141–166.

De Onis, M. and M. Blössner (2000). Prevalence and trends of overweight among preschool children in developing countries. *Amercian Journal of Clinical Nutrition 72*, 1032–1039.

Deaton, A. (1997). *The Analysis of Household Surveys*. Baltimore MD: The Johns Hopkins University Press for the World Bank.

Deaton, A. (2005). Measuring poverty in a growing world (or measuring growth in a poor world). *The Review of Economics and Statistics 87*(1), 1–19.

Deaton, A. and S. Zaidi (2002). Guidelines for constructing consumption aggregates for welfare analysis. LSMS Working Paper 135, World Bank.

Demombynes, G., C. Elbers, J. O. Lanjouw, P. Lanjouw, J. Mistiaen, and B. Özler (2004). Producing an improved geographic profile of poverty. Methodology and evidence from three developing countries. In A. Shorrocks and R. van der Hoeven (Eds.), *Growth, Inequality and Poverty: Prospects for Pro-Poor Economic Development*. New York: Oxford University Press.

Dietz, W. (1998). Health consequences of obesity in youth: Childhood predictors of adult disease. *Pediatrics 101*(3-supplement), 518–525.

DNP (2006). Metodología de medición y magnitud de la pobreza en Colombia. Mimeo, Misión para el Diseño de una Estrategia para la Reducción de la Pobreza y la Desigualdad. Departamento Nacional de Planeación (DNP-MERDP).

DNP (2008). Distribución de los recursos del Sistema General de Participaciones provenientes del crecimiento real de la economía superior al 4% de la vigencia 2006. Documento Conpes Social 115, Departamento Nacional de Planeación (DNP), Consejo Nacional de Política Económica y Social.

Duclos, J.-Y., D. E. Sahn, and S. D. Younger (2006). Robust multidimensional poverty comparisons. *Economic Journal 116*(514), 943–968.

Duclos, J.-Y. and Q. Wodon (2004). What is "pro-poor"? Cahiers de recherche 0425, CIRPEE.

Ehrlich, I. and F. Lui (1997). The problem of population and growth: A review of the literatur from Malthus to contemporary models of endogenous population and endogenous growth. *Journal of Economic Dynamics and Control 21*(1), 205–242.

Elbers, C., J. O. Lanjouw, and P. Lanjouw (2003). Micro-level estimation of poverty and inequality. *Econometrica 71*(1), 355–364.

Feres, J. C. and X. Mancero (2001). El método de las necesidades básicas insatisfechas (NBI) y sus aplicaciones en América Latina. Estudios Estadísticos y Prospectivos 7, Economic Commission for Latin America and the Caribbean, CEPAL. United Nations.

Filmer, D. and L. Pritchett (2001). Estimating wealth effects without expenditure data – or tears: An application to educational enrollments in states of India. *Demography 38*(1), 115–132.

Foster, J. E., J. Greer, and E. Thorbecke (1984). A class of decomposable poverty measures. *Econometrica 52*(3), 761–766.

González, J. I. (2001). Imparcialidad financiera y equidad. Otra lectura del informe de la Organización Mundial de la Salud. Año 2000. *Revista de Gerencia y Políticas de la Salud 1*(1), 39–47.

Grimm, M. (2004). A decomposition of inequality and poverty changes in the context of macroeconomic adjustment: A microsumulation study for Côte d'Ivoire. In A. Shorrocks and R. van der Hoeven (Eds.), *Growth, Inequality, and Poverty. Prospects for Pro-Poor Economic Development*. New York: Oxford University Press.

Grimm, M. (2007). Removing the anonymity axiom in assessing pro-poor growth. *Journal of Economic Inequality 5*(2), 179–197.

Grimm, M., C. Guénard, and S. Mesplé-Somps (2002). What has happened to the urban population in Côté d'Ivoire since the eighties? An analysis of monetary poverty and deprivation of 15 years of household data. *World Development 30*(6), 1073–1095.

Grimm, M., K. Harttgen, S. Klasen, and M. Misselhorn (2008). A human development index by income groups. *World Development 36*(12), 2527–2546.

Grosse, M., K. Harttgen, and S. Klasen (2008a). Measuring pro-poor growth in non-income dimensions. *World Development 36*(6), 1021–1047.

Grosse, M., K. Harttgen, and S. Klasen (2008b). Measuring pro-poor progress towards the non-income millennium development goals. In M. McGillivray (Ed.), *Achieving the Millennium Development Goals* (Studies in Development Economics and Policy ed.). New York: Palgrave Macmillan.

Grosse, M., S. Klasen, and J. Spatz (2005). Creating national poverty profiles and growth incidence curves with incomplete income or consumption expenditure data: An application to Bolivia. Ibero-America Institute for Economic Research Discussion Paper 129, University of Göttingen.

Grosse, M., S. Klasen, and J. Spatz (2007). Matching household surveys with DHS data to create nationally representative time series of poverty: An application to Bolivia. Centre for Statistics (ZfS) Discussion Paper 08.2007, University of Göttingen.

Grosse, M., S. Klasen, and J. Spatz (2009). Matching household surveys with DHS data to create nationally representative time series of poverty: An application to Bolivia. Courant Research Centre 'Poverty, Equity and Growth' Discussion Paper 21, University of Göttingen.

Günther, I. and M. Grimm (2007). Measuring pro-poor growth when relative prices shift. *Journal of Development Economics 82*(1), 245–256.

Günther, I. and S. Klasen (2009). Measuring chronic non-income poverty. In T. Addison, D. Hulme, and R. Kanbur (Eds.), *Poverty Dynamics. Interdisciplinary Perspectives*, Chapter 4. New York: Oxford University Press.

Günther, I., M. Marouani, and M. Raffinot (2006). La croissance est-elle pro-pauvres au Mali? Document De Travial DT/2006-15, DIAL.

Hanmer, L. and D. Booth (2001). Pro-poor growth: Why do we need it? Mimeo. Overseas Development Institute (ODI), London.

Hentschel, J., J. O. Lanjouw, P. Lanjouw, and J. Poggi (2000). Combining census and survey data to trace the spatial dimensions of poverty: A case study of Ecuador. *World Bank Economic Review 14*(1), 147–165.

Hernany, W. (1999). La pobreza en el Área urbana de Bolivia: Período 1989–1997. Tesis para la obtención de la licenciatura en economía, Universidad Católica Boliviana, La Paz, Bolivia.

INE (2004). Encuesta nacional de demografia y salud 2003. Informe Preliminar, La Paz.

INE (various issues). Información estadística. Online data base. Instituto Nacional de Estadística. www.ine.gov.bo.

INE-UDAPE (2002). Mapa de pobreza 2001. Mimeo. Instituto nacional de estadística and unidad de análisis de políticas sociales y económicas. La Paz.

Jazmín, C., M. Rivera, and M. Y. Castañeda (2004). El malestar de la salud en Colombia. Informe Especial 303, Contraloría General de la República.

Jenkins, S. P. (1991). The measurement of income inequality. In L. Osberg (Ed.), *Economic Inequality and Poverty: International Perspectives*, pp. 3–38. Armonk: M. E. Sharpe.

Jolliffe, D. and A. Semykina (1999). Robust standard errors for the Foster-Greer-Thorbecke class of poverty indices. *Stata Technical Bulletin 9*(51), 34–36.

Kakwani, N. (1993a). Performance in living standards: An international comparison. *Journal of Development Economics 41*(2), 307–336.

Kakwani, N. (1993b). Statistical inference in the measurement of poverty. *Review of Economics and Econometrics 75*(4), 632–639.

Kakwani, N. and E. M. Pernia (2000). What is pro-poor growth? *Asian Development Review 18*(1), 1–16.

Kakwani, N. and H. Son (2000). Pro-poor growth: Concept, measurement, and application. Mimeo. University of New South Wales, Sydney.

Kakwani, N. and H. H. Son (2006). New global poverty counts. Working Papers 29, International Policy Centre for Inclusive Growth.

Kanbur, R. (2002). Conceptual challenges in poverty and inequality: One development economist's perspective. Working Papers 7242, Cornell University, Department of Applied Economics and Management.

Kiely, R. and P. Marfleet (1998). *Globalisation and the Third World*. New York: Routledge.

Klasen, S. (2000). Measuring poverty and deprivation in South Africa. *Review of Income and Wealth 46*(1), 33–58.

Klasen, S. (2003). Malnourished and surviving in South Asia, better nourished and dying young in Africa: What can explain this puzzle? In FAO (Ed.), *Measurement and Assessment of Food Deprivation and Undernutrition*. Rome: FAO.

Klasen, S. (2004). In search of the holy grail: How to achieve pro-poor growth? In B. Tungodden, N. Stern, and I. Kolstad (Eds.), *Towards Pro-poor Policies – Aid, Institutions, and Globalization* (Proceedings from the Annual World Bank Conference on Development Economics – Europe 2003 ed.). Washington, D.C.: World Bank.

Klasen, S. (2008a). Economic growth and poverty reduction: Measurement issues using income and non-income indicators. *World Development 36*(3), 420–445.

Klasen, S. (2008b). Poverty, undernutrition, and child mortality: Some inter-regional puzzles and their implication for research and policy. *Journal of Economic Inequality 6*(1), 89–115.

Klasen, S., M. Grosse, R. Thiele, J. Lay, J. Spatz, and M. Wiebelt (2005). Operationalizing pro-poor growth. Country case study: Bolivia. Ibero-America Institute for Economic Research Discussion Paper 101, University of Göttingen.

Klasen, S., M. Grosse, R. Thiele, J. Lay, J. Spatz, and M. Wiebelt (2007). Analyzing pro-poor growth in Bolivia: Addressing data gaps and modeling policy choices. In S. Klasen, M. Grimm, and A. McKay (Eds.), *Determinants of Pro-Poor Growth: Analytical Issues and Findings from Country Cases*. New York: Palgrave Macmillan.

Kolenikov, S. and G. Angeles (2009). Socioeconomic status measurement with discrete proxy variables: Is principal component analysis a reliable answer? *Review of Income and Wealth 55*(1), 128–165.

Kovacevic, M. S. and D. A. Binder (1997). Variance estimation for measures of income inequality and polarization – The estimating equations approach. *Journal of Official Statistics 13*(1), 41–58.

Lanjouw, P. and M. Ravallion (1998). Benefit incidence and the timing of program capture. World Bank Policy Research Working Paper 1956.

Libhaber, M. and V. Foster (2003). Health. In M. M. Giugale, O. Lafourcade, and C. Luff (Eds.), *Colombia: The Economic Foundation of Peace*, Chapter 22, pp. 433–463. Washington, D.C.: World Bank.

Lora, E. (2001). Structural reforms in Latin America: What has been reformed and how to measure it. Working Paper 466, Inter-American Development Bank, Research Department.

Marcoux, A. (1998). The feminization of poverty: Claims, facts, and data needs. *Population and Development Review 24*(1), 131–139.

Martorell, R., K. Kettel, M. Hughes, and L. Grummer-Strawn (1998). Obesity in Latin American women and children. *Journal of Nutrition 128*(9), 1464–1473.

Mathiassen, A. (2008). The predictive ability of poverty models. Empirical evidence from Uganda. Discussion Paper 560, Statistics Norway, Division for Development Cooperation.

McCulloch, N. and B. Baulch (1999). Tracking pro-poor growth: New ways to spot the biases and benefits. ID21 insights No. 31(3). Institute of Development Studies, Sussex.

Montes, C. (2003). Results-based public management in Bolivia. Overseas Development Institute Working Paper 202.

Morales, J. A. (1994). Hiperinflación y políticas de estabilización. Serie Docente 15, CIEPLAN.

Morales, J. A. (2001). El modelo de desarrollo económico visto de nuevo. In O. Zegada (Ed.), *Bolivia: Modelo de Desarrollo Y Crisis*. La Paz: Offset Boliviana.

Moser, C. and A. Felton (2009). The construction of an asset index measuring asset accumulation in Ecuador. In T. Addison, D. Hulme, and R. Kanbur (Eds.), *Poverty Dynamics. Interdisciplinary Perspectives*, Chapter 5. New York: Oxford University Press.

Mukherjee, D. (2001). Measuring multidimensional deprivation. *Mathematical Social Sciences 42*(3), 233–251.

OECD (2001). Rising to the global challenge: Partnership for reducing world poverty. Statement by the DAC High Level Meeting. April 25-26, 2001. OECD, Paris.

OECD (2006). *Promoting Pro-Poor Growth: Key Policy Messages*. Paris: OECD.

Osberg, L. (2000). Schooling, literacy and individual earnings. Statistics Canada, Ottawa.

Ram, R. (1982). Composite indices of physical quality of life, basic needs fulfillment, and income: A 'principle component' representation. *Journal of Development Economics 11*(2), 227–247.

Ravallion, M. (2003). Measuring aggregate welfare in developing countries: How well do national accounts and surveys agree? *The Review of Economics and Statistics 85*(3), 645–652.

Ravallion, M. (2005). A poverty-inequality trade-off? *Journal of Economic Inequality 3*(2), 169–181.

Ravallion, M. and S. Chen (2003). Measuring pro-poor growth. *Economics Letters 78*(1), 93–99.

Ravallion, M. and G. Datt (2002). Why has economic growth been more pro-poor in some states of India than others? *Journal of Development Economics 68*(2), 381–400.

Republic of Bolivia (2001). Bolivia: Poverty reduction strategy, Rebublica de Bolivia. La Paz.

Roberts, J. (2003). Poverty reduction outcomes in education and health: Public expenditure and aid. Overseas Development Institute Working Paper 210.

Rodrik, D. (2003). Growth strategies. Working Paper 10050, NBER.

Rodrik, D. (2006). Goodbye Washington Consensus, Hello Washington Confusion? a review of the World Bank's *Economic Growth in the 1990s: Learning from a Decade of Reform. Journal of Economic Literature 44*(4), 973–987.

Sachs, J. and J. A. Morales (1988). *Bolivia: 1952–1986.* San Francisco: ICS Press. International Center for Economic Growth.

Sahn, D. E. and D. Stifel (2000). Poverty comparisons over time and across countries in Africa. *World Development 28*(12), 2123–2155.

Sahn, D. E. and D. Stifel (2003). Exploring alternative measures of welfare in the absence of expenditure data. *Review of Income and Wealth 49*(4), 463–489.

Sánchez, F. (2006). Descentralización y progreso en el acceso a los servicios sociales de educación, salud y agua y alcantarillado. Departamento Nacional de Planeación (DNP-MERDP).

Sarmiento, A., R. C. Angulo, and F. A. Espinoza (2005). Informe Bogotá cómo vamos. Programa Nacional de Desarrollo Humano, PNUD.

Schweickert, R. and R. Thiele (2004). From Washington to post-Washington? Consensus policies and divergent developments in Latin America and Asia. Kiel Discussion Paper 409, Kiel Institute for the World Economy.

Sen, A. K. (1979). Personal utilities and public judgements: Or what's wrong with welfare economics. *The Economic Journal 89*(355), 537–558.

Sen, A. K. (1980). Equality of what? In S. M. McMurrin (Ed.), *The Tanner Lectures on Human Values*, Volume I. Cambridge: Cambridge University Press. Delivered at Stanford University, May 22, 1979.

Sen, A. K. (1981). Public action and the quality of live in developing countries. *Oxford Bulletin of Economics and Statistics 43*(4), 287–319.

Sen, A. K. (1985). *Commodities and capabilities*. Amsterdam: North Holland.

Sen, A. K. (1987). *Standard of Living*. New York: Cambridge University Press.

Sen, A. K. (1988). The concept of development. In H. Chenery and T. Srinivasan (Eds.), *Handbook of Development Economics*, Volume 1, pp. 9–26. Elsevier.

Sen, A. K. and J. E. Foster (1997). *On economic inequality*. Clarendon Press: Oxford University Press.

Son, H. H. (2003). Approaches to defining and measuring pro-poor growth. Mimeo. World Bank, Washington, D.C.

Spatz, J. (2006). *Poverty and inequality in the era of structural reforms: The case of Bolivia*. Berlin: Springer. Kieler Studien 336.

Stifel, D. and L. Christiaensen (2007). Tracking poverty over time in the absence of comparable consumption data. *World Bank Economic Review 2*(21), 317–341.

Summer, A. (2003). Economic and non-economic well-being: A review of progress on the meaning and measurement of poverty. Paper Prepared for WIDER Conference: Inequality, Poverty and Human Well-Being, May 30-31, 2003, Helsinki.

Székely, M., N. Lustig, M. Cumpa, and J. A. Mejía (2000). Do we know how much poverty there is? IDB Working Paper 437, Inter-American Development Bank.

Thomas, V., Y. Wang, and X. Fan (2000). Measuring educational inequality: Gini coefficients of education. World Bank Policy Research Working Paper 2525.

UN (2000). United Nations millennium declaration. United Nations, A/RES55/2.

UN (2009). The millennium development goals report 2009. United Nations, New York.

UN, IMF, OECD, and World Bank (2000). *A Better World for All.* New York: International Monetary Fund, Organisation for Economic Co-operation and Development, United Nations, and World Bank.

UNDP (1990). *Human Development Report 1990: Concept and Measurement of Human Development.* New York: United Nations.

UNDP (1991). *Human Development Report 1991: Financing Human Development.* New York: United Nations.

UNDP (1995). *Human Development Report 1995: Gender and Human Development.* New York: United Nations.

UNDP (1996). *Human Development Report 1996: Economic Growth and Human Development.* New York: United Nations.

UNDP (2000). *Human Development Report 2000: Human Rights and Human Development.* New York: United Nations.

UNDP (2005). *Human Development Report 2005: International Cooperation at a Crossroads: Aid, Trade and Security in an Unequal World.* New York: United Nations.

UNDP (2006). *Human Development Report 2006: Beyond Scarcity: Power, Poverty and the Global Water Crisis.* New York: United Nations.

Van de Walle, D. (1998). Assessing the welfare impacts of public spending. *World Development 26*(3), 365–379.

Van de Walle, D. and K. Nead (Eds.) (1995). *Public Spending and the Poor: Theory and Evidence.* Published for the World Bank. Baltimore and London: Johns Hopkins University Press.

Vélez, C. E. and M. Robles (2008). Determining the paramenters of axiomatically derived multidimensional poverty indices: An application based on reported well being in Colombia. In N. Kakwani and J. Silber (Eds.), *Quantitative approaches to multidimensional poverty measurement*, Chapter 12, pp. 210–225. Houndmills, Basingstoke, Hampshire: Palgrave Macmillan.

Velez, E., D. Harding, and A. Sarmiento (2003). Education. In M. M. Giugale, O. Lafourcade, and C. Luff (Eds.), *Colombia: The Economic Foundation of Peace*, Chapter 21, pp. 611–651. Washington, D.C.: World Bank.

von Maltzahn, R. and K. Durrheim (2007). Is poverty multidimensional? A comparison of income and asset based measures in five Southern African countries. *Social Indicators Research 86*(1), 149–162.

White, H. (1980). A heteroskedasticity-consistent covariance matrix estimator and a direct test for heteroskedasticity. *Econometrica 48*(4), 817–838.

White, H. and E. Anderson (2000). Growth versus distribution: Does the pattern of growth matter? *Development Policy Review 19*(3), 267–289.

Williamson, J. (1990). *Latin American adjustment: How much has happened?* Washington, D.C.: Institute for International Economics.

Woodruff, R. S. (1971). A simple method for approximating the variance of a complicated estimate. *Journal of the American Statistical Association 66*(334), 411–414.

World Bank (2000). *World Development Report 2000/2001. Attacking Poverty.* New York: Oxford University Press.

World Bank (2003). Tertiary education in Colombia. Paving the way for reform. Country Study 26289, World Bank.

World Bank (2004). Bolivia poverty assessment: Establishing the basis for more pro-poor growth. Report No. 28068-Bo. World Bank.

World Bank (2005). *Economic Growth in the 1990s: Learning from a Decade of Reform.* Washington, D.C.: World Bank.

World Bank (2007). World development indicators. CD-ROM.

Appendix A

Table A.1: Latin America in a Comparative Perspective, 1990 and 2005

	LAC		SSA		EAP		South Asia		LLDC		MIC	
	1990	2005	1990	2005	1990	2005	1990	2005	1990	2005	1990	2005
Economic Indicators												
GDP per capita (PPP 2000 intern. $)	6035	7482	1678	1774	1857	5384	1601	2791	1053	1281	3978	6537
5-y-ave. GDP per capita growth	1.7	1.6	-1.4	-0.5	8.8	9.1	2.9	4.0	-0.8	0.1	1.7	2.4
Population growth (3-y-ave.)	1.8	1.3	2.9	2.3	1.6	0.8	2.1	1.7	2.7	2.4	1.5	0.9
Population density (per sq. km)	21.7	27.4	21.8	31.5	100.6	118.8	232.8	307.4	25.8	37.3	38.1	44.9
Inflation (3-y-ave.)	66.8	7.0	25.6	4.4	15.7	6.3	21.7	5.1	23.9	6.9	37.4	5.1
GDP shares (3-y-ave.)												
Agriculture	9	8	20	17	24	13	31	20	37	29	15	10
Industry	36	34	34	31	40	45	26	27	20	26	39	38
Services	55	58	47	52	36	42	43	53	43	45	46	53
Exports	16	25	27	32	24	43	9	18	13	23	21	34
Aid (of GNI)	0.5	0.3	5.9	5.6	1.1	0.3	1.8	0.8	n.a.	n.a.	0.8	0.5
External debt	0.4	0.4	0.6	0.4	0.3	0.2	0.3	0.2	n.a.	n.a.	0.3	0.3
Human Development and Infrastructure												
Aid per capita (current US$)	12	12	33	38	5	4	6	5	n.a.	n.a.	9	12
Life expectancy at birth (years)	68	72	49	47	67	71	59	63	50	52	68	70
Immunisation DPT (children 1–2 years)	68	91	57	65	90	84	67	65	57	76	85	88
Adult literacy, males (%)	86	91	61	70	87	95	59	70	56	70	86	93
Adult literacy, females (%)	84	89	41	53	70	87	34	45	34	50	72	87
School enrollment, primary (% gross)	104	118	71	92	118	114	91	110	63	95	110	113
Roads, paved (% of total)	21.9	23.1	16.0	12.1	17.2	20.0	37.5	30.8	16.0	13.3	50.5	46.3
Roads to land area (%)	13.6	14.9	4.7	6.2	12.9	13.7	51.9	62.6	3.9	4.8	11.8	12.1
Telephone mainlines (per 1000 people)	60	177	10	17	8	214	6	39	3	8	40	211
HDI value	0.82	0.80	0.39	0.52	0.62	0.77	0.45	0.63	0.34	0.52	0.57	0.69

Notes: All data except data on HDI (and literacy rates for LLDC in 2005) are from World Bank (2007). The 5-y-ave. GDP per capita growth is the annualized growth from 1990–1995 and 2000–2005. The indicators showing averages over 3 years (3-y-ave.) are the averages from 1989–1991 (except inflation for EAP (1990–1992)) and 2003–2005. Adult literacy rates for the second year are from 2006. Data for roads for the second year are from 1999. HDI data is from UNDP (1995) (because UNDP (1990) does not show the regional disaggregation) and UNDP (2005). HDI Data for MIC is not available, the numbers shown are for all developing countries. LAC: Latin America and the Caribbean; SSA: Sub-Saharan Africa; EAP: East Asia and Pacific; LLDC: Least Developed Countries; MIC: Middle Income Countries.
Source: Own calculations based on World Bank (2007), UNDP (1990), UNDP (1995), and UNDP (2005).

Table A.2: Bolivia and Colombia in a Comparative Latin American Perspective, 1990 and 2005

	Bolivia		Colombia		Chile		Ecuador		Peru	
	1990	2005	1990	2005	1990	2005	1990	2005	1990	2005
Economic Indicators										
GDP per capita (PPP 2000 intern. $)	2056	2508	5588	6498	5742	10700	3234	3862	3815	5373
5-y-ave. GDP per capita growth	1.7	1.6	2.1	2.1	6.8	6.7	0.6	0.1	3.6	3.7
Population growth (3-y-ave.)	2.3	1.9	2.0	1.6	1.8	1.1	2.3	1.4	2.0	1.5
Population density (per sq. km)	6.1	8.5	31.5	41.1	17.6	21.8	37.1	47.8	17.0	21.9
Inflation (3-y-ave.)	17.9	4.4	28.5	6.0	21.6	2.3	57.7	4.4	3763.3	2.5
GDP shares (3-y-ave.)										
Agriculture	17	15	17	13	9	6	14	7	8	7
Industry	34	31	38	33	41	44	37	40	30	33
Services	49	54	45	54	50	50	49	53	61	60
Exports	22	31	20	22	34	40	32	28	14	21
Aid (of GNI)	10.9	9.2	0.2	0.7	0.3	0.1	2.0	0.6	1.7	0.7
External debt	0.8	0.7	0.4	0.4	0.6	0.5	1.2	0.5	0.8	0.4
Human Development and Infrastructure										
Aid per capita (current US$)	77	85	3	14	7	6	18	14	20	17
Life expectancy at birth (years)	59	65	68	73	74	78	69	75	66	71
Immunisation DPT (children 1–2 years)	41	81	88	87	95	91	68	94	72	84
Adult literacy, males (%)	87	93	89	93	94	96	90	92	91	93
Adult literacy, females (%)	70	81	88	93	94	96	85	90	78	82
School enrollment, primary (% gross)	97	113	103	111	104	101	116	117	118	114
Roads, paved (% of total)	4.3	6.4	11.9	14.4	13.8	18.9	13.4	18.9	9.9	13.0
Roads to land area (%)	3.9	4.9	9.6	10.2	10.6	10.6	15.6	15.6	5.1	6.1
Telephone mainlines (per 1000 people)	27	70	69	168	66	211	48	129	26	80
HDI rank	81	113	44	69	23	37	55	82	56	79
HDI relative position	0.38	0.36	0.66	0.61	0.82	0.79	0.58	0.54	0.57	0.55
HDI value	0.55	0.69	0.80	0.79	0.93	0.85	0.76	0.76	0.75	0.76

Notes: All data except data on HDI (and literacy rates for Peru in 1990) are from World Bank (2007). The 5-y-ave. GDP per capita growth is the annualized growth from 1990–1995 and 2000–2005. The indicators showing averages over 3 years (3-y-ave.) are the averages from 1989–1991 and 2003–2005. Adult literacy rates for the second year are from 2006. Data for roads for the second year are from 1999. HDI data is from UNDP (1990) and UNDP (2005). The number of countries included in the HDI country list is 130 for 1990 and 177 for 2005. That is why the relative position is also given in addition to the HDI rank.

Source: Own calculations based on World Bank (2007), UNDP (1990), and UNDP (2005).

Appendix B

Table B.1: Poverty Lines for Bolivia for Various Years

	Moderate Poverty Line					Extreme Poverty Line				
	1989[a]	1994	1998	2002	2002[c]	1989[a]	1994	1998	2002	2002[c]
Urban Areas										
Chuquisaca	138.5	241.8	335.4	335.6	395.5	73.3	127.9	169.4	169.5	209.2
La Paz (City)	135.3	227.9	324.0	327.0	383.3	75.2	126.6	180.1	181.8	214.6
La Paz (El Alto)	116.6	192.6	270.4	272.6	332.9	70.7	116.7	164.1	165.5	201.8
Cochabamba	142.1	253.2	351.1	351.3	405.8	71.8	127.6	177.3	177.4	204.9
Oruro	123.0	207.1	294.7	297.4	351.1	75.2	126.6	163.9	165.3	214.6
Potosi	113.1	190.5	271.0	273.5	323.0	75.2	126.6	150.7	152.1	214.6
Tarija	144.3	257.3	356.8	351.3	412.1	71.8	127.9	178.6	177.4	204.9
Santa Cruz	141.8	237.8	354.7	343.9	404.8	72.0	120.7	180.2	174.7	205.5
Beni	141.8	237.8	354.7	343.9	404.8	72.0	120.7	180.2	174.7	205.5
Pando	141.8	237.8	354.7	343.9	404.8	72.0	120.7	180.2	174.7	205.5
Urban population weighted average	135.4	231.7	344.7	344.3	392.9	73.4	124.8	176.4	175.5	208.9
Rural Areas	96.9[b]	164.4[b]	233.6	233.4	276.6	55.2[b]	93.4[b]	131.2	133.0	157.6
Population weighted average	119.5	204.8	299.3	298.1	351.2	65.9	112.3	160.6	160.3	190.5

Notes: Numbers in current Bolivianos. [a]Since no poverty lines are available for the 2nd round (Nov. 1989) of the EIH, they are constructed as the arithmetic mean of the poverty lines for the 1st round (March 1989) and the 3rd round (Sept. 1990) of the EIH. [b]Constructed by extrapolating the relative difference between the rural poverty line and the weighted average urban poverty line of 1999. [c]1989 poverty lines inflated with the CPI.
Source: Own compilation and calculation based on unpublished data of UDAPE.

Table B.2: Sample Means from the Bolivian LSMS, 1989, 1994, 1999

	LSMS Total			LSMS City			LSMS Town			LSMS Rural		
	1989	1994	1999	1989	1994	1999	1989	1994	1999	1989	1994	1999
Demographics												
Place of Residence												
City	n.a.	n.a.	49.31	100	100	100	n.a.	n.a.	0	n.a.	n.a.	0
Town	n.a.	n.a.	15.70	0	0	0	n.a.	n.a.	100	n.a.	n.a.	0
Rural	n.a.	n.a.	34.99	0	0	0	n.a.	n.a.	0	n.a.	n.a.	100
Department												
Chuquisaca	n.a.	n.a.	6.95	4.59	4.59	5.01	n.a.	n.a.	0.92	n.a.	n.a.	12.39
La Paz	n.a.	n.a.	29.09	40.48	39.63	38.41	n.a.	n.a.	12.26	n.a.	n.a.	23.51
Cochabamba	n.a.	n.a.	18.06	14.70	14.22	15.23	n.a.	n.a.	18.77	n.a.	n.a.	21.74
Oruro	n.a.	n.a.	4.48	6.71	6.19	6.48	n.a.	n.a.	1.34	n.a.	n.a.	3.06
Potosi	n.a.	n.a.	8.95	4.30	3.81	4.55	n.a.	n.a.	6.40	n.a.	n.a.	16.3
Tarija	n.a.	n.a.	4.84	3.18	3.24	2.71	n.a.	n.a.	10.93	n.a.	n.a.	5.10
Santa Cruz	n.a.	n.a.	22.44	23.90	26.29	22.96	n.a.	n.a.	41.90	n.a.	n.a.	12.97
Beni and Pando	n.a.	n.a.	5.20	2.14	2.04	4.65	n.a.	n.a.	7.49	n.a.	n.a.	4.93
Number of												
Elderly (> 65)	n.a.	n.a.	0.09	0.10	0.09	0.08	n.a.	n.a.	0.10	n.a.	n.a.	0.11
Men (15–65)	n.a.	n.a.	1.43	1.48	1.49	1.53	n.a.	n.a.	1.42	n.a.	n.a.	1.29
Women (15–65)	n.a.	n.a.	1.63	1.76	1.74	1.73	n.a.	n.a.	1.79	n.a.	n.a.	1.42
Youngsters (6–14)	n.a.	n.a.	1.58	1.55	1.40	1.37	n.a.	n.a.	1.59	n.a.	n.a.	1.88
Children (0–5)	n.a.	n.a.	0.96	0.95	0.98	0.71	n.a.	n.a.	1.04	n.a.	n.a.	1.29
All HH members	n.a.	n.a.	5.70	5.84	5.70	5.42	n.a.	n.a.	5.94	n.a.	n.a.	5.99
Dependency of HH	n.a.	n.a.	56.33	57.18	58.74	61.94	n.a.	n.a.	56.45	n.a.	n.a.	48.37
Language (Spanish)	n.a.	n.a.	51.06	58.00	55.75	67.07	n.a.	n.a.	65.36	n.a.	n.a.	22.10
Gender (Female)	n.a.	n.a.	15.14	12.38	13.85	17.32	n.a.	n.a.	16.01	n.a.	n.a.	11.66
Age of HH Head												
≤ 24	n.a.	n.a.	4.63	3.73	4.51	4.47	n.a.	n.a.	6.74	n.a.	n.a.	3.92

continued on next page

Table B.2 continued

	LSMS Total			LSMS City			LSMS Town			LSMS Rural		
	1989	1994	1999	1989	1994	1999	1989	1994	1999	1989	1994	1999
25–34	n.a.	n.a.	21.99	26.32	25.57	21.17	n.a.	n.a.	22.05	n.a.	n.a.	23.10
35–44	n.a.	n.a.	32.28	33.37	32.60	33.85	n.a.	n.a.	29.87	n.a.	n.a.	31.16
45–54	n.a.	n.a.	26.92	20.73	22.89	26.42	n.a.	n.a.	24.48	n.a.	n.a.	28.71
55–65	n.a.	n.a.	9.48	11.52	10.31	9.91	n.a.	n.a.	11.08	n.a.	n.a.	8.14
> 65	n.a.	n.a.	4.70	4.33	4.12	4.17	n.a.	n.a.	5.78	n.a.	n.a.	4.97
Tangible Assets												
Water Source												
Inhouse Access	n.a.	n.a.	66.05	71.75	79.05	93.39	n.a.	n.a.	77.72	n.a.	n.a.	22.28
Open Water Source	n.a.	n.a.	27.12	7.62	4.93	2.02	n.a.	n.a.	18.07	n.a.	n.a.	66.55
Other Water Source	n.a.	n.a.	6.83	20.63	16.02	4.60	n.a.	n.a.	4.21	n.a.	n.a.	11.17
Toilet Facility												
No Toilet	n.a.	n.a.	31.50	32.79	25.34	11.38	n.a.	n.a.	17.55	n.a.	n.a.	66.11
Shared Toilet	n.a.	n.a.	16.66	67.21	26.24	26.99	n.a.	n.a.	12.61	n.a.	n.a.	3.94
Private Toilet	n.a.	n.a.	51.84	n.a.	48.42	61.63	n.a.	n.a.	69.84	n.a.	n.a.	29.95
House	n.a.	n.a.	67.37	58.94	56.02	56.91	n.a.	n.a.	63.35	n.a.	n.a.	83.92
Electricity	n.a.	n.a.	72.94	n.a.	95.76	98.65	n.a.	n.a.	96.54	n.a.	n.a.	26.12
Telephone	n.a.	n.a.	25.30	n.a.	20.34	43.02	n.a.	n.a.	23.91	n.a.	n.a.	0.93
Radio	n.a.	n.a.	79.57	n.a.	89.19	86.91	n.a.	n.a.	78.97	n.a.	n.a.	69.51
Television	n.a.	n.a.	66.15	n.a.	91.59	94.86	n.a.	n.a.	84.42	n.a.	n.a.	17.47
Fridge	n.a.	n.a.	35.24	n.a.	46.36	52.79	n.a.	n.a.	45.33	n.a.	n.a.	5.97
Car	n.a.	n.a.	11.48	18.82	n.a.	18.24	n.a.	n.a.	9.13	n.a.	n.a.	3.00
Family Land	n.a.	n.a.	n.a.	n.a.	n.a.	n.a.	n.a.	n.a.	n.a.	n.a.	n.a.	n.a.
Main Floor Material												
Earth	n.a.	n.a.	34.82	n.a.	11.41	7.59	n.a.	n.a.	24.76	n.a.	n.a.	77.69
Cement	n.a.	n.a.	37.67	n.a.	43.47	49.17	n.a.	n.a.	51.86	n.a.	n.a.	15.10
Brick	n.a.	n.a.	5.95	n.a.	10.79	6.80	n.a.	n.a.	10.81	n.a.	n.a.	2.56
Other Floor	n.a.	n.a.	21.57	n.a.	34.33	36.44	n.a.	n.a.	12.57	n.a.	n.a.	4.64

continued on next page

Table B.2 continued

	LSMS Total			LSMS City			LSMS Town			LSMS Rural		
	1989	1994	1999	1989	1994	1999	1989	1994	1999	1989	1994	1999
Cooking Material	n.a.	n.a.	66.56	n.a.	96.98	97.40	n.a.	n.a.	81.28	n.a.	n.a.	16.48
# Sleeping Rooms												
0–1	n.a.	n.a.	58.35	n.a.	43.28	47.18	n.a.	n.a.	57.19	n.a.	n.a.	74.61
2–3	n.a.	n.a.	35.58	n.a.	46.01	42.55	n.a.	n.a.	38.18	n.a.	n.a.	24.58
≥ 4	n.a.	n.a.	6.07	n.a.	10.71	10.27	n.a.	n.a.	4.63	n.a.	n.a.	0.81
Schooling of Adults												
Men (Partners)												
No Schooling / DK	n.a.	n.a.	5.18	2.72	1.27	0.67	n.a.	n.a.	3.75	n.a.	n.a.	11.96
Incomplete Basic	n.a.	n.a.	25.82	15.66	13.08	12.54	n.a.	n.a.	24.46	n.a.	n.a.	44.53
Complete Basic	n.a.	n.a.	11.41	11.86	10.88	8.98	n.a.	n.a.	10.15	n.a.	n.a.	15.27
Lower Secondary	n.a.	n.a.	15.33	16.60	17.55	14.39	n.a.	n.a.	15.07	n.a.	n.a.	16.74
Higher Secondary	n.a.	n.a.	28.36	32.28	35.75	39.28	n.a.	n.a.	36.01	n.a.	n.a.	10.14
Tertiary Education	n.a.	n.a.	13.90	20.89	21.47	24.14	n.a.	n.a.	10.56	n.a.	n.a.	1.36
Women (15–49)												
No Schooling / DK	n.a.	n.a.	12.52	6.35	4.52	3.82	n.a.	n.a.	4.89	n.a.	n.a.	28.22
Incomplete Basic	n.a.	n.a.	23.08	18.79	15.62	13.84	n.a.	n.a.	17.97	n.a.	n.a.	38.41
Complete Basic	n.a.	n.a.	9.43	9.36	10.24	7.62	n.a.	n.a.	9.27	n.a.	n.a.	12.04
Lower Secondary	n.a.	n.a.	14.65	14.37	15.37	15.42	n.a.	n.a.	19.27	n.a.	n.a.	11.50
Higher Secondary	n.a.	n.a.	28.52	35.79	39.89	38.57	n.a.	n.a.	39.70	n.a.	n.a.	9.35
Tertiary Education	n.a.	n.a.	11.80	15.34	14.36	20.74	n.a.	n.a.	8.90	n.a.	n.a.	0.49
Employment												
Men (Partners)												
High-skilled Admin.	n.a.	n.a.	7.54	10.50	12.12	11.90	n.a.	n.a.	6.45	n.a.	n.a.	2.04
Medium-skilled Admin.	n.a.	n.a.	8.89	8.48	11.46	13.39	n.a.	n.a.	8.76	n.a.	n.a.	2.83
Skilled Manual	n.a.	n.a.	27.49	34.32	33.33	34.94	n.a.	n.a.	37.93	n.a.	n.a.	12.84
Unskilled Manual	n.a.	n.a.	5.10	2.71	7.95	5.99	n.a.	n.a.	5.62	n.a.	n.a.	3.64
Agric.: Employed	n.a.	n.a.	5.15	1.10	0.85	1.17	n.a.	n.a.	6.02	n.a.	n.a.	10.21

continued on next page

Table B.2 continued

	LSMS Total			LSMS City			LSMS Town			LSMS Rural		
	1989	1994	1999	1989	1994	1999	1989	1994	1999	1989	1994	1999
Agric.: Self	n.a.	n.a.	23.97	2.44	0.53	0.11	n.a.	n.a.	4.48	n.a.	n.a.	64.92
Sales / Services	n.a.	n.a.	17.49	24.38	26.91	26.26	n.a.	n.a.	25.53	n.a.	n.a.	2.07
Never Worked / DK	n.a.	n.a.	4.37	16.06	6.84	6.25	n.a.	n.a.	5.21	n.a.	n.a.	1.45
Women (15–49)												
High-skilled Admin.	n.a.	n.a.	3.39	1.83	2.31	5.15	n.a.	n.a.	3.55	n.a.	n.a.	0.83
Medium-skilled Admin.	n.a.	n.a.	5.13	8.77	9.12	7.93	n.a.	n.a.	4.30	n.a.	n.a.	1.55
Skilled Manual	n.a.	n.a.	6.92	5.08	7.40	7.22	n.a.	n.a.	11.64	n.a.	n.a.	4.36
Unskilled Manual	n.a.	n.a.	6.75	0.84	9.34	9.72	n.a.	n.a.	8.27	n.a.	n.a.	1.87
Agric.: Employed	n.a.	n.a.	3.42	0.23	0.30	0.34	n.a.	n.a.	0.57	n.a.	n.a.	9.04
Agric.: Own	n.a.	n.a.	18.53	0.36	0.13	0.33	n.a.	n.a.	2.65	n.a.	n.a.	51.31
Sales / Services	n.a.	n.a.	15.48	26.89	23.45	22.30	n.a.	n.a.	17.72	n.a.	n.a.	4.87
Never Worked / DK	n.a.	n.a.	40.39	55.99	47.95	47.00	n.a.	n.a.	51.29	n.a.	n.a.	26.17
Health												
Social Security	n.a.	n.a.	23.70	34.01	n.a.	34.05	n.a.	n.a.	28.02	n.a.	n.a.	7.19
Birth in Last 12 Months	n.a.	n.a.	15.72	15.63	15.25	10.40	n.a.	n.a.	16.22	n.a.	n.a.	23.00
Attended by Doctor	n.a.	n.a.	55.47	65.00	72.26	83.65	n.a.	n.a.	82.06	n.a.	n.a.	29.00
Delivered in Hospital	n.a.	n.a.	40.97	52.53	58.36	61.35	n.a.	n.a.	55.18	n.a.	n.a.	23.52
Child under 4 Years	n.a.	n.a.	46.56	48.06	46.03	37.28	n.a.	n.a.	49.21	n.a.	n.a.	58.47
First Polio Vacc.	n.a.	n.a.	89.22	88.60	n.a.	89.30	n.a.	n.a.	93.29	n.a.	n.a.	87.60
Triple DPT Vacc.	n.a.	n.a.	71.13	33.69	n.a.	75.19	n.a.	n.a.	67.85	n.a.	n.a.	68.74
Had Diarrhea	n.a.	n.a.	31.49	16.25	8.28	22.45	n.a.	n.a.	35.09	n.a.	n.a.	38.24
Had Cough/Fever	n.a.	n.a.	48.73	16.46	16.32	45.09	n.a.	n.a.	43.55	n.a.	n.a.	53.96

Notes: DK: Don't know or no answer. Dependency of HH: Ratio of household members aged between 15 and 65 to all household members. Language spoken in the household (Spanish). Gender of household head (Female). Inhouse access: To publicly provided water supply. Family Land: One member works in agriculture on family-owned land. Cooking Material: High-quality (gas, kerosene, and electricity). Schooling and employment of men (partners) refers to only married household members in the LSMS; Admin.: white collar workers. Agric.: Agriculture. Social Security: One or more members covered by social security. Vacc.: Vaccinations.
Source: Own calculations based on ECH and EIH.

Table B.3: Sample Means from the Bolivian DHS, 1989, 1994, 1998

	DHS Total			DHS City			DHS Town			DHS Rural		
	1989	1994	1998	1989	1994	1998	1989	1994	1998	1989	1994	1998
Demographics												
Place of Residence												
City	47.55	47.96	53.46	100	100	100	0	0	0	0	0	0
Town	11.24	12.06	14.46	0	0	0	100	100	100	0	0	0
Rural	41.21	39.98	32.08	0	0	0	0	0	0	100	100	100
Department												
Chuquisaca	5.68	5.96	6.61	3.25	4.16	5.20	3.25	1.34	1.97	9.15	9.50	11.05
La Paz	36.05	31.94	30.60	42.47	40.72	38.77	21.16	13.15	11.77	32.70	27.07	25.49
Cochabamba	17.20	17.55	17.31	16.45	14.30	14.14	11.77	11.89	23.49	19.55	23.15	19.81
Oruro	6.28	6.20	4.97	6.93	7.00	6.26	5.20	7.68	4.26	5.82	4.80	3.15
Potosi	9.79	9.72	9.01	3.87	4.50	4.35	18.88	10.37	10.93	14.13	15.80	15.92
Tarija	3.90	4.50	5.31	2.93	3.15	4.32	8.04	10.07	9.30	3.88	4.43	5.16
Santa Cruz	18.25	20.91	22.04	22.44	24.49	24.77	23.25	33.83	26.57	12.06	12.72	15.45
Beni and Pando	2.87	3.22	4.14	1.67	1.67	2.20	8.46	11.67	11.70	2.72	2.52	3.97
Number of												
Elderly (> 65)	0.10	0.09	0.11	0.11	0.08	0.10	0.11	0.11	0.14	0.09	0.10	0.11
Men (15–65)	1.30	1.21	1.25	1.38	1.24	1.31	1.25	1.26	1.24	1.21	1.16	1.15
Women (15–65)	1.53	1.48	1.53	1.64	1.56	1.65	1.52	1.52	1.52	1.39	1.38	1.34
Youngsters (6–14)	1.42	1.32	1.29	1.35	1.17	1.09	1.50	1.48	1.46	1.49	1.46	1.55
Children (0–5)	1.00	1.02	0.93	0.84	0.88	0.76	0.99	1.01	0.95	1.18	1.19	1.20
All HH members	5.35	5.12	5.10	5.32	4.93	4.91	5.37	5.38	5.31	5.36	5.29	5.35
Dependency of HH	56.30	56.54	58.23	59.41	60.11	63.22	55.48	55.34	55.86	52.94	52.63	50.96
Language (Spanish)	74.13	70.04	78.46	93.30	92.79	96.27	88.14	89.50	91.05	48.18	36.88	43.09
Gender (Female)	15.14	17.15	17.45	18.17	18.38	19.08	16.02	19.78	19.71	11.40	14.89	13.71
Age of HH Head												
≤ 24	6.04	8.62	7.37	5.75	8.95	7.81	5.82	8.11	6.34	6.45	8.38	7.10

continued on next page

Table B.3 continued

	DHS Total			DHS City			DHS Town			DHS Rural		
	1989	1994	1998	1989	1994	1998	1989	1994	1998	1989	1994	1998
25–34	26.82	28.91	26.36	27.33	29.84	25.86	24.55	28.17	26.33	26.84	28.02	27.21
35–44	30.17	28.01	30.52	29.93	27.67	30.13	31.98	30.16	30.70	29.97	27.76	31.10
45–54	19.92	20.04	20.41	19.40	20.04	21.23	20.56	19.60	19.69	20.34	20.18	19.35
55-65	10.67	9.65	9.63	10.68	9.47	9.67	10.61	8.55	10.01	10.67	10.21	9.40
≥ 66	6.38	4.77	5.71	6.90	4.03	5.29	6.48	5.41	6.94	5.74	5.46	5.84
Tangible Assets												
Water Source												
Inhouse Access	47.36	56.08	69.75	67.63	77.03	88.48	58.86	79.09	84.05	20.84	24.01	32.09
Open Water Source	29.39	29.63	19.31	6.72	4.93	1.76	12.73	11.94	8.49	60.09	64.60	53.44
Other Water Source	23.24	14.29	10.94	25.64	18.04	9.76	28.40	8.98	7.47	19.07	11.39	14.48
Toilet Facility												
No Toilet	49.72	40.19	32.25	26.51	26.32	16.27	40.46	26.29	22.60	79.02	61.02	63.22
Shared Toilet	50.28	35.83	19.41	73.49	30.03	28.04	59.54	53.57	21.37	20.98	37.43	4.15
Private Toilet		23.98	48.34	n.a.	43.65	55.69	n.a.	20.14	56.02	n.a.	1.55	32.63
House	63.83	67.06	64.98	53.02	52.54	54.55	59.58	60.65	60.97	77.46	86.43	84.18
Electricity	n.a.	67.61	75.73	n.a.	95.00	98.41	n.a.	86.17	90.43	n.a.	29.16	31.31
Telephone	n.a.	10.59	24.96	n.a.	20.20	40.87	n.a.	6.66	19.89	n.a.	0.25	0.74
Radio	n.a.	85.17	88.08	n.a.	94.74	95.64	n.a.	85.74	88.93	n.a.	73.53	75.11
Television	n.a.	58.19	68.39	n.a.	88.32	93.46	n.a.	72.15	81.03	n.a.	17.83	20.91
Fridge	n.a.	29.69	37.67	n.a.	45.56	53.36	n.a.	35.91	43.32	n.a.	8.78	8.96
Car	12.07	n.a.	n.a.	19.60	n.a.	n.a.	10.80	n.a.	n.a.	3.73	n.a.	n.a.
Family Land	n.a.	28.46	21.27	n.a.	0.95	0.55	n.a.	9.77	6.63	n.a.	67.10	62.40
Main Floor Material												
Earth	n.a.	37.63	28.84	n.a.	14.56	7.42	n.a.	26.30	19.89	n.a.	68.73	68.58
Cement	n.a.	32.64	37.57	n.a.	41.62	43.51	n.a.	39.76	51.01	n.a.	19.72	21.62
Brick	n.a.	11.72	7.58	n.a.	15.98	9.36	n.a.	21.61	11.08	n.a.	3.62	3.04
Other Floor	n.a.	18.01	26.01	n.a.	27.84	39.71	n.a.	12.33	18.02	n.a.	7.93	6.76

continued on next page

Table B.3 continued

	DHS Total			DHS City			DHS Town			DHS Rural		
	1989	1994	1998	1989	1994	1998	1989	1994	1998	1989	1994	1998
Cooking Material	n.a.	64.10	71.77	n.a.	96.22	98.29	n.a.	75.18	83.92	n.a.	22.22	22.09
# Sleeping Rooms												
0–1	n.a.	53.15	59.25	n.a.	47.39	50.19	n.a.	49.94	58.85	n.a.	61.02	74.55
2–3	n.a.	41.13	34.60	n.a.	44.48	40.11	n.a.	42.87	36.57	n.a.	36.58	24.52
≥ 4	n.a.	5.73	6.16	n.a.	8.13	9.70	n.a.	7.19	4.58	n.a.	2.40	0.97
Schooling of Adults												
Men (Partners)												
No Schooling / DK	14.21	5.48	4.24	9.55	2.27	1.92	11.98	4.23	2.69	19.99	9.74	8.64
Incomplete Basic	23.99	22.84	24.18	11.33	11.10	13.69	18.90	20.12	22.28	39.39	37.79	41.84
Complete Basic	17.67	14.12	11.29	14.68	10.67	7.25	18.89	15.23	11.58	20.62	17.91	17.64
Lower Secondary	13.34	16.16	13.71	16.22	14.66	14.12	13.97	15.58	16.40	9.99	18.15	11.85
Higher Secondary	17.77	28.74	28.03	25.58	39.58	34.81	27.08	34.97	30.67	6.58	13.72	16.01
Tertiary Education	13.02	12.67	18.55	22.64	21.72	28.21	9.18	9.87	16.39	3.45	2.69	4.02
Women (15–49)												
No Schooling / DK	18.69	13.43	9.32	8.03	4.65	3.13	12.22	9.94	4.94	32.74	25.01	21.62
Incomplete Basic	29.75	27.02	23.33	21.17	18.09	14.70	26.22	22.95	18.15	40.60	38.97	40.05
Complete Basic	13.87	12.49	10.10	13.54	9.63	7.02	15.60	12.11	9.61	13.77	16.04	15.46
Lower Secondary	14.12	13.74	13.29	18.63	14.65	12.72	19.11	17.35	16.98	7.57	11.55	12.58
Higher Secondary	16.38	25.36	30.09	25.94	38.84	40.82	20.66	31.54	38.33	4.19	7.33	8.50
Tertiary Education	7.19	7.96	13.86	12.68	14.14	21.61	6.19	6.11	11.98	1.12	1.10	1.80
Employment												
Men (Partners)												
High-skilled Admin.	9.56	6.70	8.68	16.82	12.18	13.89	8.31	4.96	7.19	1.89	0.66	0.98
Medium-skilled Admin.	8.45	9.11	8.63	12.54	13.41	11.16	10.95	12.09	9.45	3.24	2.98	4.20
Skilled Manual	25.04	25.79	24.91	32.95	35.13	31.12	33.97	28.75	27.82	13.86	13.65	13.67
Unskilled Manual	5.06	4.29	4.16	6.91	5.67	5.75	6.35	4.59	4.88	2.64	2.54	1.27
Agric.: Employed	4.37	6.01	4.33	0.48	0.98	0.77	4.10	8.95	6.91	8.77	11.14	8.91

continued on next page

Table B.3 continued

	DHS Total			DHS City			DHS Town			DHS Rural		
	1989	1994	1998	1989	1994	1998	1989	1994	1998	1989	1994	1998
Agric.: Self	27.55	25.12	22.26	2.15	0.76	0.99	9.92	9.62	8.32	60.47	59.31	62.58
Sales / Services	16.85	19.34	20.29	23.50	26.54	27.71	24.87	27.21	26.11	7.32	8.19	5.81
Never Worked / DK	3.11	3.64	6.73	4.65	5.33	8.61	1.52	3.83	9.31	1.83	1.53	2.59
Women (15–49)												
High-skilled Admin.	1.43	1.42	3.07	2.58	2.39	4.93	0.67	1.34	2.40	0.31	0.30	0.28
Medium-skilled Admin.	5.39	7.14	8.17	8.38	11.30	11.29	8.29	8.90	9.37	1.16	1.61	2.41
Skilled Manual	3.58	6.53	6.99	3.93	8.25	8.18	3.43	7.10	7.53	3.22	4.30	4.76
Unskilled Manual	0.42	9.47	7.95	0.23	14.18	11.10	1.94	11.69	8.19	0.23	3.15	2.60
Agric.: Employed	0.50	6.32	0.92	0.13	0.42	0.01	0.25	1.54	0.91	1.01	14.85	2.43
Agric.: Own	0.80	15.01	12.18	0.04	0.13	0.10	0.10	2.26	1.40	1.86	36.70	37.15
Sales / Services	13.59	17.21	19.09	18.75	21.96	25.06	18.81	24.69	24.77	6.22	9.26	6.59
Never Worked / DK	74.28	36.89	41.64	65.97	41.37	39.33	66.52	42.48	45.42	85.99	29.83	43.80
Health												
Social Security	21.44	n.a.	21.31	29.19	n.a.	31.11	30.19	n.a.	23.18	10.10	n.a.	4.12
Birth in Last 12 Months	19.83	18.64	17.08	16.30	15.57	14.15	20.22	18.61	15.58	23.80	22.34	22.63
Attended by Doctor	40.29	42.06	56.73	63.31	63.20	76.54	49.36	57.50	72.66	20.00	20.50	31.24
Delivered in Hospital	36.86	31.17	42.62	56.56	46.37	51.45	50.79	40.73	60.59	17.98	16.03	27.79
Child under 4 Years	51.02	50.08	47.31	43.90	44.75	41.27	50.64	49.26	45.08	59.34	56.73	58.39
First Polio Vacc.	70.64	56.13	76.16	76.67	62.39	79.23	72.35	56.31	76.86	65.07	50.13	72.31
Triple DPT Vacc.	30.22	26.32	44.09	39.50	32.54	48.46	30.65	27.49	46.58	22.19	20.13	38.07
Had Diarrhea	29.26	21.45	20.84	28.38	21.34	19.02	30.98	24.08	19.92	29.61	20.84	23.29
Had Cough/Fever	40.93	30.35	48.17	37.31	31.80	47.13	39.71	31.85	46.78	44.29	28.56	49.89

Notes: For the explanation of the variables, see Appendix Table B.2.
Source: Own calculations based on DHS.

Table B.4: Extreme Poverty Indices Based on Observed, Predicted, and Simulated Incomes, 1989, 1994, 1998/9

	1989				1994				1998/9			
	LSMS			DHS	LSMS			DHS	LSMS			DHS
	All HH	Sample	Predicted	Simulated	All HH	Sample	Predicted	Simulated	All HH	Sample	Predicted	Simulated
Total Bolivia												
P0	n.a.	n.a.	n.a.	54.92	n.a.	n.a.	n.a.	51.99	37.19	38.29	40.53	35.43
				(0.62)				(0.40)			(1.01)	(0.42)
P1	n.a.	n.a.	n.a.	26.58	n.a.	n.a.	n.a.	30.73	15.13	15.64	16.79	14.13
				(0.34)				(0.21)			(0.49)	(0.19)
P2	n.a.	n.a.	n.a.	16.12	n.a.	n.a.	n.a.	22.44	8.24	8.59	9.08	7.48
				(0.28)				(0.16)			(0.33)	(0.12)
City												
P0	38.20	39.11	39.13	38.79	28.04	28.90	29.58	28.18	22.50	24.10	25.30	23.03
			(0.77)	(0.89)			(0.58)	(0.67)			(1.51)	(0.61)
P1	14.58	14.95	15.95	15.87	9.47	9.74	10.24	9.57	7.39	7.86	9.03	8.19
			(0.39)	(0.42)			(0.25)	(0.30)			(0.61)	(0.26)
P2	7.50	7.71	8.61	8.62	4.57	4.67	4.89	4.50	3.57	3.79	4.43	4.03
			(0.27)	(0.29)			(0.15)	(0.18)			(0.37)	(0.16)
Town												
P0	n.a.	n.a.	n.a.	61.02	n.a.	n.a.	n.a.	50.97	32.45	34.19	38.88	38.17
				(1.44)				(1.14)			(2.52)	(1.08)
P1	n.a.	n.a.	n.a.	32.27	n.a.	n.a.	n.a.	26.36	13.09	13.81	16.28	16.64
				(0.88)				(0.60)			(1.26)	(0.55)
P2	n.a.	n.a.	n.a.	20.99	n.a.	n.a.	n.a.	17.34	7.41	7.85	9.11	9.57
				(0.71)				(0.46)			(0.88)	(0.38)
Rural Areas												
P0	n.a.	n.a.	n.a.	71.87	n.a.	n.a.	n.a.	80.85	57.93	59.98	62.64	54.88
				(0.92)				(0.47)			(1.68)	(0.70)
P1	n.a.	n.a.	n.a.	37.39	n.a.	n.a.	n.a.	57.43	25.88	27.37	27.90	22.92
				(0.57)				(0.31)			(0.93)	(0.37)
P2	n.a.	n.a.	n.a.	23.45	n.a.	n.a.	n.a.	45.50	14.55	15.65	15.58	12.29
				(0.48)				(0.30)			(0.68)	(0.26)

Notes: Poverty indices are calculated using income data for cities and towns, expenditure data for rural areas, and mixed income-expenditure data for total Bolivia. Standard deviations in brackets.
Source: Own calculations based on ECH, EIH, and DHS.

Table B.5: Inequality Indices Based on Observed, Predicted, and Simulated Incomes, 1989, 1994, 1998/9

	1989				1994				1998/9			
	LSMS			DHS	LSMS			DHS	LSMS			DHS
	All HH	Sample	Predicted	Simulated	All HH	Sample	Predicted	Simulated	All HH	Sample	Predicted	Simulated
						Total Bolivia						
Gini	n.a.	n.a.	n.a.	0.550	n.a.	n.a.	n.a.	0.583	0.528	0.524	0.537	0.531
				(0.006)				(0.004)			(0.007)	(0.004)
A(0.5)	n.a.	n.a.	n.a.	0.246	n.a.	n.a.	n.a.	0.291	0.229	0.225	0.234	0.229
				(0.006)				(0.004)			(0.007)	(0.004)
A(1.0)	n.a.	n.a.	n.a.	0.427	n.a.	n.a.	n.a.	0.541	0.401	0.397	0.410	0.404
				(0.007)				(0.004)			(0.009)	(0.005)
A(2.0)	n.a.	n.a.	n.a.	0.653	n.a.	n.a.	n.a.	0.836	0.634	0.632	0.632	0.629
				(0.007)				(0.003)			(0.010)	(0.005)
						City						
Gini	0.502	0.503	0.492	0.496	0.493	0.482	0.470	0.454	0.483	0.480	0.490	0.488
			(0.006)	(0.009)			(0.005)	(0.006)			(0.011)	(0.006)
A(0.5)	0.208	0.209	0.196	0.199	0.202	0.191	0.178	0.166	0.192	0.187	0.194	0.193
			(0.006)	(0.007)			(0.004)	(0.005)			(0.009)	(0.005)
A(1.0)	0.358	0.358	0.350	0.355	0.341	0.327	0.317	0.299	0.341	0.336	0.350	0.348
			(0.008)	(0.010)			(0.006)	(0.007)			(0.013)	(0.007)
A(2.0)	0.559	0.558	0.566	0.573	0.537	0.522	0.513	0.493	0.565	0.561	0.567	0.570
			(0.009)	(0.011)			(0.006)	(0.008)			(0.015)	(0.008)
						Town						
Gini	n.a.	n.a.	n.a.	0.543	n.a.	n.a.	n.a.	0.531	0.451	0.454	0.481	0.499
				(0.016)				(0.013)			(0.020)	(0.011)
A(0.5)	n.a.	n.a.	n.a.	0.241	n.a.	n.a.	n.a.	0.234	0.168	0.170	0.189	0.203
				(0.016)				(0.012)			(0.016)	(0.009)
A(1.0)	n.a.	n.a.	n.a.	0.423	n.a.	n.a.	n.a.	0.432	0.315	0.318	0.345	0.370
				(0.019)				(0.014)			(0.024)	(0.013)
A(2.0)	n.a.	n.a.	n.a.	0.661	n.a.	n.a.	n.a.	0.736	0.584	0.587	0.579	0.614
				(0.018)				(0.014)			(0.029)	(0.013)

continued on next page

Table B.5 continued

	1989				1994				1998/9			
	LSMS			DHS	LSMS			DHS	LSMS			DHS
	All HH	Sample	Predicted	Simulated	All HH	Sample	Predicted	Simulated	All HH	Sample	Predicted	Simulated
							Rural Areas					
Gini	n.a.	n.a.	n.a.	0.484	n.a.	n.a.	n.a.	0.632	0.436	0.423	0.443	0.443
				(0.009)				(0.007)			(0.012)	(0.006)
A(0.5)	n.a.	n.a.	n.a.	0.191	n.a.	n.a.	n.a.	0.327	0.155	0.145	0.158	0.158
				(0.008)				(0.008)			(0.009)	(0.005)
A(1.0)	n.a.	n.a.	n.a.	0.334	n.a.	n.a.	n.a.	0.548	0.281	0.267	0.282	0.284
				(0.011)				(0.008)			(0.013)	(0.007)
A(2.0)	n.a.	n.a.	n.a.	0.529	n.a.	n.a.	n.a.	0.765	0.471	0.458	0.459	0.465
				(0.011)				(0.006)			(0.016)	(0.008)

Notes: Inequality indices are calculated using income data for the cities and towns, expenditure data for rural areas, and mixed income-expenditure data for total Bolivia. Standard deviations in brackets.
Source: Own calculations based on ECH, EIH, and DHS.

Table B.6: Extreme Poverty: Mobility Assumptions, 1989 and 1994

	1989					1994				
	Convergence		Divergence		No mobility	Convergence		Divergence		No mobility
	ϕ=1.1	ϕ=1.5	ϕ=0.9	ϕ=0.5	ϕ=1.0	ϕ=1.1	ϕ=1.5	ϕ=0.9	ϕ=0.5	ϕ=1.0
	Total Bolivia									
P0	75.35	75.63	75.08	73.98	76.10	72.24	72.40	72.07	71.28	72.44
	(0.47)	(0.47)	(0.47)	(0.49)	(0.53)	(0.43)	(0.42)	(0.43)	(0.45)	(0.42)
P1	43.68	45.75	42.49	39.81	44.45	46.22	48.37	44.75	40.57	45.28
	(0.33)	(0.32)	(0.34)	(0.35)	(0.35)	(0.24)	(0.24)	(0.25)	(0.26)	(0.22)
P2	29.80	32.39	28.42	25.60	30.48	35.25	38.41	33.18	27.75	33.95
	(0.29)	(0.29)	(0.30)	(0.30)	(0.31)	(0.19)	(0.19)	(0.20)	(0.21)	(0.19)
	Town									
P0	79.74	80.44	79.17	77.17	80.21	73.44	73.60	73.20	71.91	73.42
	(1.24)	(1.19)	(1.32)	(1.40)	(1.26)	(1.28)	(1.18)	(1.35)	(1.42)	(1.16)
P1	49.72	53.12	47.81	43.53	49.66	44.27	47.34	42.47	38.19	43.40
	(0.92)	(0.86)	(0.95)	(0.99)	(0.87)	(0.79)	(0.75)	(0.81)	(0.83)	(0.64)
P2	35.85	40.02	33.63	29.06	35.58	31.78	35.71	29.58	24.69	30.66
	(0.82)	(0.79)	(0.83)	(0.84)	(0.79)	(0.63)	(0.61)	(0.63)	(0.64)	(0.55)
	Rural Areas									
P0	86.49	86.96	85.97	83.86	87.96	90.34	90.68	90.00	88.40	90.23
	(0.62)	(0.57)	(0.65)	(0.79)	(0.70)	(0.44)	(0.39)	(0.48)	(0.54)	(0.43)
P1	54.90	59.01	52.54	47.22	56.35	71.35	75.82	68.21	59.06	69.86
	(0.51)	(0.46)	(0.53)	(0.58)	(0.53)	(0.26)	(0.23)	(0.28)	(0.34)	(0.28)
P2	39.31	44.45	36.57	30.96	40.54	60.82	67.53	56.30	44.18	58.66
	(0.51)	(0.48)	(0.52)	(0.52)	(0.50)	(0.25)	(0.22)	(0.27)	(0.31)	(0.28)

Notes: See Chapter 1.4 for explanation.
Source: Own calculations based on ECH, EIH, and DHS.

Table B.7: Inequality: Mobility Assumptions, 1989 and 1994

	1989					1994				
	Convergence		Divergence		No mobility	Convergence		Divergence		No mobility
	ϕ=1.1	ϕ=1.5	ϕ=0.9	ϕ=0.5	ϕ=1.0	ϕ=1.1	ϕ=1.5	ϕ=0.9	ϕ=0.5	ϕ=1.0
					Total Bolivia					
Gini	0.546	0.568	0.535	0.514	0.550	0.602	0.626	0.587	0.550	0.583
	(0.006)	(0.006)	(0.006)	(0.006)	(0.006)	(0.004)	(0.004)	(0.004)	(0.004)	(0.004)
A(0.5)	0.242	0.264	0.232	0.214	0.246	0.311	0.348	0.291	0.248	0.291
	(0.006)	(0.006)	(0.005)	(0.005)	(0.006)	(0.004)	(0.004)	(0.004)	(0.004)	(0.004)
A(1.0)	0.423	0.462	0.405	0.373	0.427	0.574	0.652	0.531	0.442	0.541
	(0.007)	(0.007)	(0.007)	(0.007)	(0.007)	(0.004)	(0.004)	(0.004)	(0.005)	(0.004)
A(2.0)	0.651	0.707	0.625	0.579	0.653	0.864	0.933	0.815	0.692	0.836
	(0.006)	(0.006)	(0.007)	(0.007)	(0.007)	(0.002)	(0.001)	(0.003)	(0.004)	(0.003)
					Town					
Gini	0.549	0.594	0.529	0.498	0.543	0.545	0.601	0.518	0.468	0.499
	(0.015)	(0.016)	(0.015)	(0.015)	(0.016)	(0.013)	(0.014)	(0.012)	(0.011)	(0.011)
A(0.5)	0.246	0.291	0.228	0.201	0.241	0.247	0.306	0.221	0.178	0.203
	(0.015)	(0.017)	(0.014)	(0.013)	(0.016)	(0.013)	(0.016)	(0.011)	(0.009)	(0.009)
A(1.0)	0.432	0.500	0.403	0.358	0.423	0.456	0.553	0.409	0.328	0.370
	(0.018)	(0.019)	(0.018)	(0.017)	(0.019)	(0.014)	(0.015)	(0.014)	(0.013)	(0.013)
A(2.0)	0.674	0.753	0.636	0.575	0.661	0.771	0.887	0.700	0.561	0.614
	(0.017)	(0.015)	(0.018)	(0.019)	(0.018)	(0.015)	(0.010)	(0.016)	(0.016)	(0.013)
					Rural Areas					
Gini	0.499	0.556	0.474	0.433	0.484	0.657	0.742	0.626	0.500	0.443
	(0.010)	(0.010)	(0.010)	(0.009)	(0.009)	(0.006)	(0.006)	(0.004)	(0.006)	(0.006)
A(0.5)	0.203	0.253	0.183	0.153	0.191	0.356	0.467	0.348	0.201	0.158
	(0.009)	(0.011)	(0.009)	(0.007)	(0.008)	(0.008)	(0.009)	(0.004)	(0.006)	(0.005)
A(1.0)	0.351	0.424	0.321	0.274	0.334	0.587	0.726	0.652	0.357	0.284
	(0.012)	(0.013)	(0.011)	(0.010)	(0.011)	(0.007)	(0.007)	(0.004)	(0.008)	(0.007)
A(2.0)	0.547	0.627	0.510	0.452	0.529	0.799	0.901	0.933	0.564	0.465
	(0.012)	(0.011)	(0.012)	(0.011)	(0.011)	(0.005)	(0.003)	(0.001)	(0.008)	(0.008)

Notes: See Chapter 1.4 for explanation.
Source: Own calculations based on ECH, EIH, and DHS.

Table B.8: Asset Endowment Among Poor and Non-Poor, 1994 and 1998

	1994			1998		
	Ext. Poor	Mod. Poor	Non-Poor	Ext. Poor	Mod. Poor	Non-Poor
Tangible Assets						
Telephone	0.06	0.30	37.81	0.31	1.26	60.62
Radio	73.15	79.73	99.58	72.89	81.33	98.25
Television	21.05	42.51	99.67	19.57	47.89	99.23
Fridge	4.08	10.82	79.60	3.92	9.75	79.67
Family Land	54.61	38.92	0.80	54.76	35.04	0.55
Electricity	36.53	55.40	99.93	34.59	59.63	99.95
Public Water	22.72	40.40	97.56	29.18	50.84	98.20
Other (Non-open) Water Source	22.58	19.23	1.22	22.12	17.38	1.26
Cooking Material	31.80	50.77	99.36	27.74	53.37	99.44
Shared Toilet	35.42	38.09	29.84	7.96	18.73	20.43
Private Toilet	1.43	8.08	66.05	27.40	30.09	75.79
Cement Floor	20.07	30.16	39.19	20.81	35.66	40.44
Brick Floor	5.12	9.14	18.54	4.47	8.17	6.69
Other (Non-earth) Floor	6.92	9.36	40.89	6.17	9.16	51.35
2-3 Sleeping Rooms	32.18	35.21	56.79	20.16	22.31	53.09
$\geq$ 4 Sleeping Rooms	1.87	1.95	15.72	0.83	0.92	14.04
Human Capital						
% of Men with						
Complete Basic	16.84	15.64	1.94	15.97	13.96	2.74
Lower Secondary	16.75	17.10	4.36	10.90	13.80	8.07
Higher Secondary	12.78	19.32	37.08	13.44	19.50	29.62
Tertiary Education	1.28	2.25	32.92	1.82	2.90	34.65
% of Women with						
Complete Basic	17.13	15.91	3.45	16.41	14.65	3.27
Lower Secondary	12.94	15.63	8.72	14.11	16.06	9.13
Higher Secondary	6.47	14.31	54.60	6.90	17.11	49.63
Tertiary Education	0.27	1.22	25.77	0.79	2.40	31.10
Number of Observations	3382	4848	1792	3571	5439	3005

Notes: For the explanation of the variables, see Appendix Table B.2. The left-out categories are: open water source, no toilet, earth floor, 0–1 sleeping rooms, no or incomplete basic schooling. The category moderately poor includes the category extremely poor, so that the number of observations of each year is the sum of moderately poor and non-poor. Numbers are in percent.
Source: Own calculations based on DHS.

Appendix C

Figure C.1: Extreme Poverty, Total Bolivia, 1989–2002

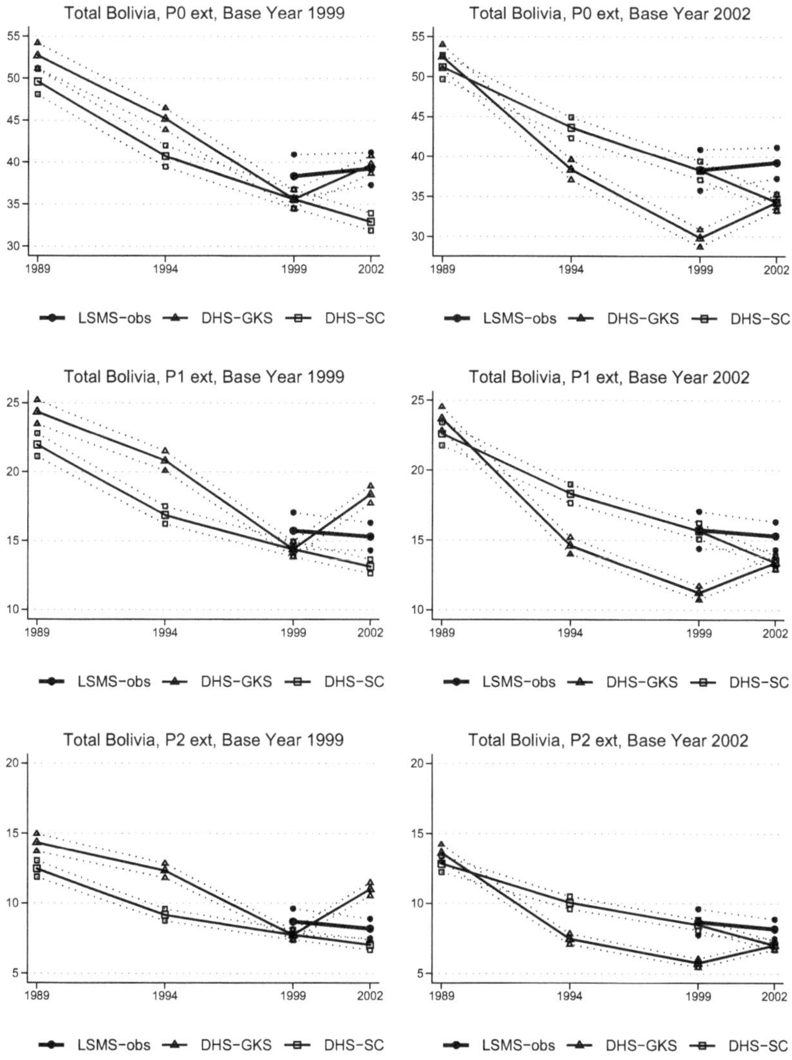

Notes: LSMS–obs: Data from LSMS using observed income; DHS–GKS: Data from DHS using GKS assumptions on dynamics; DHS–SC: Data from DHS using SC assumptions on dynamics. See notes to Figure 2.1 for details.
Source: Own calculations based on ECH, EIH, and DHS.

Figure C.2: Extreme Poverty, Cities, 1989–2002

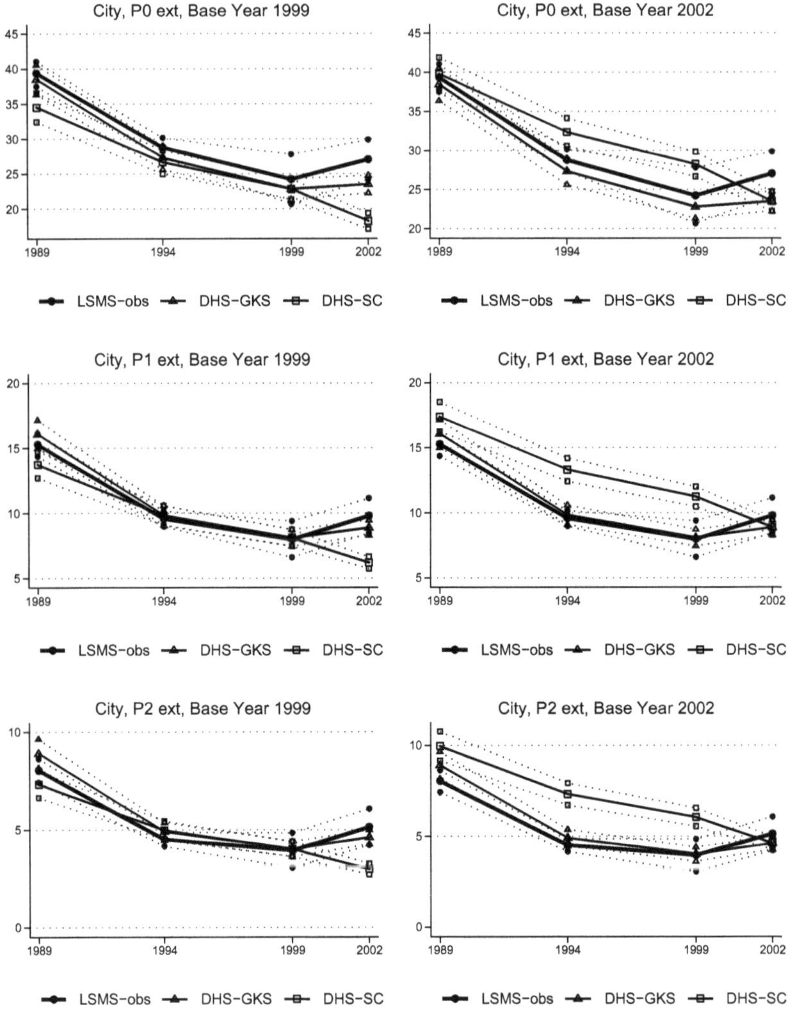

Notes: LSMS–obs: Data from LSMS using observed income; DHS–GKS: Data from DHS using GKS assumptions on dynamics; DHS–SC: Data from DHS using SC assumptions on dynamics. See notes to Figure 2.1 for details.
Source: Own calculations based on ECH, EIH, and DHS.

Figure C.3: Extreme Poverty, Towns, 1989–2002

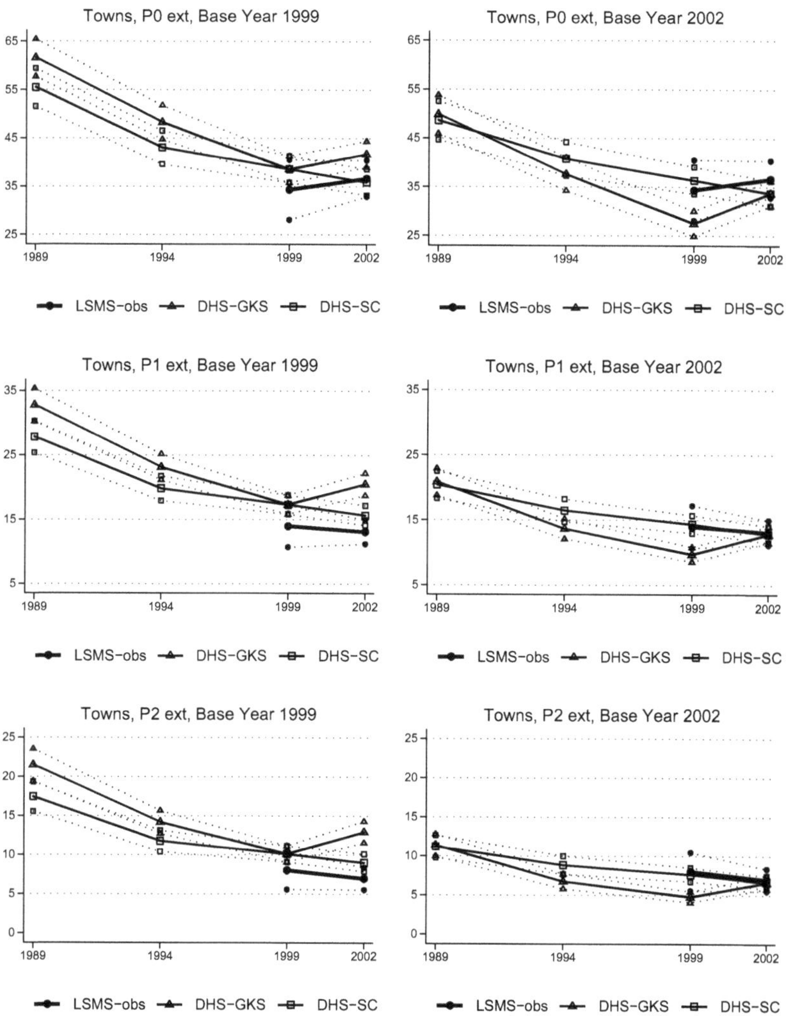

Notes: LSMS–obs: Data from LSMS using observed income; DHS–GKS: Data from DHS using GKS assumptions on dynamics; DHS–SC: Data from DHS using SC assumptions on dynamics. See notes to Figure 2.1 for details.
Source: Own calculations based on ECH, EIH, and DHS.

Figure C.4: Extreme Poverty, Rural Areas, 1989–2002

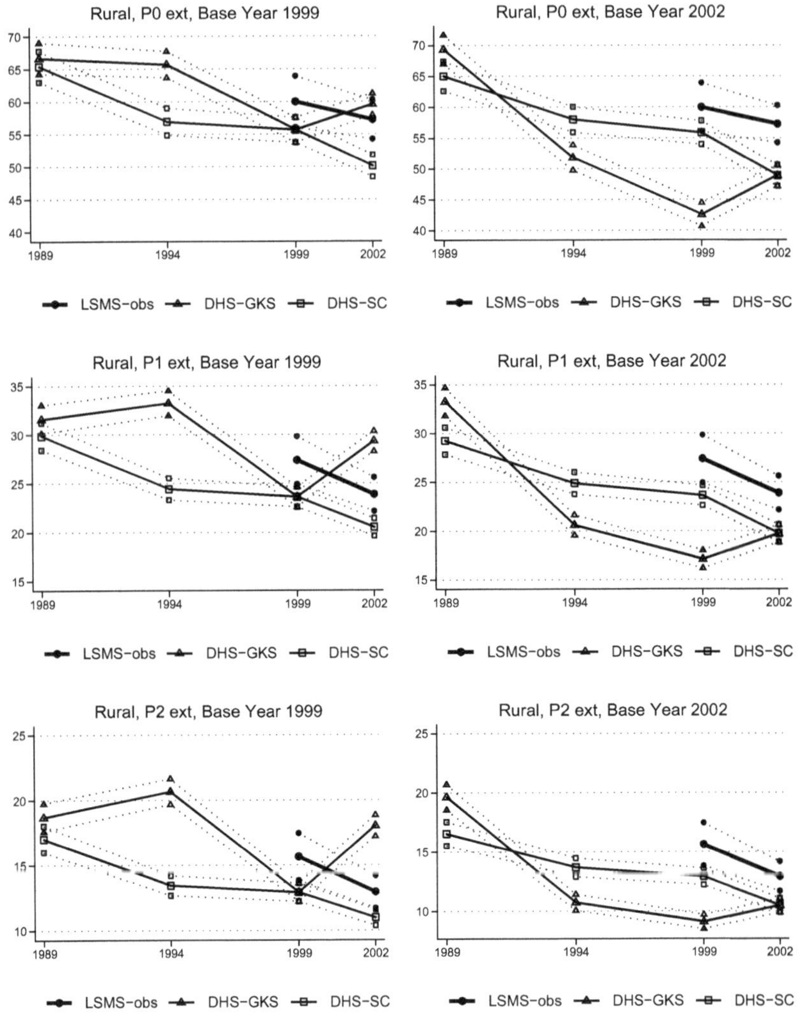

Notes: LSMS–obs: Data from LSMS using observed income; DHS–GKS: Data from DHS using GKS assumptions on dynamics; DHS–SC: Data from DHS using SC assumptions on dynamics. See notes to Figure 2.1 for details.
Source: Own calculations based on ECH, EIH, and DHS.

Table C.1: Regression Results, Log-Linear OLS, Common Model, 1989, 1994, 1999, 2002

	City								Town				Rural			
	1989		1994		1999		2002		1999		2002		1999		2002	
	β	P	β	P	β	P	β	P	β	P	β	P	β	P	β	P
La Paz	0.01	0.89	0.14	0.00	-0.02	0.88	0.00	0.98	0.11	0.81	0.23	0.17	0.25	0.00	0.23	0.00
Cochabamba	0.16	0.00	0.13	0.00	0.27	0.02	0.18	0.06	0.65	0.17	0.19	0.22	0.40	0.00	0.13	0.07
Oruro	-0.17	0.00	-0.18	0.00	-0.06	0.66	-0.22	0.05	-0.27	0.61	-0.06	0.75	0.27	0.08	0.18	0.04
Potosi	-0.25	0.00	-0.20	0.00	-0.02	0.89	-0.04	0.70	0.16	0.74	-0.02	0.92	0.06	0.57	-0.09	0.31
Tarija	-0.02	0.61	0.03	0.52	0.53	0.00	0.18	0.08	0.47	0.33	0.48	0.00	0.63	0.00	0.53	0.00
Santa Cruz	0.42	0.00	0.43	0.00	0.70	0.00	0.48	0.00	0.52	0.27	0.17	0.28	0.67	0.00	0.44	0.00
Beni & Pando	0.43	0.00	0.26	0.00	0.63	0.00	0.29	0.01	0.18	0.72	0.32	0.05	0.71	0.00	0.52	0.00
# elderly	0.01	0.84	0.04	0.29	0.11	0.41	0.07	0.58	0.09	0.73	0.09	0.39	-0.11	0.27	-0.01	0.89
# males	-0.06	0.00	-0.03	0.05	-0.07	0.03	-0.09	0.01	0.08	0.33	0.00	0.91	-0.08	0.05	-0.11	0.00
# females	-0.02	0.21	-0.05	0.00	-0.12	0.00	-0.03	0.31	-0.11	0.07	-0.01	0.80	-0.15	0.00	-0.21	0.00
# youngsters	-0.09	0.00	-0.04	0.00	-0.01	0.76	0.00	0.96	-0.08	0.16	-0.10	0.02	-0.02	0.55	-0.01	0.79
# children	-0.08	0.00	-0.05	0.00	-0.10	0.21	-0.12	0.08	-0.20	0.02	-0.08	0.08	-0.10	0.05	-0.09	0.01
# of working age / # all	0.70	0.00	1.06	0.00	1.13	0.00	1.35	0.00	0.14	0.80	0.65	0.04	0.60	0.04	1.05	0.00
gender hh head	-0.12	0.05	-0.08	0.05	0.00	0.97	0.01	0.94	0.27	0.12	0.06	0.50	0.05	0.57	-0.06	0.51
hh head age <= 24	-0.33	0.01	-0.18	0.03	-0.41	0.05	-0.09	0.65	0.04	0.91	0.00	0.99	0.04	0.83	-0.15	0.30
hh head age 25 - 34	-0.18	0.11	-0.14	0.06	-0.27	0.19	-0.05	0.81	0.05	0.90	0.21	0.22	0.06	0.73	0.00	1.00
hh head age 35 - 44	-0.10	0.34	-0.14	0.06	-0.29	0.14	-0.03	0.87	0.04	0.92	0.16	0.36	0.12	0.48	0.01	0.95
hh head age 45 - 54	-0.10	0.37	-0.12	0.10	-0.34	0.09	-0.01	0.98	0.14	0.72	0.16	0.35	-0.06	0.72	0.07	0.59
hh head age 55 - 65	-0.06	0.62	-0.07	0.40	-0.21	0.31	-0.04	0.82	0.04	0.92	0.34	0.04	0.05	0.78	-0.08	0.56
access to public water	0.14	0.00	0.03	0.23	-0.07	0.52	-0.04	0.53	0.02	0.91	0.06	0.49	0.02	0.73	0.13	0.00
has no toilet	-0.20	0.00	-0.19	0.00	-0.05	0.59	-0.04	0.58	-0.28	0.05	0.03	0.71	-0.22	0.00	-0.15	0.00
no partner in household	0.32	0.00	0.52	0.00	0.11	0.64	0.28	0.08	0.47	0.17	0.27	0.20	0.41	0.03	0.07	0.72
com. basic edu. (m.)	0.00	0.98	0.02	0.66	-0.16	0.21	-0.03	0.74	0.01	0.96	0.07	0.49	-0.05	0.55	0.13	0.02
incom. secondary edu. (m.)	0.02	0.76	0.04	0.24	-0.03	0.78	-0.08	0.47	-0.14	0.44	0.08	0.37	-0.05	0.47	0.09	0.07
com. secondary edu. (m.)	0.10	0.03	0.10	0.01	-0.06	0.52	0.09	0.31	0.26	0.10	0.07	0.42	0.03	0.77	0.17	0.02
tertiary edu. (m.)	0.51	0.00	0.31	0.00	0.35	0.00	0.38	0.00	0.01	0.97	0.34	0.01	0.56	0.01	0.33	0.05
com. basic edu. (w.)	-0.01	0.87	0.07	0.08	0.10	0.44	-0.08	0.52	0.07	0.70	-0.03	0.74	0.27	0.00	0.24	0.00

continued on next page

Table C.1 continued

	City								Town				Rural			
	1989		1994		1999		2002		1999		2002		1999		2002	
	β	P	β	P	β	P	β	P	β	P	β	P	β	P	β	P
incom. secondary edu. (w.)	0.14	0.01	0.02	0.61	0.14	0.17	0.04	0.66	0.16	0.23	0.07	0.50	0.28	0.00	0.29	0.00
com. secondary edu. (w.)	0.17	0.00	0.10	0.00	0.26	0.01	0.04	0.57	0.18	0.20	0.29	0.00	0.43	0.00	0.36	0.00
tertiary edu. (w.)	0.34	0.00	0.35	0.00	0.53	0.00	0.42	0.00	0.48	0.01	0.53	0.00	0.59	0.02	0.59	0.01
high skilled white collar (m.)	0.59	0.00	1.10	0.00	0.74	0.00	0.87	0.00	1.07	0.00	0.78	0.00	0.99	0.00	0.30	0.15
med. skilled white collar (m.)	0.32	0.00	0.55	0.00	0.37	0.09	0.38	0.01	0.95	0.01	0.53	0.00	0.64	0.00	0.18	0.43
skilled manual (m.)	0.37	0.00	0.51	0.00	0.24	0.25	0.20	0.12	0.55	0.13	0.45	0.01	0.73	0.00	0.10	0.57
unskilled manual (m.)	0.43	0.00	0.33	0.00	0.22	0.35	0.30	0.05	0.35	0.34	0.41	0.02	0.54	0.00	0.04	0.81
agr. employed (m.)	0.51	0.00	0.59	0.00	-0.32	0.48	0.38	0.07	0.46	0.25	0.75	0.00	0.57	0.00	0.53	0.02
agr. self-employed (m.)	0.38	0.00	0.39	0.02	0.27	0.29	0.09	0.68	-0.09	0.82	0.22	0.27	0.31	0.06	-0.05	0.78
sales and services (m.)	0.44	0.00	0.58	0.00	0.34	0.12	0.50	0.00	0.86	0.02	0.63	0.00	0.72	0.00	0.34	0.06
high skilled white collar (w.)	0.90	0.00	0.91	0.00	0.40	0.01	0.72	0.00	0.65	0.00	0.92	0.00	-0.06	0.83	0.68	0.00
med. skilled white collar (w.)	0.37	0.00	0.39	0.00	0.32	0.00	0.38	0.00	0.84	0.00	0.52	0.00	0.17	0.27	0.23	0.24
skilled manual (w.)	0.21	0.00	0.20	0.00	-0.07	0.53	0.09	0.33	0.44	0.00	0.18	0.06	-0.11	0.29	0.03	0.72
unskilled manual (w.)	0.43	0.01	0.34	0.00	0.31	0.00	0.33	0.00	0.63	0.00	0.15	0.12	-0.03	0.85	0.05	0.60
agr. employed (w.)	0.64	0.00	0.33	0.03	0.93	0.11	0.12	0.80	-1.02	0.06	0.00	0.00	-0.04	0.66	-0.21	0.46
agr. self-employed (w.)	0.46	0.11	-0.40	0.16	0.51	0.01	-0.08	0.79	-0.24	0.46	-0.48	0.00	-0.05	0.47	-0.05	0.37
sales and services (w.)	0.35	0.00	0.30	0.00	0.28	0.00	0.26	0.00	0.73	0.00	0.34	0.00	0.31	0.00	0.24	0.00
birth in last 12 month	-0.14	0.02	-0.14	0.01	0.18	0.39	-0.13	0.35	-0.25	0.36	-0.13	0.36	-0.08	0.27	0.02	0.81
attended by doctor	0.10	0.27	0.13	0.10	-0.16	0.51	0.06	0.72	0.61	0.07	0.04	0.82	0.21	0.07	0.03	0.83
delivered in hospital	0.01	0.94	-0.02	0.73	-0.09	0.57	-0.30	0.09	-0.25	0.25	0.15	0.34	0.10	0.45	0.13	0.32
child under 4 years	-0.02	0.62	0.00	0.88	0.07	0.48	0.18	0.08	0.12	0.48	-0.01	0.92	-0.04	0.65	0.06	0.35
has had diarrhea	-0.09	0.08	-0.05	0.42	-0.18	0.07	0.04	0.66	0.00	0.98	0.01	0.91	0.02	0.74	-0.16	0.02
has head cough/fever	-0.04	0.46	-0.12	0.00	-0.02	0.85	0.01	0.91	0.06	0.65	-0.02	0.82	0.01	0.87	0.09	0.12
c/t/r dummy/constant	4.48	0.00	4.10	0.00	4.63	0.00	4.04	0.00	3.82	0.00	3.76	0.00	3.88	0.00	4.13	0.00
# of observations	4607		5131		1037		1506		332		1120		922		1709	
R^2	41.47		49.85		46.23		42.01		43.48		42.11		45.96		40.73	

Notes: For details on the regression and variables, see text and notes of Table 2.2. β: regression coefficient; P: P-value; all: all possible covariates; common: covariates common over all 4 years.
Source: Own calculations based on ECH and EIH.

Göttinger Studien zur Entwicklungsökonomik
Göttingen Studies in Development Economics

Herausgegeben von / Edited by Hermann Sautter
und / and Stephan Klasen

Die Bände 1-8 sind über die Vervuert Verlagsgesellschaft (Frankfurt/M.) zu beziehen.

Bd. / Vol. 9 Hermann Sautter / Rolf Schinke (eds.): Social Justice in a Market Economy. 2001.

Bd. / Vol. 10 Philipp Albert Theodor Kircher: Poverty Reduction Strategies. A comparative study applied to empirical research. 2002.

Bd. / Vol. 11 Matthias Blum: Weltmarktintegration, Wachstum und Innovationsverhalten in Schwellenländern. Eine theoretische Diskussion mit einer Fallstudie über „Argentinien 1990-1999". 2003.

Bd. / Vol. 12 Jan Müller-Scheeßel: Die Privatisierung und Regulierung des Wassersektors. Das Beispiel Buenos Aires / Argentinien. 2003.

Bd. / Vol. 13 Ludger J. Löning: Economic Growth, Biodiversity Conservation, and the Formation of Human Capital in a Developing Country. 2004.

Bd. / Vol. 14 Silke Woltermann: Transitions in Segmented Labor Markets. The Case of Brazil. 2004.

Bd. / Vol. 15 Jörg Stosberg: Political Risk and the Institutional Environment for Foreign Direct Investment in Latin America. An Empirical Analysis with a Case Study on Mexico. 2005.

Bd. / Vol. 16 Derk Bienen: Die politische Ökonomie von Arbeitsmarktreformen in Argentinien. 2005.

Bd. / Vol. 17 Dierk Herzer: Exportdiversifizierung und Wirtschaftswachstum. Das Fallbeispiel Chile. 2006.

Bd. / Vol. 18 Jann Lay: Poverty and Distributional Impact of Economic Policies and External Shocks. Three Case Studies from Latin America Combining Macro and Micro Approaches. 2007.

Bd. / Vol. 19 Kenneth Harttgen: Empirical Analysis of Determinants, Distribution and Dynamics of Poverty. 2007.

Bd. / Vol. 20 Stephan Klasen / Felicitas Nowak-Lehmann: Poverty, Inequality and Migration in Latin America. 2008.

Bd. / Vol. 21 Isabel Günther: Empirical Analysis of Poverty Dynamics. With Case Studies from Sub-Saharan Africa. 2007.

Bd. / Vol. 22 Peter Dung: Malaysia und Indonesien: Wirtschaftliche Entwicklungsstrategien in zwei Vielvölkerstaaten. 2008.

Bd. / Vol. 23 Thomas Otter: Poverty, Income Growth and Inequality in Paraguay During the 1990s. Spatial Aspects, Growth Determinants and Inequality Decomposition. 2008.

Bd. / Vol. 24 Mark Misselhorn: Measurement of Poverty, Undernutrition and Child Mortality. 2008.

Bd. / Vol. 25 Julian Weisbrod: Growth, Poverty and Inequality Dynamics. Four Empirical Essays at the Macro and Micro Level. 2008.

Bd. / Vol. 26 Johannes Gräb: Econometric Analysis in Poverty Research. With Case Studies from Developing Countries. 2009.

Bd. / Vol. 27 Sebastian Vollmer: A Contribution to the Empirics of Economic and Human Development. 2009.

Bd. / Vol. 28 Wokia-azi Ndangle Kumase: Aspects of Poverty and Inequality in Cameroon. 2010.

Bd. / Vol. 29 Adriana Rocío Cardozo Silva: Economic Growth and Poverty Reduction in Colombia. 2010.

Bd. / Vol. 30 Ronald Kröker: Ansätze zur Implementierung von RSE (CSR) in einem lateinamerikanischen Entwicklungsland. Das Beispiel Paraguay – Eine wirtschafts- und unternehmensethische Untersuchung. 2010.

Bd. / Vol. 31 Maria Ziegler: Institutions, Inequality and Development. 2011.

Bd. / Vol. 32 Melanie Grosse: Measurement of Trends in Wellbeing, Poverty, and Inequality with Case Studies from Bolivia and Colombia. 2011.

www.peterlang.de